GW00362967

THE M. & E. HANDBOOK SERIES

LAW OF TORTS

J. G. M. TYAS, B.A., LL.B., A.M.B.I.M.

Principal Lecturer at the
Polytechnic of the South Bank
London

MACDONALD & EVANS LTD

8 John Street, London W.C.1
1970

First published September 1968
Reprinted 1969
Reprinted September 1970

©

MACDONALD AND EVANS LTD
1968

S.B.N. 7121 1206 5

*Printed in Great Britain by Butler & Tanner, Ltd,
Frome and London*

GENERAL INTRODUCTION

The HANDBOOK Series of Study Notes

HANDBOOKS are a new form of printed study notes designed to help students to prepare and revise for professional and other examinations. The books are carefully programmed so as to be self-contained courses of tuition in the subjects they cover. For this purpose they comprise detailed study notes, self-testing questions and hints on examination technique.

HANDBOOKS can be used on their own or in conjunction with recommended text-books. They are written by college lecturers, examiners and others with wide experience of students' difficulties and requirements. At all stages the main objective of the authors has been to prepare students for the practical business of passing examinations.

P. W. D. REDMOND
General Editor

NOTICE TO LECTURERS

Many lecturers are now using HANDBOOKS as working texts to save time otherwise wasted by students in protracted note-taking. The purpose of the series is to meet practical teaching requirements as far as possible, and lecturers are cordially invited to forward comments or criticisms to the Publishers for consideration.

AUTHOR'S PREFACE

IN this **HANDBOOK** I have tried to set out the elements of the law of Torts in a way in which my experience as a teacher suggests will make them most easily grasped by students. The primary aim of the book is to help students pass their examinations, but I should indeed be delighted if it also stimulated, in even one student, a deeper and more lasting interest in what has always seemed to me the most fascinating, as well as the most basic, of all the branches of the English common law.

The book is addressed to two categories of students: (a) Candidates for law degrees, for the qualifying examinations for Call to the Bar and Admission as Solicitors, and for the examinations leading to Membership and Fellowship of the Institute of Legal Executives; (b) those who are not primarily law students, but who have to learn some law in the process of qualifying for other professions.

Students in the latter category will find this book contains all they need. For those in the former, it should be emphasised that this book is not, and does not purport to be, a complete exposition of the law of torts. Such expositions are to be found in those great standard texts which it is scarcely necessary to remind law students they must read. I earnestly hope, however, that this **HANDBOOK**, by presenting the subject-matter in a way specifically adapted to study and revision for examinations, may do something to enable students to *read* the great works, at their own pace and without anxiety.

I wish to thank the General Editor of this series, Mr. P. W. D. Redmond, and the publishers, Macdonald and Evans Ltd., for much help and more patience. My thanks are also due to several charming and efficient ladies who typed various parts of the manuscript, but particularly to Mrs. Maureen Glover, who did the bulk of that work. I am most grateful to the Law Society and London University for permission to reproduce examination questions.

June, 1968   J. G. M. T.

CONTENTS

TABLE OF CASES

A

B

C

I

THE NATURE OF TORTIOUS LIABILITY

TORTIOUS LIABILITY

1. Importance of case law. The law of torts, like any other branch of the law, consists of certain established *principles*. Each of these principles is formed from, and rests upon, the authority of:

(*a*) propositions of law (*rationes decidendi*) laid down in judgments in decided cases; and

(*b*) rules laid down in statutes.

But many statutory rules, before they can be of practical effect, have to be interpreted in decided cases. The decided case is therefore the bedrock of English law; and this is more so in the law of torts than in any other part of the law.

2. Nature of a tort.

(*a*) A tort gives rise to a civil action for unliquidated damages. Some other remedy—injunction for example (*see* XVII, 22–25)—may be claimed in a tortious action, either jointly with, or independently of, damages: but the wrong complained of will not be a tort unless it is *capable* of giving rise to a claim for unliquidated damages.

NOTE: Damages are said to be unliquidated when they consist of such sum of money as the court, in its discretion, awards to a successful plaintiff, so as to restore him as nearly as possible to his original position: and not of a fixed—*i.e.* liquidated—sum named by the plaintiff; as, for example, when the action is one to recover a debt.

(*b*) A tort arises by *operation of law* and not by agreement of the parties. If the wrong complained of arises *exclusively* from a breach of agreement between parties it will not be a tort, but a breach of contract, or a breach of trust or other equitable obligation.

1

(c) Similarly, if a wrong gives rise *exclusively* to punishment by the State, it will not be a tort, but a crime only.

(d) However, torts, crimes and breaches of contract are not necessarily exclusive. A tort may be *also* a breach of agreement, *or* a crime, or both. For example, if a taxi driver collides with a lamp-post, he may be liable in tort to his passenger; to the person from whom he has hired the taxi; to the local authority whose lamp-post it is; or to anyone else whose person or property is injured. He may *also* be liable for breach of his contract to take his passenger to his destination; and criminally liable under the Road Traffic Acts.

3. Definition of tort. A tort may therefore be defined as: An unlawful act arising primarily from operation of law and not from breach of agreement between parties, the typical remedy for which is an action for unliquidated damages; and which is not exclusively a breach of contract, or exclusively a breach of trust or other equitable obligation, or exclusively a crime.

4. Liability in tort. The question of whether or not there exists a general principle of liability in tort is often posed in the form of the well-worn examination question: "Is there a law of tort or only a law of torts?" One school of thought says all wrongs are actionable unless they can be legally justified (a law of tort). The other school says there is simply a number of named torts—trespass, nuisance, negligence, defamation, and so on—and that a plaintiff will have no remedy unless he can bring the facts of his case within one of them (a law of torts).

5. The Forms of Action. The names of the modern torts are those of some of the old Forms of Action which thus (says the latter school, following the great legal historian Maitland) "rule us from their graves." However, since the abolition of the Forms of Action (completed by the *Judicature Acts*, 1873–6), the facts of the case are the sole determinants of liability, and the names of the various torts survive only for historical reasons and as a convenient method of classification. In this form, however, they have proved flexible and capable of apparently indefinite development; "the categories of negligence are never closed," said Lord Macmillan in the famous case of *Donoghue* v. *Stevenson* (1932).

6. No general theory of liability.

(a) *Movement towards such a theory.* The most that can be said at present, therefore, is that there is a *movement* or *tendency* towards liability in the absence of justification, but that this has not yet gone far enough to be validly described as a general principle of liability in tort.

(b) *Comparison with contract.* It is instructive to compare the situation in tort with that in contract. Every valid contract (but for a very small number of defined exceptions) must have: (*i*) offer and acceptance; (*ii*) form or consideration; (*iii*) capacity in the parties; (*iv*) the intention to form legal relations. There are no such general rules applicable to all torts.

7. The main arguments on each side.

(a) *A law of torts.* *Salmond* is the foremost representative of this school. He wrote: "Just as the criminal law consists of a body of rules establishing specific offences, so the law of torts consists of a body of rules establishing specific injuries. Neither in the one case or the other is there any general principle of liability." It is therefore for the plaintiff to bring his case under one of the recognised heads of tort, not for the defendant to prove that his action was within a recognised class of excuse or justification. Furthermore, the *names* of the various torts survive and continue to be of practical effect. It seems that every set of facts alleged to be a tort must either be brought under one of the existing names or have a new name invented for it. So, for example, the case of *Rookes* v. *Barnard* (1964) has apparently established a new tort called *intimidation*.

(b) *A law of tort.* This is the school of *Winfield*. He wrote that no action had ever been refused a hearing by the courts on the grounds that it was new. As early as 1762 *Pratt C. J.* had said in the case of *Chapman* v. *Pickersgill*, referring to counsel's argument that the plaintiff disclosed no cause of action because his case came under no recognised head of tort: "I wish never to hear this objection again. This action is for a tort. Torts are infinitely various . . . for there is nothing in nature but may be an instrument of mischief." Winfield concluded that: "All injuries done to another person are torts, unless there is some justification recognised by law."

Professor Glanville Williams wrote: "To say that the law can be collected into pigeon holes does not mean that those pigeon holes may not be capacious, nor does it mean that they are incapable of being added to."

Denning L.J. (as he then was) wrote: "The province of tort is to allocate responsibility for injurious conduct."

THE RELATIONSHIP OF DAMAGE TO LIABILITY

8. Damnum sine injuria.

(a) *Injury without legal redress.* Not every action which causes harm is actionable as a tort. Some wrongs are *damnum sine injuria*—harm done without the commission of a legal wrong. Thus, for example, if a man's business is ruined through the legitimate commercial exertions of his competitors, he has undoubtedly suffered harm, but he has not been the object of any tortious conduct for which he can seek a remedy in the courts.

(b) *Avoiding greater harm.* Harm which would otherwise be unlawful may be *damnum sine injuria* if it is done in order to avoid greater harm.

Esso Petroleum Co. Ltd. v. *Southport Corporation* (1956). The Esso Company's tanker ran aground, without negligence, in the Mersey estuary, and was in danger of breaking up. Oil was discharged to lessen the danger to life and property. The oil fouled the Corporation's foreshore, causing considerable inconvenience and expense. HELD: The Esso Company incurred no liability in tort.

(c) *Injury from lawful use of property.* Harm may be *damnum sine injuria* if it is done in the lawful exercise of a right over property.

Bradford Corporation v. *Pickles* (1895). The Corporation needed P's land for a water scheme, but would not buy at P's price. P attempted to coerce the Corporation by deliberately undermining the land so as to reduce and pollute the water supply. HELD: He had committed no tort as he was merely exercising a lawful right over his own property. His malicious motive was irrelevant.

9. Injuria sine damno. The opposite of *damnum sine injuria* is *injuria sine damno*—the right to a legal remedy although no harm has been suffered. Thus, to enter the land of another without permission is a trespass although no damage is done; and defamation by libel is actionable *per se*, *i.e.* it is enough for the plaintiff to prove that he was defamed by the libel, without going on to show that he was harmed as a result.

THE MENTAL ELEMENT IN TORT

10. Motive of the defendant. To what extent is the motive of the defendant—*i.e.* the presence or absence of *malice* on his part—relevant in deciding whether his action was a tort? Malice may be:

(a) doing a wrongful act intentionally and without lawful justification or excuse—sometimes called *malice in law*; or

(b) acting from an evil, spiteful or other improper motive —sometimes called *malice in fact*.

In general, the absence of a malicious motive will not make an unlawful act lawful; nor will the presence of malice make an otherwise lawful act unlawful: *Bradford Corporation* v. *Pickles* (1895).

11. Relevance of motive.

(a) In many torts, *e.g.* trespass, negligence, conversion, the defendant's motive is entirely irrelevant.

(b) Some torts, *e.g.* deceit, malicious prosecution, require proof of malice, in the sense of an improper motive.

(c) In other torts, *e.g.* nuisance, conspiracy, injurious falsehood, malice is *sometimes* relevant.

(d) The *absence* of malice may operate as a *defence: e.g.* in defamation, qualified privilege is a defence *unless* the defendant acted maliciously.

(e) Malice may be relevant to *damages*: if the tortfeasor aggravated his tort by acting from an improper motive, the damages may be increased.

GENERAL DEFENCES IN TORT

12. General defences. There are a number of *general defences* which may be raised, where appropriate, by a defendant in *any* tortious action: contrast with those defences—*e.g.* contributory negligence, qualified privilege—restricted to a particular type of action.

These general defences are considered in detail in **13–36** below.

13. Volenti non fit injuria.

(*a*) A person cannot be heard to complain of an injury to which he *expressly or impliedly consented*: such an injury is not actionable as a tort. For example, those injured in the course of "manly sports" have no legal remedy: and a person on a public road impliedly consents to the risk of "such mischief as reasonable care on the part of the others cannot avoid": *Holmes* v. *Mather* (1875), *per* Bramwell B.

(*b*) But he does not consent to be injured by the *negligence* of others.

Hall v. *Brooklands Auto Racing Club* (1933). Two spectators were killed when a racing car left the track. HELD: The spectators were *volens*—*i.e.* they had impliedly consented to the risk—and there had been no negligence; therefore the defendants were not liable.

14. Knowledge is not the same as consent. The test is *not* whether the plaintiff *knew* of the risk, but whether he *consented* to it. The maxim is *volenti non fit injuria* not *scienti non fit injuria*.

Smith v. *Baker & Sons* (1891). A workman in a quarry knew there was danger from a crane overhead. He had protested, but continued to work in the dangerous place. He was injured and sued his employers. HELD: His knowledge of the danger and continuing to work in spite of it did not make him a volunteer, as there was *no true consent* on his part.

NOTE: An employee will rarely be held *volens* if, when he was injured, he was obeying his employer's instructions.

Dann v. *Hamilton* (1939). A girl accepted a lift from a driver she knew was drunk. She could have gone by bus. HELD: These facts did not make her a volunteer, and she could succeed in negligence.

The above case also established that *volenti non fit injuria* cannot be used so as to claim a *licence in advance* for the commission of a tort. The maxim will not apply where the alleged consent *preceded* the subsequent tortious act.

15. The rescue principle. A plaintiff will not be a volunteer:

(*a*) if, although knowing of the risk, he went to the *rescue* of a third party *endangered by the defendant's negligence*;

(*b*) if, although knowing of the risk, he acted under a compelling *legal or moral duty*.

> *Baker* v. *T. E. Hopkins & Co. Ltd.* (1959). A doctor went down a well to help men overcome by fumes, and was killed. HELD: He was not *volens*. Per Omerod L.J.: "Dr B may well have had the knowledge of the risk he was running, but that is wholly different from saying that he freely and voluntarily took the risk. . . . . he acted under the compulsion of his instincts as a brave man and a doctor" (compelling moral duty). "The doctrine [*volenti non fit injuria*] would not . . . apply in a case of attempted rescue when the act was the natural and foreseeable result of the negligence of the defendant" (third party endangered by defendant's negligence).
>
> *Haynes* v. *Harwood* (1935). A policeman dashed from a police station and stopped runaway horses, thus averting serious danger to women and children. HELD: He freely undertook the risk, but was not *volens* because he acted under a legal and moral duty. He could recover damages from the owner of the horses.

16. Limitations of the rescue principle. *Volenti non fit injuria* would be a good defence where the plaintiff was injured through his own gratuitous act, when not engaged in a rescue.

> *Cutler* v. *United Dairies (London) Ltd.* (1933). C was injured while attempting to stop a horse on a quiet country road. He had not been asked to help and there was no danger to others. HELD: He was a volunteer.
>
> *Sylvester* v. *Chapman Ltd.* (1935). S was mauled by a leopard when he went inside a barrier to put out a cigarette end on the straw. HELD: He was a volunteer.

17. Volenti non fit injuria differs from contributory negligence. There should be no confusion with the defence of contributory negligence under the *Law Reform (Contributory Negligence) Act*, 1945. A plaintiff who is *not* a volunteer

B

(*i.e.* did not consent to the risk) may nevertheless have contributed negligence.

> *Dawrant* v. *Nutt* (1960). The plaintiff was injured while riding in a vehicle she knew was unlit. HELD: She had contributed negligence, although it was not asserted that she was *volens.*
> NOTE: *Dann* v. *Hamilton* was decided before the passing of the *Law Reform (Contributory Negligence) Act*, 1945.

18. Contract to consent. A person may *contract* to consent to a risk, but such a purported exemption will be construed strictly against the party claiming the benefit of it. Also, exemption may be prohibited by statute. Thus, the *Road Traffic Act*, 1960, provides that no exemption from liability can be claimed in respect of death or injury incurred as a passenger in a public-service vehicle.

19. Consent a question of fact. Exemption apart, however, whether or not *volenti non fit injuria* applies is a question of *fact* to be decided in the light of the circumstances of each case. The test is: Was there or was there not *a real consent* to run the risk?

20. Statutory authority.

(*a*) Statutory authority confers *statutory indemnity*. It will be a good defence in tort that the alleged tortfeasor had statutory authority to do the act complained of. In such case no compensation can be obtained unless it is provided for by the statute itself.

(*b*) The defence of statutory authority is of general application, but is particularly relevant to *nuisance.*

(*c*) Statutory authority may be *absolute* or *conditional.*

21. Absolute statutory authority. Absolute statutory authority confers immunity in respect of:

(*a*) The act itself;
(*b*) all the *necessary consequences* of the act.

A consequence is necessary if it could not have been avoided by reasonable care and skill; but "the onus of proving that the result is inevitable is on those who wish to escape liability": *Manchester Corporation* v. *Farnworth* (1930), *per* Lord Dunedin.

The House of Lords laid it down in *Geddis* v. *Proprietors of Bann Reservoir* (1878), *per* Lord Blackburn, that it was "thoroughly well established" that "no action will lie for doing that which the legislature has authorised, if it be done without negligence . . . but an action does lie for doing that which the legislature has authorised, if it be done negligently." This definition was adopted in the more modern cases of *Longhurst* v. *Metropolitan Water Board* (1948) and *Marriage* v. *East Norfolk Catchment Board* (1950).

Vaughan v. *Taff Vale Railway Co.* (1860). The defendants had statutory authority to run steam locomotives. Damage was caused by sparks from one of their locomotives. HELD: As the engines had been manufactured with all reasonable skill and care, and it was impossible entirely to prevent the escape of sparks, the statutory indemnity extended to the damage done by the sparks.

NOTE: The emission of sparks would have been an actionable nuisance at common law, but this was overriden by the statutory authority.

Pride of Derby etc. Angling Association v. *British Celanese Ltd.* (1953). The Derby Corporation were the second defendants. They admitted polluting the plaintiff's fishery but claimed statutory indemnity under the *Derby Corporation Act*, 1901, which imposed on them a duty to provide a sewerage system. HELD: A true construction of the Act revealed that it did not empower the defendants to commit a nuisance in the discharge of their statutory duty.

22. Comment on cases. The two cases above illustrate:

(a) statutory authority in the absence of negligence;
(b) the loss of statutory indemnity where negligence was present, liability for which was not expressly excluded by the Act.

23. Conditional statutory authority. This confers authority to do an act *only if* it can be done without interference with private rights.

24. The statute construed in each case. Whether statutory authority is conditional or absolute depends on the construction of the statute.

Metropolitan Asylum District v. *Hill* (1881). A statute empowered a local authority to erect a smallpox hospital. HELD: The statute gave conditional authority only. The local authority was restrained from erecting the hospital where it would cause danger to residents.

25. Imperative and permissive authority. In general, if the statutory power is *imperative,* the authority will be absolute: but authority which is merely *permissive* is *prima facia conditional*—for there is a rebuttable presumption that the legislature did not intend to take away private rights without compensation. The burden of proof is on the party asserting that Parliament *did* intend to take away private rights without compensation.

26. The difference defined. Authority to do a *particular act* is *prima facie conditional*: but authority to execute a project involving *various acts* and activities is *prima facie absolute*. The court will more readily hold that authority is absolute if the statute provides for compensation for persons adversely affected.

27. Good faith essential. An authority upon whom statutory power is conferred must act in good faith and within the scope of the power: *Marriage* v. *East Norfolk Catchment Board* (1950).

NOTE: A statute which confers a power does not (necessarily) impose a duty. If the power is *merely permissive,* no action will lie for failure to exercise it, or for doing so inadequately.

Smith v. *Cawdle Fenn Commissioners* (1938). Drainage commissioners exercised their power to build an embankment. It was too low to protect the plaintiff's land. HELD: He could not succeed in his action for negligence. The defendants could not be liable for doing negligently what they were not obliged to do at all. But he who exercises a power has a duty not to add to the damage that would have accrued if he had done nothing: *East Suffolk Catchment Board* v. *Kent* (1941).

28. Necessity. The following are the main rules governing the defence of necessity.

(a) *Avoidance of greater evil.* The necessity of doing an otherwise tortious act may be a good defence even where damage was done *intentionally* if it can be proved to have been done to avoid a greater evil—to the Realm; to a third party; or to the defendant himself.

The Case of the King's Prerogative in Saltpetre (1606): It is a good defence that it was necessary for the Crown or a subject to trespass on the land of another in order to take measures (*e.g.* erect fortifications) for the defence of the Realm.

Cope v. *Sharpe* (1912). A gamekeeper, in order to save his master's young birds, set fire to the heather of an adjoining landowner. HELD: No trespass had been committed. Despite the fact that the birds would not have been harmed had the heather not been fired, it was *reasonable in the circumstances* for the gamekeeper to think his action necessary to avert a greater evil.

Esso Petroleum Ltd. v. *Southport Corporation* (1956). In this case it was necessary to do what was *prima facie* tortious in order to avert danger to *life and property*.

(*b*) *Life and property,* A different scale of values applies to the saving of life than to the saving of property. *Per* Devlin J. in the *Esso Petroleum Case:* "The two are beyond comparison and the necessity for saving life has at all times been considered a proper ground for inflicting such damage as may be necessary to another's property."

(*c*) *Destruction of animals:* When *property* is in real danger, necessity will be a good defence to an action for the destruction of animals: *Hamps* v. *Darby* (1948), homing pigeon; *Goadway* v. *Beecher* (1951), dog.

However, the courts do not favour the defence of necessity. In *Andrae* v. *Selfridge & Co. Ltd.* (1936) the court rejected the defence of the necessity of carrying on noisy building operations in order to save time and money.

29. Effect of defendant's negligence. The defence of necessity is not available if the defendant's predicament is due to his own negligence. Thus in *Esso Petroleum Co. Ltd.* v. *Southport Corporation* (1956) the Esso Company could not have succeeded with the defence of necessity *if* the ship had gone aground through negligence.

30. Inevitable accident. It is a good defence that an accident was one which could not have been avoided by any care, precaution or forethought that a reasonable man could have taken in the circumstances of the case.

Stanley v. *Powell* (1891). The plaintiff and defendant were both members of a shooting party. The plaintiff was wounded by a pellet which had been fired in a proper manner by the defendant, but had glanced off a tree almost at right angles. HELD : The accident was inevitable and the defendant not liable.

National Coal Board v. *Evans* (1951). In this case the Court of Appeal held that inevitable accident was a good defence to an action for trespass to chattels. The colliery company which preceded the N.C.B. had buried an electric cable in the County Council's land. This fact was unknown to, and could not have been reasonably discovered by, either the Council or its contractor. The contractor damaged the cable while excavating the land. HELD : The accident arose mainly from the wrongful act of the plaintiff's predecessors in burying cables on another's land. Therefore the defendants were without fault, and could escape liability through the defence of inevitable accident.

NOTE: Inevitable accident is probably *not* a defence to a claim under the rule in *Rylands* v. *Fletcher*, for which (it seems) only the more stringent defence of Act of God would suffice (*see* VIII, 17).

ACT OF GOD

31. Human forethought excluded. This defence applies only to accidents or injuries which *no* human care or forethought could have avoided, and in which there was *no human intervention*.

Nicholas v. *Marsland* (1876). This was an action under the Rule in *Rylands* v. *Fletcher*. The defendant constructed a series of artificial pools by damming a natural stream. The pools were well constructed and adequate in all normal circumstances. However, they were destroyed by a storm of quite exceptional violence, with resultant damage to the plaintiff's bridges. HELD : No one had been negligent and the accident was due entirely to Act of God.

32. Limitations of the defence. Act of God is a defence of very limited application, imposing a heavy onus on the defendant. There are *dicta* in a number of cases to the effect that heavy rainfall and violent snowstorms were *not* Acts of God, *i.e.* the resultant damage could have been avoided by *human* care and forethought.

The following points should also be noted.

(a) An accident is not an Act of God unless it is the direct result of natural causes without human intervention. This does not mean, however, that human activity must have been completely absent. The *direct and immediate cause* of the accident must be looked at to determine whether it was caused by Act of God or act of man. Thus, an aeroplane may be destroyed in the air by Act of God notwithstanding that it could not have been in the air except by human action.

(b) An act need not necessarily be violent or exceptional to be an Act of God. The test is: Could the harm have been prevented by human care? For example, if an accident is caused by the sudden death of a lorry driver from a disease he did not know he had or against the effects of which he could not have guarded, it will be an Act of God: *Ryan* v. *Youngs* (1938). But this would not be so if, for instance, the driver was a diagnosed diabetic who had neglected to take his treatment.

PLAINTIFF A WRONGDOER

33. Plaintiff acting unlawfully. Can a plaintiff succeed if, at the time of the allegedly tortious act, he was himself acting unlawfully? This point has not been finally decided and remains obscure, but the position seems to be as follows. The *general rule* is that "plaintiff a wrongdoer" is no defence. So, for example, if A unlawfully takes possession of wine belonging to B, B will not be debarred from succeeding in an action for conversion, merely by the fact that he broke the licensing laws when purchasing the wine.

34. Plaintiff's injury and conduct directly connected. It will be otherwise, however, if the harm suffered by the plaintiff was *directly connected* with his own unlawful conduct.

In *National Coal Board* v. *England* (1954) it was said that a wrongdoer would not be debarred from sueing "unless some unlawful act or conduct on his own part is connected with the harm suffered by him as part of the same transaction."

35. Common unlawful purpose. Probably no cause of action could arise between persons who had engaged in a *common* unlawful purpose. Thus, if two men injured each other in the illegal activity of prize-fighting, there would be no cause of action *inter se*.

36. Limitations of the defence.

(*a*) "Plaintiff a wrongdoer" ought not to be equated with *ex turpi causa non oritur actio* (a base cause cannot found an action). This maxim belongs to the realm of contract and probably has no application in tort. A contract is by definition a joint activity, in which the unlawful conduct of each party will be *directly connected* with the harm done him by the other, but this is not necessarily so in tort.

(*b*) "Plaintiff a wrongdoer" should not be confused with *volenti non fit injuria*, contributory negligence, or remoteness of damage, none of which depend primarily upon the allegation that the plaintiff was acting unlawfully. It has been suggested that there is no need to recognise the defence of "plaintiff a wrongdoer" because, in the exceptional cases in which it might be applicable, the facts would always bring the defence within one of the three categories mentioned.

TORTS COMMITTED ABROAD

37. Foreign torts actionable in Great Britain.
A tort committed abroad will be actionable in Great Britain only if the following conditions apply:

(*a*) The wrong must have been actionable as a tort if committed in England.

(*b*) It must have been *unjustifiable* by the law of the country where it was committed. But it need not be classified as a *tort* in that country. For example, our courts would regard a wrong as "unjustifiable" if it gave rise to *criminal liability* in the country of commission, although merely tortious here.

But our courts will not entertain an action concerning rights over, or trespass against, foreign *land*.

38. Defences.
When an action brought here is based on a wrong committed abroad, the defendant may raise *any defence available here* although it would not be available in the country of commission.

Phillips v. *Eyre* (1870). "Two conditions must be fulfilled. First, the wrong must be of such a character that it would have been actionable if committed in England . . . secondly, the act must not have been justifiable by the law of the place where it was done": *per* Willes J.

The Halley (1868). An English and a Dutch ship collided in Dutch waters because of the negligence of the pilot of the English ship. By *Dutch law* (a) the ship was obliged to take a pilot; and (b) the owners of a ship causing damage were liable in respect of it *although* the compulsory pilot was in charge at the time. This was *not* the case according to English law. HELD: The defendants were not liable. An English court will not enforce foreign municipal law in respect of an act not unlawful by English law.

Machado v. *Fontes* (1897). Action was brought here in respect of a libel published in Brazil. By Brazilian law libel is a crime but not a civil wrong. HELD: The court would hear the case. The wrong was tortious here and unjustifiable in Brazil.

NOTE: The rule as to foreign torts has been criticised on the grounds that damages may be obtained here for an act which would give no right to damages in the country of commission.

PROGRESS TEST 1

1. Define "tort."   (1–3)
2. Can a tort be also—and if so which—other forms of legal wrong?   (2)
3. What is meant by the question: "Is there a law of tort or only a law of torts?"?   (3–4)
4. Summarise the arguments for (a) a law of tort; (b) a law of torts.   (4–7)
5. What is (a) a tort *damnum sine injuria*; (b) a tort *injuria sine damno*?   (8–9)
6. Summarise the relationship of motive and malice to liability in tort.   (10–11)
7. Illustrate with decided cases the meaning of *volenti non fit injuria*.   (13–19)
8. Explain "the rescue principle."   (15–16)
9. Outline the defence of statutory authority. What are the differences between absolute and conditional statutory authority?   (20–27)
10. State the main rules governing the defence of necessity. Does the defendant's negligence make any difference to the application of this defence?   (28–29)
11. Summarise the defence of inevitable accident.   (30)

12. Summarise the defence of Act of God. How does it differ from inevitable accident?   (31–32)

13. Can a plaintiff succeed if, at the time of the allegedly tortious act, he was himself acting unlawfully?   (33–36)

14. Summarise the conditions under which a tort committed abroad will be actionable here.   (37, 38).

CHAPTER II

TRESPASS TO LAND

TRESPASS GENERALLY:
DEFINITION AND CHARACTERISTICS

1. Trespass of three kinds. Trespasses may be committed:

(*a*) to land (*see* **4-29** below);
(*b*) to chattels (*see* III);
(*c*) to the person (*see* IV).

2. Trespass a direct injury. For hundreds of years, the action for trespass has been the main remedy for *direct* injury, *consequential* injuries being dealt with by an action on the case, *e.g.* for *nuisance* or *negligence*. Thus, even today, a trespass consists of a *direct* unlawful injury to, or interference with, the land, goods or person of the plaintiff.

3. Proof of damage not required. For the same historical reasons trespass is actionable *per se*, *i.e.* without proof of special damage. It is a trespass to go on another's land without lawful authority, even if no damage is done.

WHAT CONSTITUTES TRESPASS TO LAND?

4. A wrong against possession. Any unlawful entry upon land or buildings in the *possession* of another is actionable as a trespass. Even a person in *wrongful* possession can bring trespass against anyone *without a better title*.

5. Possession defined. Possession means *the right to exclude others*, whether or not the possessor is physically present. A person who leaves his house for a long period, but intends to return, retains this right of general exclusion, and therefore possession.

6. No jus tertii. Because trespass is a wrong to possession, a trespasser cannot raise the defence of *jus tertii*, *i.e.* that a

17

third person has a better title than the plaintiff in possession. It is a good defence, however, that the defendant was entitled to immediate possession *as against the plaintiff*.

7. Trespass by relation. Furthermore, when a person with a better title thus enters the land, the first occupier immediately becomes a trespasser; also the person with the better title can sue for any trespass to the land committed since his right of entry accrued, as his possession will be held to *relate back* to that time—although he must be in *actual* possession when the action is brought. This is the doctrine of *trespass by relation*.

8. Trespass without personal entry. Trespass to land does not necessarily involve personal entry, but may consist, *e.g.*, of placing objects on the land: *Gregory* v. *Piper* (1829); or the release of oil: *Esso Petroleum Ltd.* v. *Southport Corporation* (1956); or gas: *McDonald* v. *Associated Fuels* (1954), so that the plaintiff's land is damaged.

9. Trespass by abuse of authority. A person who has authority to enter another's land *for a particular purpose* becomes a trespasser if he *goes beyond that purpose*. This applies particularly to abuse of public and private rights of way.

NOTE: The public's right on the highway is that of passing and repassing; anything beyond this is *prima facie* a trespass.

Hickman v. *Maisey* (1900). Plaintiff owned the soil of a highway, and occupied adjoining land, on which racehorses were trained. Defendant traversed the highway for two hours so as to observe the form of the horses. HELD: This was not an ordinary and reasonable use of the highway. Defendant had abused his right of entry and was therefore a trespasser.

10. Continuing trespass. If a trespasser *remains* on the land, or allows things he has unlawfully placed on it to remain there, such trespass can be the subject of a fresh action *for each day that it continues*; but this must be carefully distinguished from *the continuing consequences of a past and completed trespass*, *e.g.* digging a hole on the land, which gives rise to one action only.

11. The air above and the soil beneath. A possessor of land also possesses—and may also own—the soil beneath and the column of air above it—*cujus est solum est usque ad coelum et usque ad inferos;* unless, *e.g.*, he has conveyed the mining rights.

12. Rights of removal. An occupier may *remove* things obtruding upon his air space, even though they do no harm. Thus, he may, *e.g.*, lop overhanging branches: *Lemmon* v. *Webb* (1895); or remove unauthorised telegraph wires: *Wandsworth Board of Works* v. *United Telephone Co.* (1884).

13. Has the occupier a right of action in trespass? This point seems unsettled. In *Lemmon* v. *Webb* the Court of Appeal took the view that an occupier has *no* right of action *unless he suffered damage;* but in *Kelsen* v. *Imperial Tobacco Co. Ltd.* (1957) it was held that an obtruding advertising sign was a trespass, and the plaintiff obtained an injunction for its removal. However, this seems inconsistent with *Pickering* v. *Rudd* (1815), in which a projecting board was held *no* trespass.

NOTE: There is ample authority for saying that such projections are actionable in *nuisance* (*see* V, **13**).

14. Trespass by aircraft. Section 40 (I) (*k*) of the *Civil Aviation Act,* 1949, provides that: "No action shall lie in respect of trespass or . . . nuisance, by reason only of the flight of an aircraft over any property at a height above the ground which . . . is reasonable, or the ordinary incidents of such flight." However, the Act also provides that damages are recoverable, *without proof of negligence,* for damage caused by the flight, by the taking off or landing of an aircraft, or by things or persons falling from an aircraft. Note carefully, however, that the Act does *not* apply to aircraft on Her Majesty's service.

WHO MAY SUE IN TRESPASS TO LAND?

15. The importance of possession. As trespass is a tort against possession, it follows that, in order to succeed in his action, a plaintiff must establish his right of possession.

(*a*) An owner *not in possession* cannot sue except for permanent damage to his *reversionary interest.*

Baxter v. *Taylor* (1832). Plaintiff sued for trespass to his land, in possession of tenants, when defendant unloaded stones upon it. HELD: Plaintiff could not maintain trespass, as his reversion was not injured.

(b) Possession, to give a right of action in trespass, must be *exclusive*. Thus, *e.g.*, a guest or servant cannot sue for trespass to his room, as he lacks such exclusive possession.

(c) Possession is not confined to actual physical possession. It includes possession through servants or agents; and it may be *constructive*, *e.g.*, where one leaves his house unoccupied for a long time but intends to return.

> *Wuta-Ofie* v. *Danquah* (1961). Plaintiff acquired land in Ghana, which she did not physically occupy, but marked with pillars according to custom. Some years later defendant built on the land. HELD: The plaintiff could succeed in trespass, the "slightest amount of possession" being sufficient.

(d) A purchaser of *standing crops* acquires a right to bring trespass for damage to them, although not in possession.

> *Wellaway* v. *Courtier* (1918). Defendant's sheep ate growing turnips which plaintiff had bought from the farmer in occupation of the land. HELD: Plaintiff could bring trespass because, although not in occupation, he had *the exclusive right of possession* of the crop.

(e) If there is *more than one possessor—e.g.* A owns the subsoil and B occupies the surface—each can sue for trespass to his portion. But tenants in common and joint tenants cannot sue in trespass *inter se*.

16. Trespass ab initio.

If a person enters the land or premises of another in the exercise of a right conferred by law, but subsequently does some wrongful act there, then, subject to the conditions set out below, his original (lawful) entry will be regarded as a trespass, for which the occupier may recover damages additional to those for the wrongful act.

The *conditions* which must obtain are as follows:

(a) The entry must be in pursuance of a *right conferred by common or statute law*, *e.g.* not merely by leave of the occupier, or under contract.

(b) The wrongful act must be a *misfeasance*, not merely a nonfeasance.

> *The Six Carpenters Case* (1610). Six carpenters refused to pay for wine they had drunk in an inn. HELD: They had abused their lawful right to enter a common inn, but were

not trespassers *ab initio*, as their refusal to pay was a non-feasance only.

(*c*) For the doctrine to apply, the (subsequent) wrongful act must make the defendant's presence *totally unjustifiable*. He will not be a trespasser *ab initio* if, despite the wrongful act, his presence is still legally justified.

> *Elias* v. *Pasmore* (1934). Police officers entered plaintiff's premises to make a lawful arrest, but also wrongfully seized certain papers. HELD: They were not trespassers *ab initio*, their presence before and after the wrongful seizure being justified by their duty to arrest.

REMEDIES

17. Usual remedies. A plaintiff in trespass normally sues for damages, or for an injunction to prohibit or restrain the trespass, or both (*see* XVII).

18. Other remedies. Subject to certain conditions, the following remedies are also available.

(*a*) *Reasonable force.* An occupier may eject with reasonable force a trespasser who refuses to leave. Similarly, a person legally entitled to do so may enter or re-enter land, and will not be *civilly* liable if he uses the minimum force necessary; but he may be *criminally* liable under various statutes.

(*b*) *Distress damage feasant.* This is the common-law right of an occupier to detain trespassing animals, or other chattels which *do damage* on the land. The following conditions apply:

(*i*) *The thing unattended.* The thing doing the damage must be *unattended* when distrained: *e.g.* a cow cannot be distrained if the drover is present.

(*ii*) *No power of sale.* The distrainor cannot sell distrained chattels, and must take proper care of them: *e.g.* feed animals.

(*iii*) *No retrospective power.* A trespassing chattel cannot be distrained for damage done during a *previous* trespass. Furthermore, the chattel must be distrained *while trespassing*; there is no power to bring it back after it has left.

(*iv*) *Compensation ends distraint.* The distrainor must release the chattel when its owner tenders proper compensation —the amount of which is a question of fact.

(*v*) *Distraint excludes damages.* Distress damage feasant is an *alternative* to an action for damage.

Boden v. *Roscoe* (1894). Pony distrained when it entered plaintiff's field and kicked his filly. HELD: The distraint was lawful, but while it continued no action for damages would lie.

(*vi*) *Damage limits restraint.* Only a chattel which *does damage* may be seized: *e.g.* not the whole flock for damage by one sheep.

19. Wild animals.

(*a*) *Wild animals without an owner.* Such animals clearly cannot be distrained damage feasant, but can be killed or captured by the occupier, unless protected by statute.

(*b*) *Wild animals with an owner.* Such animals may be killed for good cause, *e.g.* for damaging crops; but the onus is on their killer to establish the reasonable necessity of his action.

Hamps v. *Darby* (1948). A farmer, without first trying to drive them away, shot plaintiff's homing pigeons which were eating his peas. HELD: The plaintiff could sue for trespass to the pigeons, the farmer having acted unreasonably in the circumstances.

20. Ejectment. Ejectment is the historical name for the action to *recover* land. Originally available only to leaseholders, it was extended to freeholders by elaborate fictions (abolished in 1852) involving Messers R. Roe and J. Doe. The main thing to note about the modern action is that the onus is entirely on the plaintiff claiming possession *to show a better title than the person in possession, i.e.* the plaintiff *cannot rely merely on the weakness of the defendant's title.* Furthermore, the plaintiff must be *out of possession* when the action is brought, and must show entitlement to *immediate* possession. The onus on the plaintiff may not be heavy. In *Asher* v. *Whitlock* (1865) an action for possession succeeded by one whose title rested on *seizure* of the land, the person in possession being nevertheless unable to show a better title.

21. Action for mesne profits. This is an action by a plaintiff claiming possession for the damage suffered by being kept out of possession, *e.g.* for rent, depreciation and the costs of the action.

22. Joint action. The action for mesne profits may be joined with that for possession; indeed, since mesne profits is an action for *trespass*, it can be brought separately only by a plaintiff in possession.

23. Action for an account. Where a person profits by using the land of another, *e.g.* by working mines, an action for an account may be the appropriate remedy.

DEFENCES

24. Authority of law. There may be the authority of law for entries which would otherwise be trespasses, as in the following examples.

(*a*) A *police officer* may enter premises to prevent a breach of the peace.

Thomas v. *Sawkins* (1935). Police officers entered a private meeting against the organisers' wishes. HELD: No trespass, as the officers reasonably apprehended a breach of the peace.

(*b*) A *statutory right* is granted by the *National Parks and Access to the Countryside Act*, 1960, *s.* 60, which provides that, under certain conditions, people going on land for outdoor recreation shall not be treated as trespassers.

(*c*) Entry may be justified on the grounds that it was made *to abate a nuisance*: but note that abatement forfeits the right to an action for damages.

25. Entry by licence. The classic definition of licence is that of Sir Frederick Pollock: "That consent which, without passing any interest in the property to which it relates, merely prevents the act for which consent is given from being wrongful."

(*a*) *Licence without consideration.* A "bare" licence, *i.e.* one for which no valuable consideration was given, may be revoked at will.

(*b*) *Licence by contract.* A contractual licence *not coupled with an interest* is revocable at will, subject to an action for breach; but there are the following exceptions:

(*i*) Where construction clearly reveals that the parties meant the licence to be irrevocable.

(*ii*) Where the licence was granted for a specific purpose and a limited time. In this case it is irrevocable until the purpose has been accomplished.

Jones v. *Tankerville* (1909). Injunction granted to prevent the revocation of a licence to fell and remove timber which had been sold to the plaintiff. See also *Winter Garden Theatre* v. *Millenium Productions* (1948) and *Hurst* v. *Picture Theatres* (1916). In the former case Lord Greene M.R. said (*obiter*) that "it is the settled practice of the Courts of Equity to do what they can by an injunction to preserve the sanctity of a bargain."

NOTE: The law on this point does not seem entirely clear. What is the position where there is not time to get an injunction or the plaintiff seeks damages only?

(*c*) *Remaining after revocation.* To remain on land after one's right of entry has ended is a trespass. Therefore the licensee becomes a trespasser immediately on revocation; but he must be given reasonable time to remove himself and his property.

(*d*) *Executed licences.* An *executed* licence cannot be revoked: *e.g.* X may revoke Y's licence to dump rubbish on X's land, but cannot merely by so doing oblige Y to remove rubbish already dumped.

26. Licence and interest. A licence coupled with an interest is a *grant*, and irrevocable; for, although permission to enter is merely a right *in personam*, it confers a right *in rem*—which will be protected by equity—to do something after entry. Thus as Vaughan C.J. said in *Thomas* v. *Sorrel* (1672), a man may have a bare licence to enter land to hunt, but a *grant* to carry away the deer.

27. Retaking goods. It is a good defence that the defendant entered the land to retake his goods placed there by the plaintiff—or by anyone feloniously.

28. Involuntary and accidental trespass.

(*a*) *Involuntary trespass.* It is no defence that the trespass was *involuntary*—*e.g.* because defendant honestly believed he had the right to enter, or did so under an inevitable mistake of fact or law—if the entry was nevertheless *intentional*.

Basely v. *Clarkson* (1682). Defendant mowed grass on adjoining land, honestly believing it was his own land. HELD: He was a trespasser.

(*b*) *Accidental trespass.* It is uncertain whether this is a defence, there being no authority directly in point. *Salmond* proposes that, as inevitable accident is a defence in trespass to goods and the person, it ought logically to be so in trespass to land as well.

29. Danger to life.

An act which would otherwise be a trespass may be justified if done to avert danger to life.

Esso Petroleum Co. Ltd. v. *Southport Corporation* (1956). Oil jettisoned from tanker washed up on Corporation's foreshore. HELD: No trespass, as the crew's lives were in danger.

PROGRESS TEST 2

1. What is the modern significance of the difference between trespass and case? **(2–3)**

2. What is the meaning and significance of possession to the law of trespass? How does this affect the defence of *jus tertii*? **(4–6)**

3. Explain "trespass by relation." **(7)**

4. Explain (*a*) trespass without personal entry; (*b*) trespass by abuse of authority; (*c*) continuing trespass. **(8–10)**

5. Explain *cujus est solum ejus est usque ad coelum et usque ad inferos.* To what extent, if at all, can an occupier sue in trespass for an intrusion into his air space? **(11–13)**

6. State the main effects of the *Civil Aviation Act*, 1949. **(14)**

7. In what circumstances (if at all) can an owner not in possession sue in trespass? **(15)**

8. Explain the significance of "exclusive possession" from the point of view of a potential plaintiff in trespass. **(15)**

9. What is "trespass *ab initio*"? Illustrate by decided cases. **(16)**

10. What remedies are available in respect of trespasses to land? **(17–18)**

11. Define "distress damage feasant" and explain the rules which govern it. **(18)**

12. Explain the rules governing trespass by wild animals. **(19)**

13. Explain the modern applications of the actions for (*a*) ejectment; (*b*) mesne profits; (*c*) an account. **(20–23)**

14. Outline the defence of "authority of law" against an action for trespass to land. **(24)**

15. Explain the term "licence by contract." When (if at all) can a licence by contract be revoked? **(25)**

16. What is "a licence coupled with an interest"? Can it be revoked? Give reasons for your answer. **(26)**

17. To what extent (if at all) is it a defence that the trespass was involuntary or accidental? **(28)**

CHAPTER III

TRESPASS TO CHATTELS

DEFINITION AND CHARACTERISTICS

1. Definition. Trespass to chattels consists of a *direct* and unlawful injury to, or interference with, a chattel in the *possession* of another.

2. Direct interference. Trespass to chattels is actionable *per se, i.e.* proof of the direct and unlawful application of force suffices, and it is unnecessary to prove damage. However, direct application of force does not necessarily involve physical contact, *e.g.* it is a trespass to drive away cattle.

NOTE: A trespass to chattels which involves moving them from one place to another may or may not also amount to conversion (*see* **14** below).

3. Proof of intention or negligence necessary. The plaintiff in an action for trespass to goods must prove intention or negligence by the defendant. This was not always so, but has been established at least since the decision of the Court of Appeal in *N.C.B.* v. *Evans* (1951) that inevitable accident is a good defence in trespass to goods.

NOTE
  (*i*) Carefully distinguish an action in *trespass* for a *direct* injury due to negligence from an action in *negligence* arising from breach of a duty of care (*see* VI).
  (*ii*) Do not be misled by the above into thinking that *mistake* is a defence. The general rule that mistake is no defence in tort applies to trespass to goods.

4. Four actions. Possession of chattels is protected by the following actions:
  (*a*) Trespass to goods.
  (*b*) Conversion.
  (*c*) Detinue.
  (*d*) Replevin.

27

TRESPASS TO GOODS

5. Definition and meaning.

(a) *Possession is essential* because it is the sole basis of the plaintiff's right. *Only* the person in possession of the goods at the time of the alleged trespass can bring the action.

NOTE: Because possession is the sole basis of the plaintiff's right, the defence of *jus tertii* is excluded.

Armory v. *Delamirie* (1921). A boy *found* a jewel, which he gave to a goldsmith to be valued. The goldsmith refused to return the jewel. The boy sued him in trover. HELD: The boy, as possessor of title to the goods, could maintain the action. The goldsmith could not raise the *jus tertii, i.e.* the better title of the original owner.

The "Winkfield" (1902). The *Winkfield* negligently sank a mailship. The Postmaster General sued the *Winkfield's* owners in respect of the lost mails. HELD: The P.M.G., although not the owner of the mails, could nevertheless sue as *bailee in possession*. "As between bailee and stranger possession gives title": *per* Collins M.R.

(b) Possession *normally* means personal physical custody by the possessor. However, a master has legal possession of goods in the custody of his servant, *except* where the servant receives them from a stranger and withholds them from the master's possession. An *executor* or *administrator* is treated as having possession of the deceased's goods between his death and the grant of probate or letters of administration. A *trustee not in possession* is also treated as having possession for the purpose of bringing trespass against third parties.

6. Defences to trespass to goods.
The defences to an action for trespass to goods are as follows:

(a) *Protection of persons or property.* A direct injury to goods is not a trespass if done to avert immediate danger to persons or property. The onus is on the defendant to justify his conduct. He must show (*i*) that the danger was real and imminent; (*ii*) that he acted reasonably in the circumstances: *Creswell* v. *Sirl* (1947), *Hamps* v. *Darby* (1948).

(b) *Exercise of a legal right.* It is no trespass to interfere with goods in levying lawful distress for rent, or distress damage feasant, or in carrying out any legal process.

CONVERSION

7. Definition. Conversion consists of *a wilful and wrongful interference* with the goods of one *entitled to possession* of them, in such a way as to *deny his right* to that possession, or in a manner *inconsistent with such right*. The right to immediate possession is the determining factor: *i.e.* if the *right* exists, *actual* possession is unnecessary.

North Central Wagon and Finance Co. Ltd. v. *Graham* (1950). One C instructed the defendant G to sell his (C's) car, in breach of a hire-purchase agreement, thus entitling the finance company to terminate the hiring. When G sold the car the company sued him for conversion. HELD: They could succeed, as they became entitled to immediate possession of the car as soon as C broke the hire-purchase agreement.

8. Two or more claimants. Possession for the purpose of conversion may be difficult to determine where more than one person claims it. The court must then decide which claimant had the *greater degree of control* at the material time. There is no general rule, cases being treated on their merits according to the circumstances. The following cases are illustrative.

Bridges v. *Hawksworth* (1851). The plaintiff found some bank-notes on the floor of a shop, and gave them to the proprietor for him to return to the true owner. The latter was never discovered. HELD: The finder of goods in a shop open to the public has a good title against everyone but the true owner.

Elwes v. *Brigg Gas Co.* (1886). The Gas Company were lessees of land. They discovered a prehistoric boat beneath its surface. HELD: A lessee has a good title against his lessor of ownerless things found on the land.

Hannah v. *Peel* (1945). A soldier found a valuable brooch in a requisitioned house in which he was billeted. The owner of the house had never occupied it, and had no knowledge of the brooch, the true owner of which could not be found. HELD: In these circumstances the finder (the soldier) had a better title than the owner of the house.

NOTE: Although in the case of dispute between the finder of goods and the lessee, the lessee has a better title, the *owner* may have an *equitable* title better than that of the lessee: *London Corporation* v. *Appleyard* (1963).

9. Denial of possession essential. Mere possession of goods without title does not constitute their conversion *unless* possession is thereby denied to the person entitled to it—by refusal to surrender them to him, or by wrongfully disposing of them. Thus, it is not in itself conversion to receive goods in good faith by way of pledge or deposit.

10. Innocent delivery not conversion. It is not conversion if an innocent holder of goods (*e.g.* a carrier or warehouseman), who receives them in good faith from one whom he believed to have lawful possession of them, delivers them, on the latter's instructions, to a third party. The test is: Did the innocent holder merely transmit the goods, without affecting the property in them? *Hollins* v. *Fowler* (1875).

11. Reception by purchase. At common law conversion *is* committed by one who *buys and takes delivery of* goods from a seller without title to them. This is in accordance with the rule that acts of ownership are exercised at the doer's peril.

12. Who can sue? It follows from the above that anyone in actual possession or entitled to immediate possession can sue in conversion. Thus a bailee and his bailor can sue, as can a person with a lien on the goods: but an owner out of possession cannot sue.

13. The interference must be wilful and wrongful. If the defendant's conduct is less than such interference, *e.g.* is merely negligent, it will not amount to conversion.

> *Ashby* v. *Tolhurst* (1937). Defendant's car-park attendant negligently allowed a stranger to remove plaintiff's car. HELD: No conversion by the car-park proprietor, as his servant had not wilfully and wrongfully interfered with plaintiff's goods, nor acted inconsistently with his title to them.

14. Types of conversion. Conversion may be committed in the following ways:

(a) *By wrongfully taking the goods.* To amount to conversion, the taking must be accompanied by an *intention to exercise temporary or permanent dominion* over the goods.

Foulds v. *Willoughby* (1841). Plaintiff's horses were removed by defendant from his ferry boat, whereby plaintiff lost possession of the horses. HELD: Plaintiff could not succeed in trover as the defendant's act, being unaccompanied by an intention to exercise dominion, was not conversion, but merely trespass *de bonis asportatis*.

(*b*) *By wrongfully detaining the goods.* Detention constitutes conversion only if accompanied by an intention to keep the goods from the person entitled to possession of them. Thus it is not conversion if the finder of a chattel, or a bailee after the expiry of the bailment, merely refrains from returning it to the person entitled to possession. For conversion to be committed there must be *some positive denial of possession to the person entitled to it*, *e.g.* by refusing to surrender the chattel to him.

(*c*) *By wrongfully destroying the goods.* Destruction amounts to conversion if (*i*) one person *wilfully* destroys the chattel of another; (*ii*) the chattel either ceases to exist or changes its identity, as, *e.g.*, when yarn is made into cloth. Mere damage cannot be conversion.

(*d*) *By wrongfully disposing of the goods.* Conversion by wrongful disposition consists of so dealing with chattels as to confer a good title to them on someone other than the person originally entitled to it, adversely to the latter. Thus, since the *Hire Purchase Act*, 1964, if a person with a motor car on hire purchase sells it to another without revealing that it is on hire purchase, the buyer gets a good title adverse to the hirer, and the seller commits conversion.

(*e*) *By wrongfully delivering the goods.* Conversion by wrongful delivery occurs when one denies possession of goods to the person lawfully entitled to it, by wrongfully delivering them to another.

Hollins v. *Fowler* (1875). After complicated dealings, cotton lawfully belonging to F came into the hands of H, a broker. H, genuinely but mistakenly believing that he had a good title to the cotton, delivered it to a client, who spun it into yarn. HELD: H had converted the cotton.

15. Conversion of documents. The *value* of a cheque is not a *chattel*, and therefore incapable of conversion. The difficulty is avoided by regarding the cheque itself, *i.e.* the piece of paper as the converted chattel: *Lloyds Bank* v. *Chartered Bank*

(1929). Note that this rule is not confined to negotiable instruments.

16. Effectual defences.

(a) A defendant in conversion may traverse, *e.g.* aver that he had mere custody of the goods.

(b) He may show that the plaintiff had *no or insufficient possession* to maintain conversion, *e.g.* that he was an owner out of possession, or that his right to possession was not immediate.

(c) *Contributory negligence* is also probably a defence (*see* VI, **30**).

17. Ineffectual defences.

(a) *Mistake.* Mistake is no defence, on general principles.

(b) *Plaintiff's default.* The general rule is that the plaintiff's negligence is no defence in conversion, unless it amounted to a breach of a duty of care owed to the defendant. However, the authorities for the rule are all pre-1945, and the *Law Reform (Contributory Negligence) Act,* 1945, probably applies to conversion, although the point is not settled.

(c) *Damage too remote.* It is immaterial that the defendant did not intend to deprive the plaintiff of his goods, or that such was not the natural or probable result of his act: *Hiort* v. *Bott* (1874). However, an involuntary bailee commits conversion only if his wrongful dealing with the goods was also negligent: *Elvin and Powell Ltd.* v. *Plummer, Roddis Ltd.* (1933).

(d) *Defendant acted for another.* A person may be liable in conversion although he wrongfully interfered with the goods merely as the servant or agent of another—unless he was "a mere conduit pipe": *Hollins* v. *Fowler* (1875).

> *Consolidated Co.* v. *Curtis* (1892). A lady assigned furniture to the plaintiffs by bill of sale, but subsequently instructed the defendants (auctioneers) to sell the furniture—which they did, in ignorance of the assignment. HELD: The defendants were liable in conversion, as they knowingly affected the title to the goods.
>
> NOTE: It is no defence that the plaintiff was not permanently deprived of the goods. The duration of the dispossession is relevant to damages only.

DETINUE

18. Definition.

(a) *The goods must be withheld.* The essence of detinue is the fact of *withholding* the goods from the person entitled to immediate possession of them. The element of *detention* is essential.

> NOTE: Detention means refusal to allow repossession by one entitled to take it. Detinue is not committed merely by refusal to *return* the goods.

(b) *Regaining chattels.* Detinue is the appropriate action when *return of the chattel* is desired, rather than damages. However, damages can be obtained for failure to allow repossession; and also damages for the *detention* in any case.

> *General & Finance Facilities Ltd.* v. *Cook's Cars (Romford) Ltd.* (1963). "An action in detinue today may result in a judgment in one of three different forms: for the value of the chattel as assessed and damages for its detention; for return of the chattel or recovery of its value as assessed and damages for its detention; or for return of the chattel and damages for its detention": *per* Diplock L.J.

19. Detinue distinguished from conversion. Detinue or conversion may be used in the alternative where there is a *denial of title* (which is essential for conversion), *e.g.* when a bailee refuses to deliver up the goods. However, because there can be no conversion unless there is a denial of title, detinue (but not conversion) will lie for the act of a bailee (*e.g.* damaging the goods) which does not deny the plaintiff's title.

20. Present possession by defendant not essential. Detinue will lie against one who had possession of the chattel adversely to the plaintiff, but wrongfully parted with it before the action was brought: *Jones* v. *Dowle* (1841). It is a good defence, however, that the defendant lost possession through no fault of his own, but the onus is on him to show this affirmatively.

RECAPTION AND REPLEVIN

21. Recaption. At common law a person may retake, with the minimum necessary force, goods of which he was wrongfully deprived. For this purpose he may peaceably enter upon the land of one who took the goods.

22. Replevin. This lies where goods have been wrongfully taken or detained by way of distress for rent or distress damage feasant—although it is not, in theory, confined to such cases. The object of replevin, which is now practically obsolescent, was to secure return of the goods pending the trial of the action.

PROGRESS TEST 3

1. Of what does trespass to chattels consist? What effects had *N.C.B.* v. *Evans* (1951) on the rules governing trespass to chattels? **(1–3)**

2. Outline the essentials of the action for trespass to goods. Illustrate by decided cases. What defences are there to such an action? **(5–6)**

3. Define conversion. **(7)**

4. Explain the importance of *possession* in the rules governing conversion. Illustrate by decided cases. **(7–9)**

5. Can innocent delivery be conversion? What is the test of innocent delivery? **(10)**

6. Can a bailee sue for conversion? **(12)**

7. In what ways may conversion be committed? Outline the rules governing each of these ways. **(14)**

8. Can a cheque be converted? **(15)**

9. List (a) the effectual, (b) the ineffectual, defences in conversion. **(16, 17)**

10. (a) To what extent (if at all) does the *Law Reform (Contributory Negligence) Act*, 1945, apply to conversion? (b) Can an involuntary bailee commit conversion? (c) What are the effects of *Hollins* v. *Fowler* (1875) and *Consolidated Co.* v. *Curtis* (1892)? **(17)**

11. What are the essentials of detinue? How is it distinguished from conversion? **(18, 19)**

12. What are the essentials of recaption and replevin? **(21, 22)**

CHAPTER IV

TRESPASS TO THE PERSON

DEFINITION AND CHARACTERISTICS

1. Definition. Trespass to the person may consist of:

(*a*) assault and battery;
(*b*) false imprisonment.

2. Assault and battery.

(*a*) Assault and battery may be distinguished in this way. Battery is the application of unlawful force to the person of another; assault is the putting of any person *in reasonable fear of immediate battery*.

(*b*) An act may be an assault although the defendant lacked the power to inflict violence, *e.g.* defendant pointed gun which he, but not the plaintiff, knew was unloaded.

(*c*) An act will not be an assault unless it causes *reasonable fear of immediate violence*. There is no assault where, *e.g.* the plaintiff could not see the threatening action, but merely learnt of it afterwards. Similarly, if the defendant was so far distant from the plaintiff that he could not inflict an *immediate* battery, there is no assault.

(*d*) Must a plaintiff in assault and battery show *intention* or *negligence* by the defendant? Battery derives from trespass, not case, so that its incidence depends on whether the injury was *direct*, not on whether it was accompanied by intention or negligence.

However, it was held in *Fowler* v. *Lanning* (1959) that proof of intention or negligence *is* essential to success in trespass to the person; but in view of the fact that *Fowler* v. *Lanning* was settled at first instance, and its approval by the Court of Appeal in *Cooper* v. *Letang* (1964) was merely *obiter*, the point cannot be regarded as finally settled.

(*e*) *Assault and battery are crimes.* In general, civil and criminal proceedings can take place concurrently: but *summary* conviction or acquittal for an assault or battery bars civil proceedings in respect of it.

3. False imprisonment

(a) False imprisonment consists of *wrongful deprivation of personal liberty* in *any* form, *i.e.* not necessarily by force or incarceration. Unlawful prevention of egress suffices; so does restraint by merely moral pressure.

Warner v. *Riddiford* (1858). Defendant, after dismissing plaintiff as resident manager of a beer-house, prevented his going upstairs to collect belongings. HELD: This amounted to false imprisonment.

(b) *The deprivation must be complete.* It is not false imprisonment if the plaintiff had any *reasonable* means of leaving, *e.g.* if his path was barred in one direction, but not in another. It would be *unreasonable* restraint if, *e.g.* a person was physically free to leave, but had been deprived of his clothes.

Bird v. *Jones* (1845). Defendants blocked one side of Hammersmith Bridge to form a grandstand for a boat race, thus preventing plaintiff's passage. Plaintiff remained in the enclosure for some time, and refused to cross by the opposite path. HELD: No false imprisonment, as he had reasonable means of leaving.

(c) Mere failure to facilitate the egress of persons on one's premises is not in itself false imprisonment.

Herd v. *Weardale Steel, Coke & Coal Co.* (1915). A miner, in breach of his contract of service, demanded to be taken out of the mine. Defendants denied him use of the lift, thereby detaining him against his will. HELD: *Volenti non fit injuria* applied, and there was no false imprisonment.

(d) Plaintiff need not know he is restrained. A person may be falsely imprisoned without his knowledge.

Meering v. *Grahame White Aviation Co. Ltd.* (1919). Employee of respondent company, who was suspected of theft, agreed to wait in a room with two security officers. He was not told he was free to leave, although such was in fact the case. HELD: False imprisonment. A person can be imprisoned without knowing it.

(*e*) A person who enters a police station, on his own initiative or by invitation of police officers, will be falsely imprisoned if detained against his will except by lawful arrest, *e.g.* by a false pretence that he is not free to go.

DEFENCES

4. Self-defence.

(*a*) A person may use *reasonable*, *i.e.* necessary and *proportionate* force to defend himself or *any other person* against unlawful violence. Note, however, that "necessary" and "proportionate" are not synonymous. Force may be disproportionate although necessary. Thus, trivial violence cannot be warded off by a fatal blow, even though it could not be repelled in any other way; but "if you are attacked with a deadly weapon you can defend yourself with a deadly weapon": *Turner* v. *M.G.M. Pictures Ltd.* (1950), *per* Lord Oaksey.

(*b*) It is not necessary, in order to justify violent self-defence, to warn of one's intention to use it. Furthermore the defender, if in reasonable fear of immediate battery, may lawfully strike the first blow.

5. Preservation of the public peace.
What would otherwise be a trespass to the person may be justified if done to support the law or maintain the peace. The onus is on the defendant to prove that he acted for those objects.

(*a*) *Lawful arrest*. Force may be justified if used to affect a lawful arrest. The rules are as follows.

(*i*) *Any person* may arrest without warrant for a breach of the peace *committed in his presence*—or if he reasonably anticipates a renewal of such breach. A *police officer* may forcibly arrest without warrant if he reasonably apprehends an *imminent* breach of the peace. In cases of unlawful assembly or riot *any subject* has a duty to use such force—even fatal force—as is *reasonably* necessary to restore the peace.

(*ii*) *Any subject* has the right to arrest with reasonable force for felony, for treason, or to preserve life; but the onus is on the arrester to show *reasonable and probable* cause.

(*iii*) A *constable* can justify an arrest with reasonable force by showing *reasonable* suspicion of felony. A private person can justify such an arrest only by showing that the felony was *committed*.

(*iv*) There is no *common-law power* to arrest without warrant for misdemeanour, although numerous statutes confer such power on police officers.

(*b*) *Other justifiable force.* A private person may lawfully use force in the following circumstances:

(*i*) to arrest a person escaping from lawful custody;

(*ii*) to arrest a mentally deranged person endangering himself or others;

(*iii*) in aid of police or other law officers performing their duties.

6. Prevention of trespass. An occupier of land (*i.e.* one having exclusive possession) may use reasonable force to repel, eject or control a trespasser.

Harrison v. *Duke of Rutland* (1893). The plaintiff owned the soil of a highway which traversed his grouse moor. The plaintiff remained for some time on the highway for the purpose of diverting grouse from the butts. Defendant's servant restrained him with minimum force. HELD: Plaintiff's unreasonable use of the highway made him a trespasser thereon, therefore the forcible restraint was justified.

7. Consent of the plaintiff. On general principles, it is a good defence that the plaintiff consented to the trespass; but consent to personal violence (especially if unilateral) is difficult to establish.

8. Reasonable chastisement.

(*a*) It is no trespass for a *parent* to administer *reasonable* chastisement to his child under 21. Furthermore, parental authority is delegated to schoolteachers, who may therefore also administer reasonable chastisement or other punishment.

(*b*) The master of a ship may arrest or imprison with reasonable force if he *reasonably* believes it necessary to preserve order or safeguard passengers.

Hook v. *Cunard Steamship Co. Ltd.* (1953). The captain of the *Queen Mary* imprisoned the plaintiff (a steward) on suspicion of his having indecently assaulted a child passenger.

HELD: The plaintiff could succeed for false imprisonment, the captain having failed to establish that his action was reasonably necessary to preserve order and safety.

9. Inevitable accident. It is well established that inevitable accident is a good defence in trespass: see *Stanley* v. *Powell* (1893) and *N.C.B.* v. *Evans* (1951). Note, however, that these decisions have been heavily criticised, and that the point has not been submitted to the House of Lords.

PROGRESS TEST 4

1. What is the distinction between assault and battery? Must the defendant have been capable of inflicting violence? Must the plaintiff have been in fear? **(2)**

2. To what extent (if at all) must a plaintiff in trespass to the person show intention or negligence by the defendant? **(2)**

3. Is there any bar to civil proceedings for assault and battery? **(2)**

4. What constitutes false imprisonment? What was decided by (a) *Bird* v. *Jones* (1845); (b) *Herd* v. *Weardale Steel etc. Co.* (1915)? **(3)**

5. List the possible defences against an action for trespass to the person. **(4–9)**

6. What are the rules governing self-defence? **(4)**

7. Outline the rules governing the use of force in making arrests. Are there any other circumstances in which force is justifiable? **(5)**

8. Explain the defences of (a) prevention of trespass; (b) consent of the plaintiff; (c) exercise of parental authority; (d) inevitable accident, as they apply to trespass to the person. **(6–9)**

CHAPTER V

NUISANCE

NATURE OF NUISANCE

1. Public or private nuisance. A nuisance may be *public* or *private*.

(*a*) A public nuisance, *e.g.* obstructing a highway, keeping a brothel, is a crime.

(*b*) A public nuisance may *also* be a private nuisance and a tort: but to prevent multiplicity of actions a public nuisance is actionable as a tort only by one who has suffered *particular* damage over and above that suffered by the public at large.

> *Campbell* v. *Paddington Corporation* (1911). The Corporation committed the public nuisance of obstructing the highway with a grandstand from which to view the coronation procession of Edward VII, thus preventing the plaintiff letting her windows for that purpose. HELD: She could recover damages for private nuisance.

(*c*) A nuisance will not be public *unless* the number of persons affected is sufficiently large to constitute a *class*. This is a question of *fact*—which may be decided by enquiring whether the nuisance was "so widespread in its range or indiscriminate in its effects that it would not be reasonable to expect one person to take steps to put a stop to it." *A.-G.* v. *P.Y.A. Quarries Ltd.* (1957), *per* Romer L.J. (widespread nuisance from blasting and other quarrying operations).

> NOTE: Some nuisances are forbidden by statute, *e.g. Public Health Act*, 1936; *Clean Air Act*, 1956; *Noise Abatement Act*, 1960.

2. Essence of nuisance. Nuisance is governed by the common-law maxim: *sic utere tuo ut alienum non laedas*—"So use your own property as not to injure your neighbour's." The

essence of the tort of nuisance, therefore, is that the plaintiff
is adversely affected in his use or enjoyment of *land*, or of some
right over or interest in land: except that a plaintiff who
alleges particular damage arising from a public nuisance need
have no interest in land. Thus, for instance, *smoke, smells,
noise and vibration may all be actionable* as nuisances; but this
will depend on the circumstances and the nature of the
defendant's conduct. Not every such phenomenon is an
actionable nuisance, for the law requires reasonable give and
take among neighbours.

3. **Examples of actionable nuisances.** Only a few can be
noted here.

(*a*) Tree roots grew under neighbouring land: *Butler* v.
Standard Telephones and Cables Ltd. (1940).

(*b*) Overhanging branches grew over neighbouring land:
Lemmon v. *Webb* (1895).

(*c*) Smoke: *Crump* v. *Lambert* (1867).

(*d*) Destructive animals: *Farrer* v. *Nelson* (1885).

(*e*) Unreasonable noise: *Christie* v. *Davey* (1893).

(*f*) Vibration: *Hoare & Co.* v. *McAlpine* (1923).

The list is well-nigh inexhaustible—"*Nocumenta
infinita sunt*" (Bracton).

NOTE: *Injuries to servitudes.* An activity may be actionable
as a nuisance if it adversely affects a servitude, such as a
right to light, air or support. It is submitted, however, that
this is a matter of real-property law rather than tort.

4. **Nuisance distinguished from other torts.**

(*a*) For historical reasons nuisance and trespass are
mutually exclusive. Trespass lies only for *direct* interference
with land; nuisance only for *indirect* interference.

(*b*) Nuisance and negligence overlap. Although many
actions in nuisance arise from intentional acts, for which
negligence does not lie, many also arise from the defendant's
inadvertence; and in these cases both nuisance and negligence may be relied on.

(*c*) Nuisance also overlaps with the Rule in *Rylands* v.
Fletcher (*see* VIII, **6**).

5. Nuisance and damage. Nuisance is not actionable *per se*. Therefore the plaintiff must prove damage, except in the following cases:

(*a*) Where the facts are such that damage can be presumed, the presumption will suffice; *e.g.* where a roof projects over adjoining land, damage from dripping water may be presumed. *Fay* v. *Prentice* (1845).

(*b*) In the case of nuisance affecting a servitude proof is not required; for, if the plaintiff were debarred from action merely by lack of proof of damage, his acquiesence for twenty years might, by creating a prescription in favour of the servient tenement, permanently extinguish the right of action.

(*c*) Where a nuisance affects a right absolutely protected, then, by analogy with the rule in trespass, proof of damage is not essential. *Nicholls* v. *Ely Beet Sugar Factory Ltd.* (1949), *per* Lord Wright.

(*d*) An injunction (*see* XVII, **23**) may be had in a *quia timet* action where imminent danger is reasonably feared.

PRIVATE NUISANCE

6. Definition. Private nuisance consists essentially of *damage* to the plaintiff arising from *unlawful interference* with his use or enjoyment of *land* of which he is the owner or occupier.

Spicer v. *Smee* (1946). Plaintiff's bungalow was destroyed through defective wiring in defendant's adjoining bungalow. HELD: Plaintiff could succeed in nuisance. "Private nuisance arises out of a state of things on one man's property whereby his neighbour's property is exposed to danger": *per* Atkinson J.

7. Interference must be unreasonable and substantial.

(*a*) Interference will be unlawful only if it is *unreasonable*; for "a balance has to be maintained between the right of the occupier to do what he likes with his own, and the right of his neighbour not to be interfered with": *Sedleigh–Denfield* v. *O'Callaghan* (1940), *per* Lord Wright.

(*b*) However, interference will *not* be unreasonable unless it is *substantial*, "not merely according to elegant or dainty modes and habits of living, but according to plain and sober and simple notions among the English people": *Walter* v. *Self* (1851), *per* Knight–Bruce V.C.

> NOTE: The requirement of reasonableness is *not* the same as that of reasonable care in negligence (*see* VI, 15). One who takes reasonable (or even extreme) care may nevertheless commit nuisance if, despite his care, another's use or enjoyment of his land is adversely affected.

8. Reasonableness a question of fact.

The reasonableness of an act is a question of *fact* to be determined in accordance with the circumstances, *e.g.* time, place and manner of commission, the presence or absence of malice, whether the effects are transitory or permanent, the state of scientific knowledge at the time.

> *Manchester Corporation* v. *Farnworth* (1930). Escape of fumes. "The onus of proving that the result is inevitable is on those who wish to escape liability for nuisance, but the criterion of inevitability is . . . what is possible, according to the state of scientific knowledge at the time, having also in view a certain commonsense appreciation, which cannot be rigidly defined, of practical feasibility in view of situation and of expense": *per* Lord Dunedin.

> *St. Helens Smelting Co.* v. *Tipping* (1863). Physical damage to property by the emission of fumes. "The law does not regard trifling inconveniences; everything must be looked at from a reasonable point of view. . . . the time, locality and all the circumstances should be taken into consideration": *per* Lord Westbury L.C.

9. Abnormal sensitivity.

Abnormal sensitivity of property or persons is immaterial to the question of reasonableness (*see* VIII, 14).

> *Robinson* v. *Kilvert* (1889). Defendant heated a cellar, thereby damaging plaintiff's unusually sensitive brown paper on the floor above. The heat would not have damaged paper generally. HELD: No nuisance.

> *Heath* v. *Mayor of Brighton* (1908). The incumbent of a church alleged nuisance by noise from adjacent power station. The noise was not excessive and the congregation had neither diminished nor complained. HELD: No nuisance; injunction refused.

But carefully distinguish the effect of abnormal sensitivity *before* and *after* nuisance has been established: for, although abnormal sensitivity is not taken into account in deciding whether the interference was substantial, *once the nuisance has been established*, the remedies of damages and injunction will extend to abnormally delicate or sensitive operations, *e.g.* the growing of orchids: *McKinnon Industries Ltd.* v. *Walker* (1951), a Privy Council case.

10. Duration of the interference. The duration of the interference is relevant—*but only* in conjunction with the other circumstances—to whether it was substantial. In general, the fact that the interference was merely temporary or intermittent will be evidence (but no more) that it was reasonable. But a permanent or continuous interference may be lawful; and a transitory or intermittent (even a momentary) interference may be a nuisance. In fact, however, most private nuisances consist of a lengthy interference with the enjoyment of property.

Leeman v. *Montague* (1936). Cocks crowed for weeks in a residential area. HELD: A nuisance; damages and injunction.

Castle v. *St. Augustines Links* (1922). Golf balls were repeatedly hit into the highway. HELD: *A public* nuisance. Plaintiff, who had lost an eye, recovered for *private* nuisance.

Bolton v. *Stone* (1951). Cricket balls were hit into highway about six times in thirty years. HELD: No nuisance (or negligence).

Dollman v. *Hillman Ltd.* (1941). Plaintiff injured by slipping on a piece of fat outside defendant's shop. HELD: Although it was a single occurrence, defendant liable in nuisance and negligence.

Midwood v. *Mayor of Manchester* (1905). An isolated and instantaneous occurrence may be a nuisance. The defendant corporation allowed gas to accumulate. HELD: The resultant explosion was a nuisance.

11. Malice in nuisance.

(*a*) An act not otherwise a nuisance may become one if done *maliciously* in order to annoy the plaintiff.

Christie v. *Davey* (1893). Defendant created a din whenever his neighbour gave music lessons. HELD: A nuisance, because defendant acted deliberately and maliciously to annoy the plaintiff; injunction.

Hollywood Silver Fox Farm Ltd. v. *Emmett* (1936). Defendant, out of spite, fired guns near the fox farm, thereby damaging breeding vixens. HELD: although defendant fired the guns on his own land, he was liable in nuisance because he acted maliciously; damages and injunction.

Palmer v. *Loader* (1962). Perpetual injunction to restrain noise maliciously intended to interfere with plaintiff's enjoyment of her flat.

Stoakes v. *Brydges* (1958). Defendant, because of a grievance against the plaintiff, persistently telephoned the latter. HELD: A nuisance, for "you are not entitled to abate a nuisance by creating another": *per* Bramwell B. in *Barnford* v. *Turnley* (1862).

(*b*) At first sight, these cases may seem difficult to reconcile with *Bradford Corporation* v. *Pickles* (1895), in which it was held that a malicious motive does not make a lawful act unlawful; but in the cases above the effect of the defendant's malice was to make his conduct *unreasonable* and therefore a nuisance.

NOTE: Although malice may sometimes make an otherwise innocent act a nuisance, malice by the defendant is *not essential* to an action in nuisance—as it is, for example, in malicious prosecution (*see* XVIII, 2–7).

NUISANCE TO HIGHWAYS

12. Who is responsible?

(*a*) *The duty to repair.* At common law, this duty lay on the inhabitants of the parish; but the *Highways Act*, 1959, finally transferred it to the Minister of Transport or the appropriate local authority. By *s.* 59 notice to repair may be served on the authority; and application may be made to a magistrates' court for an order to the authority to repair.

(*b*) *Former immunities abolished.* The *Highways* (*Miscellaneous Provisions*) *Act*, 1961, abolished the immunities of the Minister of Transport and local authorities from civil liability arising from:

(*i*) public nuisance on a highway;

(*ii*) *non-feasance* in the repair of a highway.

These provisions came into effect on 3 August 1964 (but do not apply to damage due to an occurrence before that date).

Noble v. *Harrison* (1926): Defendant's tree, which overhung the highway, collapsed and damaged plaintiff's motor coach. HELD: No liability in nuisance; to grow trees is a natural use of land, and the defendant could not reasonably have known or discovered the latent defect. Thus "*Noble* v. *Harrison* saved the beautiful hedgerows of the English countryside."

13. Artificial projections. The liability of an occupier for injury to persons on the highway through the collapse of, *e.g.*, a lamp or sign is not entirely settled, but is certainly stricter than in the case of a natural projection. The present position is apparently as follows:

Tarry v. *Ashton* (1876). This was a case in which a projecting lamp injured plaintiff on highway. It was decided that if the defendant knew of the latent defect he is liable in nuisance, even though he employed a seemingly competent independent contractor to repair the defect. *Tarry* v. *Ashton* was considered by the Court of Appeal in *Wringe* v. *Cohen*.

Wringe v. *Cohen* (1940). This was a case of similar facts but not directly in point as it concerned a projection over private property. *Dicta* in this case, however, strongly suggested that the defendant in *Tarry* v. *Ashton* would have been liable even if she had not known of the defect. It seems to be the better opinion, therefore, that liability in nuisance in respect of artificial projections is almost as strict as in the Rule in *Rylands* v. *Fletcher*.

14. Trees. An owner of land is liable in nuisance if his trees encroach upon adjoining land, the occupier of which may abate the nuisance by lopping branches or curtailing roots: *Davey* v. *Harrow Corporation* (1958).

(a) The immunity in respect of non-feasance applied only to those authorities which were the successors of the inhabitants at large; it did not apply, for example, to dock, railway and canal companies.

(b) The 1961 Act further provides that it shall be a defence to an authority alleged to have inadequately maintained a highway that the authority had taken *all reasonable care* to ensure the highway was safe for traffic. In deciding this, the court shall take account, *inter alia*, of the character of the highway; the traffic normally to be expected on it; the appropriate standard of maintenance; whether the authority could reasonably have known the highway was

defective; whether adequate warning had been given when
repairs could not be done at once.

15. Nuisance by obstruction of the highway.
A temporary
obstruction, *e.g.* by a delivery van or repairs to mains services,
is not a nuisance, if it is reasonable in amount and duration.
A permanent obstruction is not *necessarily* a nuisance.

NOTE: There will be no nuisance *unless* there is an *obstruction*.
In the absence of obstruction, liability (if any) will be in negligence. "Where the law of negligence will suffice to determine
liability the less one hears of nuisance the better": *per* Adams J.
in *Everitt* v. *Martin* (1953), a New Zealand case.

Trevett v. *Lee* (1955). Householder laid half-inch hosepipe
across road to supply water during a drought. HELD: No
nuisance, as user reasonable in the circumstances.

16. Loss of custom.
An obstruction may be a nuisance
because it causes loss of custom to a tradesman; but only if the
person affected suffers *special* harm. He will have no action
in nuisance if the harm he suffers is no greater than that of
other occupiers adjacent to the highway.

The authorities on this point, which go back to *Wilkes* v.
Hungerford Market Co. (1835)—a case in which a bookseller
recovered damages for private nuisance on the grounds that
an obstruction diverted his customers—are somewhat con-
flicting; but the better modern opinion seems to be that
nuisance is maintainable in these circumstances. *Unreasonable
obstruction by a queue* constitutes a nuisance by one outside
whose premises it forms.

Lyons, Sons & Co. v. *Gulliver* (1914). Long queues, five deep,
remained outside a theatre for lengthy periods. HELD: A
nuisance to the proprietor of adjoining premises.
Fabri v. *Morris* (1947). A queue is an obstruction if due to an
unusual method of selling—in this case, the sale of ice-cream
through a shop window.

But a proprietor of premises will not be liable for obstruction
by a queue for which he was not responsible: *e.g.* in *Dwyer* v.
Mansfield (1947) the queue was due to wartime shortages.

17. Passage along a highway.
The *public* right of passage
along a highway is a higher right than the *private* right of

access from adjoining premises; but the former will not automatically or invariably prevail; the reasonable exercise of *both* rights is legally permissible. Note that the same interference may affect *both* the public right of passage *and* the private right of access: *Rose* v. *Groves* (1843).

(*a*) The mere fact that something *projects* over the highway from adjacent land does not, in itself, constitute a private nuisance. This rule does not apply, however, to a projection over private property, as the rights of the occupier are much wider.

(*b*) Where a user of the highway is injured by something *naturally* on adjacent land, *e.g.* a tree, the occupier will not be liable *unless* he knew or ought reasonably to have known of the defect which caused the projection to collapse.

WHO CAN SUE?

18. Who can sue in nuisance? It follows from the fact that a nuisance is essentially an interference with the use or enjoyment of *land* that only one with some *title* to the property affected can sue. Possession or occupation is therefore the test: "The plaintiff in order to maintain an action must show some title to the thing to which the nuisance is alleged to be": *Cunard* v. *Antifyre Ltd.* (1933).

(*a*) *The occupier.* The owner in possession can always sue in nuisance.

(*b*) *Tenants.* A tenant for a term of years can sue in nuisance, subject to the following:

(*i*) He cannot sue if he has *assigned* the lease: *Metropolitan Properties Ltd.* v. *Jones* (1939).

(*ii*) A *yearly* tenant under notice to quit cannot get an injunction except for very substantial damage, but is restricted to an action for damages.

(*iii*) Possibly even a *weekly* tenant can get an injunction (in addition to damages) for a substantial injury to health or comfort.

(*c*) *Reversioners.* A reversioner can sue for a *permanent* injury to his property, *e.g.* structural damage through vibration—*Colwell* v. *St. Pancras Borough Council* (1904)—but not for temporary interference, *e.g.* by smoke or smells.

(*d*) *Persons on the highway.* A person on the highway can

sue in nuisance if he suffers special damage. A few examples of nuisances affecting the highway may be noted: *Dollman* v. *Hillman Ltd.* (1941)—Fat from butcher's shop a nuisance on pavement.

Holling v. *Yorkshire Traction Co. Ltd.* (1948) Smoke and steam from coke ovens adjoining the highway.

See also *Bolton* v. *Stone* (1950) and *Castle* v. *St. Augustine's Links* (1921).

19. Who cannot sue? A person with neither possession nor proprietory interest in the land affected, *e.g.* members of the occupier's family, servants, guests or lodgers, cannot sue in nuisance: *Malone* v. *Laskey* (1907).

WHO CAN BE SUED?

20. The creator of the nuisance. One who creates a nuisance by *misfeasance* is *strictly* liable in respect of its creation and continuance, *even if not in occupation* of the land from which it emanates. It is no defence that he could not abate the nuisance without trespassing: nor is it a defence to a continuing nuisance that all possible care and skill had been directed to its prevention: *Rapier* v. *London Tramways Ltd.* (1893).

21. An occupier who fails to repair. An occupier (and sometimes the owner) is *strictly* liable for nuisance due to failure to repair premises adjoining the highway, *i.e.* in such a case he will be liable whether or not he knew or ought to have known of the danger.

Wringe v. *Cohen* (1940). Part of respondent's house, which abutted on the highway, had collapsed because of disrepair and damaged appellant's adjoining property. Respondent did not occupy the premises, but was responsible for repairs. HELD: Respondent liable although he neither knew nor had the means of knowing of the disrepair.

22. An occupier who himself creates a nuisance. He is liable during his occupancy. He may also be liable for a nuisance created by *someone else* on the premises, or by a previous occupier (*see* **23** below).

23. Nuisance created by other persons lawfully on the premises. The occupier is responsible for:

　　(a) nuisances created by his servants or agents;

　　(b) nuisances due to *anyone under his control*, *e.g.* his family and guests; independent contractors and their servants; those whom he allows on the premises: *A.-G.* v. *Stone* (1895), in which an occupier was liable for nuisance created by gypsies permitted to camp on his land.

24. Independent contractors. One who orders work to be done which in the ordinary course of events is likely to cause nuisance cannot by employing another exempt himself from his responsibility to take reasonable steps to prevent the nuisance. This is one of the exceptions to the general rule that a person is not responsible for the torts of his independent contractor.

The exception applies particularly to dangerous or extraordinary interferences with highways, creating a risk clearly greater than those arising from normal repairs.

Hole v. *Sittingbourne Railway* (1861). The railway company had statutory authority to build a swing bridge. Their independent contractor built it so badly it would not open. HELD: The railway company was liable.

Matania v. *N. P. Bank Ltd* (1936). Nuisance from building operations carried on by defendant's independent contractor. HELD: Defendant liable. "Unless precautions were taken there was a great and obvious danger that nuisance would be caused"; *per* Finlay J.

NOTE: An occupier has an *absolute* right to lateral support from his neighbour's building; therefore the neighbour is liable if his contractor infringes the right. *Bower* v. *Peate* (1876).

25. Nuisance created by a trespasser. An occupier is not liable for nuisance created by a trespasser *unless*:

　　(a) the occupier, knowing of the nuisance, takes no reasonable steps to abate it; or

　　(b) the occupier *adopts* the nuisance: *e.g.* a trespasser interferes with a chimney, causing it to smoke excessively; the occupier continues to use the chimney.

Sedleigh–Denfield v. *O'Callaghan* (1940). A trespasser laid a pipe in a ditch in such a way that adjoining land was flooded.

The occupier of the land on which the ditch was situated ought reasonably to have discovered and prevented the danger. HELD: He was liable for the nuisance.

26. Nuisances created by predecessors in title. One who acquires land from which a nuisance emanates will be liable only if he knew of or ought reasonably to have discovered the nuisance.

St. Anne's Well Brewery Co. v. *Roberts* (1929). Adjoining building collapsed because of ancient excavations which the present owner could not reasonably have discovered. HELD: He was not liable.

27. Landlord and tenant. The general rule is that the *tenant*, as occupier, is liable for a nuisance on the premises: but the *landlord* is liable if he authorises the nuisance, when he is concurrently liable with the tenant on the ordinary principles of vicarious liability.

Harris v. *James* (1876). The landlord let a field to be worked as a lime quarry, blasting from which created a nuisance. He knew blasting was inevitable. HELD: He had impliedly authorised the nuisance.

But, if the tenant has a harmless alternative, the landlord does not authorise the nuisance *merely because* he knows it would be possible for the tenant to create one. The test is: Could the tenant have avoided the nuisance? *Rich* v. *Basterfield* (1847).

EFFECTUAL DEFENCES

28. Rebuttal. It is an adequate defence to prove that the activity complained of is not a nuisance, *i.e.* not an unreasonable interference with the use or enjoyment of land, or with health or comfort.

29. Consent. The consent of the plaintiff is a good defence, provided the defendant was not negligent. But it is no defence that the plaintiff came to the nuisance, *i.e.* consent will not be implied by his coming to the premises with knowledge of the nuisance: except that where the interference is with *comfort* the nature of the locality may be relevant—"What would be a nuisance in Belgrave Square would not necessarily be so in Bermondsey": *Sturgess* v. *Bridgman* (1879): *see* I, **13.**

30. Prescription. A *private* nuisance is legalised after twenty years: but time begins to run only when the plaintiff becomes aware of the nuisance.

Sturgess v. *Bridgman* (1879). The defendant for more than twenty years caused noise and vibration, which were not, however, complained of as a nuisance. Then his neighbour, a physician, built a consulting room adjacent to the site of the noisy operations, which the physician now alleged were a nuisance. HELD: A prescriptive right had not been established, as the activity was not previously a nuisance. Injunction granted.

31. Statutory authority. Activities which would be a nuisance at common law may be sanctioned by statute. But the authority will be lost if the conduct goes beyond the limits permitted by the statute.

32. Other defences. The following defences have also succeeded against a plea of nuisance (*see* I, **13–27, 30–36**):

(*a*) Contributory negligence by the plaintiff: *Trevett* v. *Lee* (1955).

(*b*) Inevitable accident: *Esso Petroleum Co. Ltd.* v. *Southport Corporation* (1956).

(*c*) Act of a stranger, of which the plaintiff had neither actual nor constructive notice: *Sedleigh–Denfield* v. *O'Callaghan* (1940).

(*d*) Act of God, seems, on general principles, as if it would be a good defence in nuisance.

INEFFECTUAL DEFENCES

33. Public benefit. If the nuisance injures the plaintiff, it is no defence that it benefits the public generally, even if the public benefit is substantial and the injury to the plaintiff relatively slight: *Adams* v. *Ursell* (1913).

34. That the defendant used all possible skill and care. Nuisance is not merely a branch of negligence, therefore the defendant cannot excuse himself by showing that he took reasonable (or even extreme) care—although proof of care may have *evidential* value in determining whether an ordinary user of land is actionable as a nuisance.

> *Adams* v. *Ursell* (1913). A fried-fish shop was held a nuisance in a residential street. It was no defence (*a*) that it benefited the poor; (*b*) that all possible care and "the most approved appliances" were used.

At *common law* an activity which cannot be prevented from being a nuisance cannot be carried on at all, except by the consent of those affected. Note, however, that many common-law nuisances are authorised by statute.

> *Powell* v. *Fall* (1880). Nuisance by sparks from traction engine; they could not be prevented and there was no consent or statutory authority. HELD: The machine could not lawfully be operated.

35. Volenti non fit injuria.

It is well established that it is no defence that the plaintiff came to the nuisance.

> *Bliss* v. *Hall* (1838). The plaintiff took a house near a tallow chandlery, which emitted fumes and smells. HELD: No defence that these activities had been carried on for three years, before the plaintiff's arrival.

However, the nature of the locality is relevant to the application of this rule. For instance, one who chooses to reside in a manufacturing district cannot expect more immunity from its disadvantages than the other inhabitants. But note that the local standard is confined to nuisance causing personal discomfort, and has no application to cases involving damage to property.

> *St. Helens Smelting Co.* v. *Tipping* (1865). The appellant's house was in a manufacturing district. His vegetation was damaged by fumes. HELD: A nuisance, the situation of the house being no defence.

36. Suitable place.

It is no defence that the place from which the nuisance emanates is a suitable one for the purpose of carrying on the activity complained of, and that no other place is available. Again, if the business cannot be carried on without creating a nuisance, then it cannot be carried on at all, except by consent of those affected or by statutory authority.

37. Contributory acts of others. It is no defence that the defendant's act was in itself too negligible to amount to a nuisance, and that the nuisance arose only from the aggregate effect of a number of similar activities. In such a case, each contributor is liable (*a*) for the nuisance, (*b*) for his proportion of the total damages.

> *Pride of Derby, etc. Angling Association* v. *British Celanese Ltd.* (1953). A number of defendants polluted the plaintiff's fishery. HELD: Jointly and severally liable as above.

38. Reasonable use of property. Reasonable use of his own property cannot be a defence to the creator of a nuisance; for the creation of a nuisance is unreasonable by definition. "If a man creates a nuisance he cannot say that he is acting reasonably. The two things are self-contradictory": *A.-G.* v. *Cole* (1901), *per* Kekewich J.

Nor is the nature of the defendant's act to be tested by enquiring whether he could foresee the damage. The matter must be looked at from the point of view of the victims of the alleged nuisance: the criterion is—was the activity to which the victim was exposed tolerable in all the circumstances of the case?

PROGRESS TEST 5

1. Explain the difference between public and private nuisance. **(1)**

2. Give some examples of statutes which create actionable nuisance. **(1)**

3. Give some examples, from decided cases, of actionable nuisances. **(3)**

4. What is the relationship of (*a*) nuisance and trespass; (*b*) nuisance and negligence? **(4)**

5. In what circumstances (if at all) is nuisance actionable *per se*? **(5)**

6. How does "reasonableness" affect liability in nuisance? Is this the same as "reasonable care" in negligence? **(7)**

7. Is "reasonableness" a question of law? **(8)**

8. What is the effect on liability for nuisance of abnormal sensitivity of persons or property? **(9)**

9. What is the effect of malice on liability in nuisance? Illustrate by decided cases. **(11)**

10. Who has the legal duty to repair highways? What was the effect of the *Highways (Miscellaneous Provisions) Act*, 1961? **(12)**

11. What is the extent of the liability in nuisance with respect to (a) an artificial projection; (b) trees? **(13, 14)**

12. When (if at all) is a temporary obstruction of a highway an actionable nuisance? Is a permanent obstruction always a nuisance? **(15)**

13. Under what circumstances will an obstruction be a nuisance because it causes loss of custom to a tradesman? Illustrate by decided cases. **(16)**

14. When will an occupier be liable for injury done by something naturally on his land to a person on the highway? **(17)**

15. List the persons who can sue in nuisance. Under what circumstances can (a) a reversioner; (b) a tenant for a term of years, sue in nuisance? **(18)**

16. Can (a) a servant; (b) a lodger, sue in nuisance? **(19)**

17. List the persons who can be sued in nuisance. What is the position of one who creates a nuisance by misfeasance? **(19, 20)**

18. What is the extent of the liability in nuisance of (a) an occupier; (b) other persons lawfully on the premises; (c) independent contractors? **(20–24)**

19. What (if any) is the liability of an occupier for a nuisance created by (a) a trespasser; (b) a predecessor in title? **(25–26)**

20. What are the respective liabilities in nuisance of landlord and tenant? **(27)**

21. List the effectual defences in nuisance. **(28–32)**

22. Are any of the following effectual defences in nuisance: (a) contributory negligence; (b) inevitable accident; (c) act of a stranger; (d) Act of God? **(32)**

23. List the ineffectual defences in nuisance. **(33–38)**

24. To what extent (if at all) is it relevant for a defendant in nuisance to plead that he used all possible skill and care? **(34)**

25. Is it ever a good defence that "the plaintiff came to the nuisance"? Has the nature of the locality any bearing on this? **(35)**

CHAPTER VI

NEGLIGENCE

DEFINITION AND CHARACTERISTICS

1. Two meanings of negligence. Negligence may be:

(a) a mode of committing other torts;

(b) an independent tort.

This chapter deals only with negligence as an independent tort.

2. Origins of negligence. Negligence derives from trespass by way of the action on the case, and, like all derivatives of case, it is actionable only on proof of damage, *i.e.* not *per se*. However, the modern tort of negligence, arising from breach by the defendant of a legal duty of care owed by him to the plaintiff, takes its origin only from the early nineteenth century. Since then it has developed in "disconnected slabs"—*Candler* v. *Crane Christmas & Co.* (1951)—so that even today it exhibits relatively little generality.

3. Definition difficult. This lack of generality makes negligence somewhat difficult to define, but the definition of Alderson B. in *Blyth* v. *Birmingham Waterworks Co.* (1856) is generally regarded as classic: "Negligence is the omission to do something which a reasonable man . . . would do, or doing something which a prudent and reasonable man would not do."

It has also been said that negligence "properly connotes the complex concept of duty, breach and damage thereby suffered by the person to whom the duty was owing": *Lochgelly Iron & Coal Co.* v. *M'Mullan* (1934), *per* Lord Wright. This is the modern definition.

4. Test of negligence objective. Negligence is an *objective* concept. No moral blame necessarily attaches to a negligent tortfeasor.

NOTE: Wilful wrongdoing and negligence are mutually exclusive. A negligent tortfeasor does not intend the harm, but is indifferent as to whether it occurs or not.

WHAT THE PLAINTIFF MUST PROVE

5. Three "incidents of negligence." A plaintiff who alleges negligence must prove:

   (a) that the defendant owed the plaintiff a *legal duty of care*;
   (b) that the defendant *broke* his legal duty of care;
   (c) that the plaintiff suffered damage *in consequence of the breach*.

6. Advertent and inadvertent negligence. Negligence is not the same thing as carelessness—although often accompanied by it. Negligence may be *advertent* or *inadvertent*:

   (a) *Advertent.* The tortfeasor knows of the risk but disregards it; he displays "an attitude of mental indifference to obvious risks": *Hudston* v. *Viney* (1921), *per* Eve J.
   (b) *Inadvertent.* The tortfeasor is merely careless—the possibility of consequential harm does not occur to him.

THE DUTY OF CARE

7. Existence a question of law. Whether a duty of care is owed in any given circumstances is a question of *law*, to be decided by the judge.

8. To whom is the duty of care owed? The "neighbour principle." Lord Atkin's celebrated leading judgment in *Donoghue* v. *Stevenson* (1932) ("the snail in the ginger-beer bottle") established the general rule that the duty of care is owed to one's "neighbour." His lordship said that "you must take reasonable care to avoid acts or omissions which you can reasonably foresee would be likely to injure your neighbour."

   (a) *Definition of neighbour.* Lord Atkin asked the rhetorical question: "Who then, in law, is my neighbour?"—to which he gave the answer: "*Persons who are so closely and directly affected by my act that I ought reasonably to have them in contemplation as being so affected when I am directing my mind to the acts or omissions which are called in question.*"
   (b) *Limits of the neighbour principle.* Lord Atkin's reply was "restricted" in the sense that a plaintiff in tort cannot

succeed *merely* by showing that he was the defendant's "neighbour" when the alleged wrong was committed. The exact extent of the "neighbour principle" is uncertain; but, broadly speaking, it is restricted to the tort of negligence.

9. No general principle established. Although Lord Atkin's famous judgment undoubtedly introduced a considerable degree of generality into the concept of the duty of care (and therefore into the tort of negligence), his lordship nevertheless pointed out that it did *not* establish a "general conception of relations giving rise to a duty of care, of which the particular cases found in the books are but instances."

NOTE

(i) The "neighbour principle" is the *ratio decidendi* of Lord Atkin's leading judgment; but, as Lords Macmillan and Thankerton did not specifically endorse it, it is probably not the *ratio* of the *case*.

(ii) *Donoghue* v. *Stevenson* is also authority for the propositions (a) that a manufacturer owes a duty of care to the ultimate consumer or user of his product; (b) that the absence of privity of contract between plaintiff and defendant is no bar to an action in tort.

LIABILITY FOR NEGLIGENT MIS-STATEMENTS

10. The "Hedley Byrne Case." An important extension of the duty of care arose from the unanimous decision of the House of Lords in *Hedley Byrne & Co. Ltd.* v. *Heller & Partners Ltd.* (1963) that there may be liability for financial loss arising from *negligent mis-statements*. Such liability had previously been possible in respect of *physical* loss or damage: but before *Hedley Byrne* the rule was that, in the absence of a fiduciary or contractual relationship, and, except where physical loss was sustained, there was no general duty to refrain from careless mis-statements. This was emphasised as recently as 1951 in *Candler* v. *Crane, Christmas & Co.*, which *Hedley Byrne* overruled.

Hedley Byrne & Co. Ltd. v. *Heller & Partners Ltd.* (1963). The appellants, advertising agents, accepted the instructions of E & Co. Ltd. to place substantial television advertising contracts. The defendants, Heller & Partners Ltd., were bankers who, in reply to an enquiry from the plaintiff's bankers as to the financial standing of E & Co. Ltd., replied "without responsibility" that E & Co. Ltd. could meet their ordinary business commitments. However, E & Co. Ltd. failed, causing the plaintiffs, as *del credere* agents, to lose £17,000. HELD: The plaintiffs could not succeed in respect of the defendant's negligent statement, the defendants having successfully protected themselves by giving the reference "without responsibility." However, the House of Lords made it clear that, under certain circumstances, there would be liability for negligent mis-statements.

11. Two conditions. The liability will exist if the following conditions obtain:

(a) *A special relationship exists between the parties.* A special relationship will exist where the person who was asked for information or an opinion:

(i) was a person on whose statement it would be reasonable to rely, *e.g.* an expert or professional adviser; and
(ii) knew or ought to have known that the enquirer intended to rely on the information or opinion.

"If someone possessed of a special skill undertakes, quite irrespective of contract, to apply that skill for the assistance of another person who relies on such skill, a duty of care will arise": *per* Lord Morris in *Hedley Byrne*.

NOTE: Such a duty of care already existed where there was a *fiduciary relationship* between the parties. *Hedley Byrne* extends the ambit of such liability to include a *special relationship*.

(b) *The defendant has not disclaimed responsibility.* The defendants in *Hedley Byrne* escaped liability through their effective disclaimer. It seems that the ordinary rules governing disclaimers and exemptions apply, the effectiveness of the disclaimer being a matter of fact in each case.

THE EXTENT OF THE DUTY OF CARE AT COMMON LAW

12. Two determining factors. The extent of the duty of care depends on the following:

(a) *Reasonable foresight.* The defendant will owe a duty of care if he could *reasonably foresee* that his act or omission would cause loss or damage to his neighbour.

(b) *Reasonable care.* The defendant will break his duty of care if, reasonably foreseeing loss or damage to his neighbour, he did not take reasonable care to avoid it.

Reasonable foresight therefore tests: (a) whether a *new duty* should be added to the list of existing duties; and (b) the *scope and extent* of an existing or admitted duty.

NOTE
  (i) The concepts of reasonable care and reasonable foresight are relevant also to those of *standard of care* and *remoteness of damage.* Duty of care, standard of care and remoteness of damage (XVII, **15–18**) frequently intermingle; but it is important (although often difficult) carefully to distinguish them.
  (ii) Duty of care is often governed by *statutory rules, e.g.* those contained in the *Factories Acts.*

13. Cases in which a duty of care was held to exist. Two examples may be cited:

Buckland v. *Guildford Gas, Light & Coke Co.* (1948). A duty of care will be owed only if the likelihood of injury was *probable,* not merely possible. A girl of thirteen climbed a tree and was electrocuted by touching an overhead wire close to the tree and concealed by its branches. HELD: In these circumstances the defendants ought reasonably to have foreseen the *likelihood* of injury.

Farrugia v. *Great Western Railway* (1947). Part of an insecure load fell off defendant's lorry, injuring plaintiff, who was illicitly riding on the lorry. HELD: Defendant's liable; plaintiff was *within the area of potential danger* created by them, and they therefore owed him a duty of care.

14. Cases in which a duty of care was held not to exist. Again, two examples may be cited.

Bourhill v. *Young* (1942). A pregnant fishwife alighted from a tram and was made ill by hearing (but not seeing) a fatal accident to a motor cyclist some fifty yards away. HELD: The motor cyclist could not, in the circumstances, reasonably have foreseen the likelihood of injury to the plaintiff and therefore owed her no duty of care; his personal representatives incurred no liability in negligence.

King v. *Phillips* (1953). A taxi driver, in reversing, slightly injured a child. His mother, from seventy-five yards away, saw the child's damaged cycle under the taxi and suffered severe shock. HELD: In the circumstances, the driver owed her no duty of care.

THE STANDARD OF CARE

15. An objective standard. The standard of care demanded is an *objective* one, *i.e.* that of *the ordinary reasonable man* ("the man on the Clapham Omnibus") *in the circumstances of the case.* A defendant who fails to observe this standard will be held to have been negligent.

The ordinary reasonable man is a notional person, conceived of as being neither unduly apprehensive nor over-confident. The application of the reasonable-man standard is said to ensure objectivity and uniformity, in that it "eliminates the personal equation and is independent of the idiosyncrasies of the particular person whose conduct is in question":—*Glasgow Corporation* v. *Muir* (1943), *per* Lord Macmillan.

NOTE: The reasonable-man standard has been criticised on the grounds that there have been wide variations in judicial interpretation of this hypothetical creature. Thus, *Winfield* said of Lord Bramwell that he sometimes credited the reasonable man with "the agility of an acrobat and the foresight of a Hebrew prophet."

16. Particular knowledge or skill. The standard expected is that of the ordinary practitioner. It follows from the fact that the standard of care varies with the circumstances that a person who holds himself out as possessing particular knowledge or skill (*e.g.* a surgeon or a plumber) must exhibit the degree of knowledge or skill reasonably to be expected of an ordinarily skilled member of that profession or vocation. But he need not exhibit the highest degree of skill, nor avoid every risk inherent in the particular task he is carrying out.

Roe v. *Minister of Health* (1947). A patient was paralysed because an experienced anaesthetist injected contaminated nupercaine. The contamination arose in a way which could not, at that time, have been reasonably foreseen or discovered. HELD: The anaesthetist had shown *normal* competence, therefore he was not negligent.
NOTE
(*i*) A person cannot be liable for harm resulting from his lack of a particular attribute if he had no choice but to occupy a

position in which the lack caused the harm, *e.g.* if a one-armed man is obliged to work a machine the operation of which with one arm by a normal man would be negligent, the one-armed man will not be judged by the same standard as the normal man.

(*ii*) Barristers are immune from suits for professional negligence in respect of their conduct of cases in court. This has recently been reaffirmed by the House of Lords in *Rondel* v. *Worsley* (1967).

17. The standard of care to be regarded as reasonable. This depends also upon the following four criteria.

(*a*) The extent to which the risk could have been foreseen (*see* **18–19** below).

(*b*) The magnitude of the risk (*see* **20** below).

(*c*) The importance of the object to be attained, relative to the measures necessary to eliminate the risk (*see* **21** below).

(*d*) Usual and approved practice (*see* **22–23** below).

18. The extent to which the risk could have been foreseen. There is a duty to take *reasonable care* to guard against *reasonably foreseeable risks*. "People must guard against reasonable probabilities, not fantastic possibilities": *Fardon* v. *Harcourt-Rivington* (1932), *per* Lord Dunedin.

Fardon v. *Harcourt-Rivington* (1932). A dog, without vicious propensities, jumped up inside a car and splintered the window, thereby injuring the plaintiff. HELD: Defendant not negligent in failing to foresee and guard against this "fantastic possibility."

Bolton v. *Stone* (1950). Plaintiff, standing outside cricket ground, was injured by a ball which travelled a hundred yards and cleared a seventeen-foot fence. Similar hits had occurred six times in thirty years. HELD: The risk of injury was so small that defendants not negligent in failing to take further precautions. The event was foreseeable but not reasonably probable. "There must be sufficient probability to lead a reasonable man to anticipate [injury]": *per* Lord Porter.

19. Foresight not the same as balance of probability. Foreseeability is not determined by a balance of probabilities. It may be unreasonable—and therefore negligent—not to guard against a rare, or even a unique, event if, *in the circumstances of the case,* the likelihood of damage is such that a reasonable man would take precautions against it.

Protheroe v. *Railway Executive* (1951). An action is not necessarily reasonable merely because it has been frequently and safely performed. "I should not consider it to be conclusive, to show that a platform was reasonably safe, that it has been used by hundreds and thousands of passengers without injury to anyone": *per* Parker J.

Carmarthenshire County Council v. *Lewis* (1955). A unique risk may be reasonably foreseeable. A lorry driver was killed through swerving to avoid a 4-year-old child who had strayed from defendant's school. HELD: Although this particular risk had never arisen before, the defendants ought in the circumstances reasonably to have foreseen and guarded against it.

However, the plaintiff need not show that the *particular* accident or damage was foreseeable, but only that it was *of a kind* the defendant ought reasonably to have foreseen.

20. The magnitude of the risk.

Proportionate care is required. The law does not require the highest possible degree of care, but that which is commensurate with (*a*) the seriousness of the injury risked; and (*b*) the likelihood of its occurring. This standard varies with the circumstances, so that, for example, a higher degree of care is owed to children or the disabled; or to a man on a roof than to one on the ground. On the other hand, necessity may justify the taking of greater risks, *i.e.* a lower standard of care (*see* IX, 6).

Paris v. *Stepney Borough Council* (1951). P, a one-eyed man, was employed where there was danger from splinters, but where, by long-established practice, the employer did not provide goggles. A splinter blinded P's remaining eye. HELD: The employers were negligent in not providing him with goggles. They owed him a higher duty of care because of the greater seriousness of an eye injury in his case.

Yachuck v. *Oliver Blaise Co. Ltd.* (1949). A Privy Council case. A high standard of care is owed to children. A boy of nine was burned through playing with petrol he got from a garage by pretending it was for his mother. HELD: In the circumstances, the garage proprietor was negligent in selling him the petrol.

Watt v. *Hertfordshire County Council* (1954). A fireman employed by the Council was injured because, in an emergency, a heavy jack was carried in an unsuitable lorry. HELD: No negligence; the emergency justified the risk.

21. The importance of the object to be attained relative to the measures necessary to reduce the risk.

Here a varying standard

obtains. In the case of a very great risk which no precautions can substantially reduce, the duty of care may be discharged only by ceasing the dangerous operations altogether; but, where the risk is slight, slight precautions (or even none) will suffice. Between these two extremes, the duty will be met by precautions proportionate to the risk.

> *Latimer* v. *A.E.C. Ltd.* (1953). Exceptionally heavy rain caused floor of defendant's factory to be covered with oil and water. Sawdust was immediately put down, but supplies ran out before the whole floor could be covered. Plaintiff slipped and was injured on uncovered portion. HELD: No negligence, as all reasonable precautions had been taken. Reasonable prudence did not demand the closing of the factory in these circumstances.

NOTE
  (i) Any risk involved in setting up the precautions should be taken into account.
  (ii) A person who fails in his duty to take precautions cannot excuse himself by showing that the accident would still have happened if he *had* taken them.

22. Usual and approved practice. The defendant may be able to show that, in the circumstances, he discharged his duty of care by following the usual and approved practice, even if his act or omission would, in isolation, have amounted to negligence. In the case of inherently dangerous work, for example, a defendant employer need not show that he took every possible precaution, but "can clear his feet if he shows that he has acted in accordance with the general and approved practice": *Vancouver General Hospital* v. *McDaniel* (1934), *per* Lord Alnes.

23. Usual and approved practice and reasonableness. It should be stressed, however, that "usual and approved practice" does *not* supersede the test of reasonableness. The rule is that failure to follow the usual and approved practice will be negligent *only if a reasonably prudent man would have followed it.* Nor will proof that a neglected precaution is *not* usual and approved practice avail as a defence if the precaution is such that "a reasonable and prudent man would think it so obvious that it was folly to omit it": *Paris* v. *Stepney Borough Council* (1951), *per* Lord Normand.

A usual and approved practice does not necessarily become reasonable *merely because* it has been long continued: "Neglect of duty does not cease by repetition to be neglect of duty": *Bank of Montreal* v. *Dominion Guarantee Co.* (1930), *per* Lord Tomlin.

PROOF OF NEGLIGENCE AND 'RES IPSA LOQUITUR'

24. The burden of proof. It is for the plaintiff to prove that the defendant was negligent *except* where the maxim *res ipsa loquitur* applies.

25. Law and fact: functions of judge and jury. The *judge* decides *as a matter of law* whether the *plaintiff's* evidence is such that a reasonable man might conclude from it that the defendant was negligent. If the judge decides this question in the negative, he withholds the case from the jury; or, if sitting alone, he does not go on to hear the issues of fact argued by the parties.

(a) *The issue of law defined.* The question of law for the judge to decide, therefore, is whether the plaintiff has adduced *facts*—as distinct from mere *conjecture*—from which a *reasonable inference* of negligence could be drawn.

(b) *The issue of fact defined.* If the judge decides that the plaintiff has established negligence *prima facie*, he leaves the case to the jury (notionally if sitting alone) which decides *as a matter of fact*, and on the evidence of *both* parties, whether the defendant was negligent.

Metropolitan Railway Co. v. *Jackson* (1877). "The judge has to say whether any facts have been established by evidence from which negligence *may be* reasonably inferred; the jurors have to say whether, from those facts, when submitted to them, negligence *ought to be* inferred": *per* Lord Carus L.C.

Wakelin v. *London & S.W. Railway Co.* (1886). In this instance the House of Lords held that there had been no case to go to the jury. A man was killed by a train which had a headlight but did not whistle. It was not known why he was on the line. Lord Halsbury L.C. said: "One may surmise, and it is but surmise and not evidence, that the unfortunate man was knocked down by a train; but . . . is there anything to show that the train ran over the man rather than that the man ran against the train?"

26. Res ipsa loquitur. *Res ipsa loquitur* ("the thing speaks for itself") is *a rule of evidence,* the effects of which are twofold:

(*a*) If the rule applies, *negligence is presumed,* and the onus of disproving it is thrown onto the defendant.

(*b*) If the rule applies, *the plaintiff is entitled to have his case put to the jury;* so that, if the court of first instance decides for the defendant on the grounds that negligence could not reasonably be inferred, a new trial will be ordered on appeal.

NOTE: In *Scott* v. *London & St. Catherine Docks Co.* (1865) and *Byrne* v. *Boadle* (1863), both tried before 1873, new trials were ordered, on the ground that the maxim applied, after the plaintiffs had been non-suited at first instance.

27. Lack of explanation essential. *Res ipsa loquitur* applies typically to cases in which the facts indicate negligence, but where there is *no apparent explanation* and the plaintiff cannot show the cause of the accident. These conditions will apply when:

(*a*) "there is reasonable evidence of negligence";

(*b*) "the thing is shown to be under the management of the defendant or his servants";

(*c*) "the accident is such as in the ordinary course of things does not happen if those who have the management use proper care."

Then: "It affords reasonable evidence, in the absence of explanation by the defendants, that the accident arose from want of care": *per* Erle C.J. in *Scott* v. *London & St. Catherine's Docks Co.* (1865), a case where bags of sugar fell, without apparent cause, from an upper warehouse onto a passer-by.

Res ipsa loquitur will *not* apply where there is an explanation.

Barkway v. *South Wales Transport Co. Ltd.* (1950). Plaintiff was injured when defendant's bus left the road. However, there was an explanation in term of speed and a defective tyre. HELD: *Res ipsa loquitur* did not apply.

28. Res ipsa loquitur restated. In *Barkway's case* Lord Radcliffe restated the maxim: "An event which in the ordinary course of things is more likely than not to have been caused by negligence is by itself evidence of negligence."

Sochaki v. *Sas* (1947). Furniture caught fire in a room in which an ordinary domestic fire was left unattended. HELD: *Res ipsa loquitur* did *not* apply, nor was there evidence of negligence. "Everybody knows fires occur through accidents which happen without negligence on anybody's part": *per* Lord Goddard C.J.

29. Defendant may rebut the presumption. When *res ipsa loquitur* applies, the defendant may rebut the presumption of negligence:

(*a*) by showing that the accident could reasonably have occurred without his negligence;

(*b*) by showing that he was not personally negligent—in which case he need not go on to show how the accident happened. In *Woods* v. *Duncan* (1946) it was said that *res ipsa loquitur* "only shifts the onus of proof, which is adequately met by showing that [the defendant] was not in fact negligent. He is not to be held liable because he cannot prove exactly how the accident happened": *per* Viscount Simon L.C.

CONTRIBUTORY NEGLIGENCE

30. The present position outlined. Contributory negligence is governed by the *Law Reform (Contributory Negligence) Act, 1945*, which provides that the damages recoverable by the plaintiff shall be reduced proportionately to the extent to which his own negligence contributed to his injury. However, an outline knowledge of the common-law rules which preceded that Act is necessary for a proper understanding of the present position.

31. Contributory negligence at common law. The basic common-law rule was that, if the plaintiff had contributed by his own negligence, however slightly, to his own injury, he could not succeed in respect of the negligence of the defendant, notwithstanding that the defendant's negligence was the effective and major cause of the harm suffered by the plaintiff.

Butterfield v. *Forrester* (1809). Plaintiff was injured because defendant wrongfully obstructed a road. HELD: Plaintiff could not succeed because, although defendant had acted unlawfully,

plaintiff had contributed to his injury by his own negligence—
"One person being in fault will not dispense with another's
using ordinary care for himself": *per* Lord Ellenborough C.J.

32. An unsatisfactory position. The attempt to alleviate the
injustice implicit in the common-law rule gave rise to what
Lord Du Parcq described (in a lecture to the Holdsworth Club
in 1948) as "a mass of verbal refinements, of logic-chopping, of
. . . pointless microscopical research" and caused *Salmond* to
write of contributory negligence that "no more baffling and
elusive problem exists in the law of torts" (6th edition, 1923).

**33. Effect of the Law Reform (Contributory Negligence) Act,
1945.** Since the passing of this Act, however, such subtleties
and complexities as "the Principle in *Davies* v. *Mann*" and the
so-called "last-opportunity rule" have ceased to bedevil contributory negligence, which is now "approached broadly,
avoiding those fine distinctions which were apt to be drawn
when some slight act of negligence on the part of the plaintiff
might defeat his claim altogether": "*Boy Andrew*" (*owners*) v.
"*St. Rognvald*" (*owners*) (1948), *per* Lord Porter.

34. Main provision of the Act. Section 1 (*i*) provides that,
"where any person suffers damage as a result partly of his own
fault and partly of the fault of any other person or persons, a
claim in respect of that damage shall not be defeated by reason
of the fault of the person suffering the damage, but the damage
recoverable in respect thereof shall be reduced to such extent
as the court thinks just and equitable having regard to the
claimant's share in the responsibility for the damage."

35. Previous statutory provision. By the 1945 Act the common-law rules of contributory negligence were brought into
line with those of Admiralty law; for the *Maritime Conventions
Act*, 1911, enabled the court *at its discretion* to apportion the
loss according to the respective degrees of negligence of the
parties. The 1945 Act does not apply to a claim governed by
the *Maritime Conventions Act*, 1911.

NOTE: The 1945 Act does not apply only to negligence. Section 4
defines "fault" as "negligence, breach of statutory duty or other
act or omission which gives rise to a liability in tort."

36. No reciprocal duty of care. A defendant who pleads contributory negligence need *not* prove breach of a duty of care owed to him *by the plaintiff*, but only that the plaintiff *failed to take reasonable care for his own safety in respect of the risk to which the defendant's negligence exposed him.* This is an exception to the principle that the plaintiff's contributory negligence is to be judged by the same standard as the defendant's negligence.

37. The plaintiff's negligence must contribute to his injury. The Act will not affect a negligent plaintiff *unless* his negligence was *operative, i.e. contributed to his injury.*

Davies v. *Swan Motor Co. (Swansea) Ltd.* (1949). "It is not necessary to show that the [plaintiff's] negligence constituted a breach of duty to the defendant. It is sufficient to show lack of reasonable care by the plaintiff for his own safety": *per* Bucknill L.J.

The plaintiff's negligence will be inoperative, *i.e. not contributory,* if it was the *sole* cause of the accident. For the Act to apply, not only must *both* parties have been negligent, but the *negligence of each* must have contributed to the harm suffered by the plaintiff.

Jones v. *Livox Quarries Ltd.* (1952). Plaintiff worked in defendant's quarry. He was injured when, through the negligence of another employee, he was crushed between two vehicles, when thrown off a tow-bar on which he was riding against express orders. He answered defendant's plea of contributory negligence by asserting that his own negligence was inoperative, as the risk he ran was not the one the orders were intended to guard against, and therefore not the one to which the defendant's negligence had exposed him. He argued that he had exposed himself to the risk of being thrown off, but not to the risk of being crushed. HELD: His negligence was operative, and his damages would be reduced by one-fifth.

38. Operative negligence limited. Nevertheless *Jones* v. *Livox Quarries Ltd.* stresses that the plaintiff's negligence, to be operative, must be *in respect of the risk to which the defendant's negligence exposed him,* and not some other risk. Singleton L.J. observed that the plaintiff's negligence would not have been contributory if "he had been hit in the eye by a shot from a negligent sportsman."

NOTE: The onus on the defendant to show that the plaintiff failed to take reasonable care in respect of the risk to which he was exposed is discharged by showing that he failed to anticipate danger of *that class*, not necessarily the particular danger he actually encountered. It has been said, for example, that pedestrians ought reasonably to anticipate danger from "the class of legitimate road users—which includes a tame elephant but not a helicopter": *Moore* v. *Nolan* (1960), *per* Kingsmill Moor J. (*obiter*).

39. Plaintiff must incur some duty. A plaintiff cannot contribute negligence if he incurs *no* duty towards the defendant, *e.g.* because the plaintiff was entitled to assume the absence of danger. Thus, a driver can assume that others will obey the traffic regulations, except perhaps where experience shows they are often broken. It has been held, *e.g.*, that he may rely on others obeying traffic lights, but not "slow" signs. Furthermore, a plaintiff will not contribute negligence if the defendant misled him into thinking there was no danger.

THE PRINCIPLE OF ALTERNATIVE DANGER

40. The rule still sometimes operative. Since the Act of 1945 the importance of this common-law rule has been diminished by the power of the court to apportion the loss. However, it may still be relevant in deciding whether the plaintiff (or the defendant, to whom it also applies in respect of the plaintiff's contributory negligence) took reasonable care in all the circumstances of the case.

41. The principle defined. The doctrine of alternative danger may be shortly stated as follows: The plaintiff will not have contributed negligence if, by the *defendant's* negligence, he was placed in a *dilemma*, and "in the agony of the moment", he chose the wrong alternative, *e.g.* to jump from or remain in a runaway vehicle: *Jones* v. *Boyce* (1816).

42. Other applications of the doctrine.

(*a*) The doctrine of alternative danger will also apply, if otherwise appropriate:

(*i*) where the emergency was created by a third party, or Act of God;

(*ii*) where the property only (not persons) was endangered.

(*b*) The plaintiff will not necessarily contribute negligence if, *as the only alternative* to forfeiting his freedom of action, he chooses to take the risk the defendant has created.

Clayards v. *Dethick and Davis* (1848). Defendants obstructed the only entrance to plaintiff's stable, so that one of his horses was killed when he attempted to lead it out. HELD: The danger was not so obvious that a reasonably prudent man would not have incurred it, and defendants had deprived plaintiff of any alternative course of action.

43. The doctrine qualified.

(*a*) The doctrine does *not* apply where the plaintiff took a disproportionate risk to avoid a mere inconvenience.

Adams v. *Lancashire & Yorkshire Railway Co.* (1869). Plaintiff was a passenger on defendant's train. Because of defendant's negligence the carriage door would not stay closed. In attempting to close it, plaintiff fell out. The carriage was not crowded, and the train almost at a station. HELD: Plaintiff failed, the risk taken being disproportionate to the inconvenience suffered.

(*b*) A plaintiff, although placed in a dilemma, may nevertheless contribute negligence if his work, trade or profession is such that he might reasonably be expected to cope with the emergency.

NOTE: The principle of alternative danger is also known as the Rule in the Bywell Castle.

44. Contributory negligence of children and servants.

(*a*) *Age and capacity of the child.* Whether a child plaintiff can be held to have contributed negligence depends on the age and capacity of the child and the other circumstances of the case (*see* IX, 6).

Yachuk v. *Oliver Blaise Co. Ltd.* (1949). Child of 9 HELD not sufficiently capable of taking care of himself to have contributed negligence.

(*b*) *No contribution through adult.* A child plaintiff does not contribute negligence through the negligence of an adult in charge of him.

D

Oliver v. *Birmingham & Midland Omnibus Co. Ltd.* (1933). Child of 4 was injured through the combined negligence of the defendants' driver and the child's grandfather, who was in charge of him. HELD: The grandfather's lack of care was not contributory negligence by the child.

(c) *Presence of an adult may obviate duty of care.* However, one who injures a child may owe him no duty of care *because* an adult was in charge of the child at the material time. In such a case the defendant disproves negligence, so no question of contributory negligence arises.

NOTE: These rules apply to others incapable of looking after themselves, *e.g.* the very old and the mentally retarded.

45. Contributory negligence of servants and agents.

A plaintiff can contribute negligence through his servant or agent in all circumstances in which he himself could do so: but a plaintiff cannot contribute negligence through his independent contractor, or other agent for whom he is not responsible.

46. Apportionment under the 1945 Act not automatic.

The Act of 1945 does *not* mean that, whenever both parties were to blame, the loss should always and automatically be apportioned. One party may be held solely liable despite the other's fault, if the former's action was *sufficiently separated in time, place or circumstances for it to be regarded as the sole cause* of the accident. "Sometimes it is proper to disregard all but one [fault] and to regard that one as the sole cause": *Stapley* v. *Gypsum Mines Ltd.* (1953), *per* Lord Read.

NOTE: This is the modern application of the Principle in *Davies* v. *Mann* (1843), which should not be confused with the discredited "last-opportunity" rule.

47. Rules of apportionment.

(a) The proportion by which the claimant's damages are to be reduced is a *question of fact* in each case.

(b) The court determines the total damages which would have been awarded if the claimant had not been at fault. It then finds and subtracts the proportion attributable to his contributory negligence. This is more advantageous to the claimant than if the final figure were determined by a single calculation.

(c) The Act has no application to costs.

(d) An appellate court will not alter the apportionment merely because its own would have been different.

PROGRESS TEST 6

1. Define negligence. **(3)**

2. Outline what a plaintiff in negligence must prove. **(5)**

3. What is "the neighbour principle"? Define "neighbour." **(8)**

4. What is the significance of *Hedley Byrne & Co. Ltd.* v. *Heller & Partners Ltd.* (1963)? **(10)**

5. What is a "special relationship" with regard to liability for negligent mis-statements? **(11)**

6. On what factors does the extent of the duty of care at common law depend? **(12)**

7. Define "standard of care." Who is "the man on the Clapham omnibus"? **(15)**

8. What are criteria of reasonableness in standard of care? **(17)**

9. Explain the concept of "foreseeability." **(18–19)**

10. How does the magnitude of the risk affect the standard of care? **(20)**

11. Define and explain "usual and approved practice." **(22–23)**

12. Explain *res ipsa loquitur*. **(24–28)**

13. How may the defendant rebut *res ipsa loquitur*? **(29)**

14. What was the effect of contributory negligence at common law? **(31–32)**

15. Outline the present position with regard to contributory negligence. **(33–39)**

16. Explain the qualifications on contributory negligence. **(37–38)**

17. To what extent (if at all) can a child contribute negligence? **(44)**

18. Explain how damages are apportioned when contributory negligence has been established. **(46–47)**

CHAPTER VII

BREACH OF STATUTORY DUTY

1. The nature of the duty. Breach of a statutory duty is *prima facie* actionable by one who is injured thereby: but the success of his action will depend on whether *on a construction of the statute*, in the light of the facts and circumstances of the case, he can discharge his onus of proof.

BURDEN OF PROOF

2. The onus of proof.

(a) The plaintiff must make good his case by the ordinary standard of proof in civil actions, *i.e.* on a balance of probabilities: *Bonnington Castings Ltd.* v. *Wardlaw* (1956).

(b) The plaintiff must prove:

(*i*) that the statute was broken (*see* **3** below);

(*ii*) that the breach caused the injury (*see* **4** below);

(*iii*) that he was a person or one of a class of persons the statute was intended to protect (*see* **5** below);

(*iv*) that the injury of which he complains is one the statute was intended to prevent (*see* **6** below).

3. That the statute was broken. It may appear on the facts that there was no breach of statutory duty.

Ebbs v. *James Whitson & Co. Ltd.* (1952). The plaintiff pleaded that his skin disease arose from his employment in sand-papering wood, and was caused by the defendant's breach of *ss.* 4 and 47 of the *Factories Act,* 1937. HELD: A construction of the Act revealed that the defendants incurred no liability under either section.

4. That the breach caused the injury or damage. It is essential for the plaintiff to prove *causality*.

Bonnington Castings Ltd. v. *Wardlaw* (1956). The plaintiff, because of the defendant's breach of the Factories Acts with respect to ventilation, was injured by inhaling silica dust. The defendants admitted the breach but denied it caused the plaintiff's injury. The House of Lords rejected this plea but nevertheless emphasised the obligation to prove causality. Lord Reid stressed that an employee cannot succeed *merely because* there was a breach of duty which could possibly have caused his injury, but that he must prove *causation*—"The employee must, in all cases, prove his case by the ordinary standard of proof in civil actions; he must make it appear at least that, on a balance of probabilities, the breach of duty caused, or materially contributed to, his injury."

5. That the plaintiff was a person or one of a class the statute was intended to protect.

(a) *Prosecution.* The statutory duty on which the plaintiff relies may turn out to be one which is owed to the public at large, the remedy being a criminal prosecution, or an injunction at the suit of the Attorney-General; and one where it was not Parliament's intention to provide a civil remedy for individuals. An example is the duty to provide a system of education under the *Education Act*, 1944.

(b) *Negligence.* Furthermore, a construction of the statute may reveal that a breach of a duty it imposes may not, in itself, entitle a person so injured to a civil remedy for breach of the statutory duty, but that the appropriate remedy is an action for negligence.

Clarke v. *Brims* (1947). The plaintiff was injured through defendant's failure to comply with the statutory regulations requiring a red rear light on a vehicle. HELD: No right of action merely because of the breach of statutory duty, as the plaintiff was adequately protected by an action for negligence.

(c) *Sole remedy.* Conversely, the court may hold that the remedy or penalty provided by the statute is intended to be the only one, resort to common law being consequently precluded.

Atkinson v. *Newcastle & Gateshead Waterworks Co.* (1877). Plaintiff's timber yard was destroyed by fire because of defendants' failure to discharge their duty under the *Waterworks Clauses Act*, 1847, to maintain minimum pressures in water mains. The statute provided for a penalty of £10 for each day that the pressures were not maintained. HELD: This was intended to be the only penalty, therefore the plaintiff could not recover damages in a common-law action.

(*d*) However, the fact that the statute provides a remedy or penalty does not necessarily mean that resort to an action for damages is precluded.

Monk v. *Warbey* (1935). The defendant lent his car to another, the negligence of whose driver injured the plaintiff. The defendant was not insured against this risk, and was, therefore, liable to a criminal penalty under *s.* 35 of the *Road Traffic Act*, 1930. HELD: He was nevertheless also liable in damages to the plaintiff for breach of statutory duty; otherwise the object of the statute (to protect persons injured by impecunious drivers) would have been defeated.

NOTE: This is an exception to the general principle that penal statutes should not be interpreted so as to create torts.

6. That the injury of which he complains is one the statute was intended to prevent. This rule is clearly demonstrated by the following example:

Gorris v. *Scott* (1874). Plaintiff's sheep were washed overboard because defendant failed in his statutory duty to provide pens on the ship's deck. HELD: The action could not succeed, as the object of the statute was to prevent the spread of disease among sheep.

NOTE: The fact that a statute gives no remedy for a particular injury does not extinguish the common-law duty to take reasonable care to avoid such injury, unless the statute excludes the common-law duty by express words or necessary implication.

NATURE OF DUTY

7. When is a statutory duty absolute?

(*a*) *Question of construction.* Whether a statute imposes an absolute duty, or one the breach of which is actionable only on proof of negligence or wrongful intent, is a *question of construction* in each case.

Hammond v. *Vestry of St. Pancras* (1874). The plaintiff was injured by the defendants' breach of their statutory duty to repair sewers. HELD: No liability in the absence of proof of negligence.

Groves v. *Lord Wimborne* (1898). The plaintiff was injured by breach of statutory duty to fence dangerous machinery.

HELD: The duty was absolute, *i.e.* independent of proof of negligence.

NOTE: Breaches of absolute duties imposed, *e.g.* by the Factories Acts, often involve negligent or intentional misconduct. In such cases proof of the negligence or misconduct is not necessary *in itself*, but may constitute the *evidence* for the breach of the statute.

(b) *Where duties not absolute.* In the case of a *statutory duty which is not absolute*, but where the statute requires that all "practicable" or "reasonably practicable" measures be taken, the general rule is that *the risk has to be balanced against the practicability of the measures needed to obviate it.* Cost is the criterion most likely to be irrelevant; but what is required must be "practicable" according to the knowledge and resources available at the time.

Adsett v. *K. & L. Steelfounderers & Engineers Ltd.* (1953). "In deciding whether all practicable measures were taken one must have regard to the state of knowledge at the material time, and, particularly, to the knowledge of scientific experts": *per* Singleton L.J.

8. "Statutory negligence."

(a) *Scope of statutory duties.* In some instances, *e.g.* many of the duties imposed by the *Factories Acts*, the statutory duty *includes* the duty to take care not to cause harm. In other statutes, *e.g.* the *Road Traffic Acts*, this is not the case. The former type of duty was described by Lord Wright in *Lochgelly Iron & Coal Co.* v. *McMullan* (1934) as "statutory negligence"—by which his lordship seems to have meant that in these cases the criteria of common law negligence and breach of statutory duty largely coincide. Lord Wright subsequently made it clear, however, in *London Passenger Transport Board* v. *Upson* (1949), that he regarded negligence and breach of statutory duty as distinct torts. This is generally accepted—the differences being as follows:

(*i*) In negligence the standard of care is decided by the court; but in breach of statutory duty it is laid down in the statute.
(*ii*) The application of *volenti non fit injuria* differs in the two cases.

(*iii*) In practice and pleading they are treated as distinct and separate causes of action.

(*iv*) A defendant alleged to be in breach of his statutory duty need not necessarily prove, in order to avoid liability, that he did not break his common-law duty.

(*b*) *Overlapping.* However, the two torts coincide to the extent that, when a plaintiff has pleaded both, his success in the one claim also settles the other.

DEFENCES AGAINST CLAIMS FOR BREACH OF STATUTORY DUTY

9. Volenti non fit injuria (or consent): *see* I, **13**. Because contracting out of a statutory duty is forbidden as against public policy, the consent of the plaintiff cannot be a defence to a breach of statutory duty whereby he was injured.

For the same reason, however, employees who injure themselves and each other by embarking on a joint enterprise in breach of a statutory duty imposed upon them cannot make their employer vicariously liable for such breach; for it would be clearly against public policy if an employee could evade the legal consequence of his own breach by causing a fellow employee to join him in it.

I.C.I. Ltd. v. *Shatwell* (1964). Two qualified shot-firers were injured through testing a circuit without taking shelter, although they knew it was dangerous and against both the company's orders and statutory regulations. HELD: *Volenti non fit injuria* was a complete defence to the company in respect of its alleged vicarious liability.

10. Contributory negligence (*see* VI, **30**). Contributory negligence is a good defence to an action for breach of statutory duty: *Caswell* v. *Powell Duffryn Collieries Ltd.* (1940). The damages may be apportioned under the *Law Reform (Contributory Negligence) Act*, 1945. Note that the relevant part of the decision in *Caswell* v. *Powell Duffryn etc.*, although unanimous was also *obiter*.

Contributory negligence may not be easy to establish where a workman sues his employer for breach of statutory duty, for the standard to be expected is only that of an ordinary prudent workman—"It is not for every risky thing that a work-

man in a factory may do . . . that the plaintiff ought to be held
guilty of contributory negligence": *Flower* v. *Ebbw Vale etc.
Steel Co.* (1934), *per* Lawrence J.

NOTE: As in negligence, the onus is on the *defendant* to prove the
plaintiff's contributory negligence. A plaintiff who has established that the breach caused his injury need not show exactly
how the accident happened.

11. Delegation of the statutory duty. In the case of the
breach of an *absolute* statutory duty (*see* **7** above) it is no
defence that it was delegated to a reasonably competent
person. Furthermore, although delegation is still in theory a
defence where the delegation was to the plaintiff himself,
who was injured solely because of his own disobedience,
the defence is in practice obsolete. The modern test is—was
the plaintiff's own negligence so great as to absolve the defendant altogether? If not, then the damages are apportioned
under the *Law Reform (Contributory Negligence) Act*, 1945.

NOTE: This position should be contrasted with that in which two
or more servants are involved: *I.C.I. Ltd.* v. *Shatwell* (1964).

PROGRESS TEST 7

1. What is the onus of proof in an action for breach of statutory
duty? **(2–6)**
2. What must the plaintiff prove? **(2)**
3. What are the appropriate remedies for a breach of statutory
duty owed to the public at large? **(5)**
4. For what proposition is *Atkinson* v. *Newcastle and Gateshead
Waterworks Co.* (1877) authority? **(5)**
5. In what circumstances will a breach of statutory duty be
(*a*) absolute; (*b*) actionable only on proof of special damage or
wrongful intent? **(7)**
6. What is meant by the term "statutory negligence"? What are
the differences between negligence and breach of statutory duty?
(8)
7. To what extent (if at all) is *volenti non fit injuria* a good
defence to an action for breach of statutory duty? **(9)**
8. Is contributory negligence a defence? **(10)**
9. When (if ever) is it a good defence that the statutory duty
was delegated to a competent person? **(11)**
10. What is the position where the delegation was to the plaintiff himself? **(11)**

CHAPTER VIII

THE RULE IN RYLANDS *v.* FLETCHER

A RULE OF STRICT LIABILITY

1. Strict liabilities defined. The Rule in *Rylands* v. *Fletcher* is a rule of *absolute* or *strict* liability, *i.e.* it does not require proof of negligence, or lack of care, or wrongful intention, by the defendant.

2. The original statement. The rule was originally formulated by Blackburn J. when the case was heard in the Court of Exchequer chamber in 1866 (*sub nom Fletcher* v. *Rylands*), in the following terms: "The person who for his own purposes brings on his land and collects and keeps there anything likely to do mischief if it escapes, must keep it in at his peril and, if he does not do so, is *prima facie* answerable for all the damage which is the natural consequences of its escape." This was approved by the House of Lords when the case was finally settled in 1868.

3. The facts of Rylands v. Fletcher. The facts of the case were that the defendant employed an independent contractor to construct a reservoir on his (the defendant's) land. The defendant did not know of, and could not reasonably have discovered the existence of disused mine shafts on the site. When the reservoir was filled, the plaintiff's adjoining coal mine was flooded.

4. Plaintiff restricted by the Forms of Action. The plaintiff, for various reasons, could not bring his action in Trespass, Nuisance or Negligence. In consequence he could make the defendant liable only if he could establish that, in the circumstances, the defendant's liability was strict or absolute. The House of Lords eventually upheld that proposition, thus establishing the separate and distinct form of tortious liability since known as the Rule in *Rylands* v. *Fletcher*.

NOTE: *Rylands* v. *Fletcher* established a new *rule* but it did not originate the *principle* of absolute liability, which had already existed for at least three hundred years.

5. The extent of the rule

(*a*) *Effect of strict liability.* Because liability under the rule is strict, the courts have always been vigilant to contain its operation within the limits originally laid down. It is therefore essential to grasp the exact nature and extent of these limits; and also of the exceptions to the rule (*see* **12** below).

(*b*) *Limits of the rule established.* Since 1868 the limits of the rule have been defined and established by certain propositions laid down in decided cases. They may be summarised as follows:

(*i*) There must have been an *escape* from the defendant's land of a "thing likely to do mischief."

(*ii*) There must have been a *non-natural use* of the defendant's land.

6. There must be an "escape"

(*a*) *Analogy with nuisance.* The rule in *Rylands* v. *Fletcher* is analogous with nuisance to the extent that the thing doing the damage must escape from *the land* of the defendant. Thus, damage occurring *outside* the boundaries of the land from which the thing doing the damage emanated is actionable in nuisance or *Rylands* v. *Fletcher*: but damage caused wholly *within* the land or premises concerned is not, the appropriate action being, *e.g.*, for negligence or breach of statutory duty.

Thus, in *Read* v. *J. Lyons & Co. Ltd.* (1947), it was said that *escape*, for the purposes of applying the proposition in *Rylands* v. *Fletcher*, means "escape from a place where the defendant has occupation of or control over land to a place which is outside his occupation or control": *per* Lord Simon; and "there must be the escape of something from one man's close to another man's close": *per* Lord Macmillan.

Read v. *J. Lyons & Co. Ltd.* (1947). The plaintiff, a Munitions Inspector of the Ministry of Supply, was injured while on defendant's premises by the explosion of a shell in process of manufacture. She did not allege negligence but sued in *Rylands* v. *Fletcher*. HELD: *Rylands* v. *Fletcher* did not apply as there had been *no escape of a dangerous thing* from the premises—"The doctrine of *Rylands* v. *Fletcher* . . . derives from a conception of mutual duties of adjoining or neighbour-ing landowners and its cogeners are trespass and nuisance": *per* Lord Macmillan.

(*b*) *Damage a natural consequence of the escape.* Further-more, the plaintiff must prove, not only that there was an *escape* of the dangerous thing, but also that the damage was the *natural consequence of the escape*.

7. Things likely to do mischief

(*a*) *A question of fact.* Whether a "thing" which has been brought and kept on the defendant's land is one which is likely to do mischief if it escapes is a question of *fact*. Consequently, a particular "thing" may come within the rule in one case but not in another. This has applied, *inter alia*, to trees, water, motor vehicles and guns: on the other hand electricity and chemicals have always been held to come under the rule.

(*b*) *What is a "thing"?* Again, it is a question of fact in each case; for such a wide variety of animate and inanimate objects and phenomena have been held to come under the rule that neither a concise nor an exhaustive definition is possible.

(*c*) *"Rylands* v. *Fletcher objects."* Examples:

    (*i*) Electricity: *Eastern and South African Telegraph Co.* v. *Capetown Tramways Co.* (1902).
    (*ii*) Gas: *Northwestern Utilities Ltd.* v. *London Guarantee and Accident Co.* (1936).
    (*iii*) Sewage: *Jones* v. *Llanrwst U.D.C.* (1911).
    (*iv*) Vibration: *Hoare and Co.* v. *McAlpine* (1923).
    (*v*) Projecting trees: *Crowhurst* v. *Amersham Burial Board* (1878).

There are many more: it seems that *Rylands* v. *Fletcher* objects are, like nuisances, infinite.

CONDITIONS OF LIABILITY

8. A question of fact. It is impossible to say with certainty when such an object will give rise to liability. It seems, however, that it will do so if it is "dangerous" or "potentially dangerous"; albeit these descriptions, although often invoked, are difficult to define and have been much criticised. The most that can be said is that an object is dangerous if, the defendant having brought and kept it upon his land, it will *do damage if it escapes therefrom*. Thus anything which will do damage if it escapes, whether or not it is harmless while confined, comes under the rule.

9. "Things" widely defined. The very wide definition of "things" for the purpose of the rule is illustrated by the decision in *A.-G.* v. *Corke* (1933) that it includes persons.

The defendant allowed caravan dwellers to camp on his land. They "escaped" and committed nuisances on adjacent land. HELD: Defendant liable in *Rylands* v. *Fletcher*. Injunction granted to prevent further "escapes" and depredations.

10. The rule as it affects highways. Things on the highway form an exception to the general rule that the dangerous object must have escaped from land occupied or controlled by the defendant. There is strict liability for dangerous things which have been brought upon the highway, or interfered with while there, so that they escape and do damage on adjacent property.

Charing Cross Electricity Supply Co. v. *Hydraulic Power Co.* (1914). Both companies were statutory licensees on the highway. The defendant's water escaped, damaging plaintiff's cables. HELD: Defendant liable in *Rylands* v. *Fletcher*.

11. The land itself and things naturally upon it.

(*a*) *The thing must be brought and kept on the land.* *Rylands* v. *Fletcher* applies only to things *brought and kept* on the land for the defendant's own purposes—and therefore not to the land itself and *things naturally upon it*. Such things as water, weeds and destructive wild animals have been held *not* to come within the rule. There is no common-law duty to prevent the escape of such things, but there may be a statutory duty, *e.g.* under the *Weeds Act* (1959).

Giles v. *Walker* (1890). Defendant ploughed waste land, thereby causing thistles to grow on adjoining land. HELD: No liability in nuisance or *Rylands* v. *Fletcher*.

(*b*) *Artificial accumulation.* But distinguish carefully between things naturally on the land and the artificial accumulation of natural things, *e.g.* rainwater in a reservoir. There will be liability in the latter type of case.

(*c*) *Liability for causation.* A person will be liable who *causes* the escape of things naturally on the land.

> *Whalley* v. *Lancashire and Yorkshire Rly.* (1884). Rain-water accumulated on defendant's land, but was contained by an embankment. The company removed part of the embankment in order to save the remainder, thus flooding plaintiff's land. HELD: Liable in *Rylands* v. *Fletcher.*

But the defendant must *cause* the escape, *i.e.* the defendant is not necessarily liable *merely because* he removes an artificial barrier from his own land, whereby adjoining land is flooded. Furthermore, *Smith* v. *Kenrick* (1849) established that a mine-owner will not be liable where the ordinary working of his mine caused water to flow by gravitation into an adjoining mine.

(*d*) *No liability for prevention.* A person who *prevents* flood water coming onto his land will not be liable if he thereby sends the water upon adjoining land: but *aliter* if defendant's preventive operations divert water *already upon* his land onto that of the plaintiff.

EXCEPTIONS TO THE RULE

12. Non-liability. In the following instances the occupier is not liable under the Rule in *Rylands* v. *Fletcher*—although he may be liable for negligence.

    (*a*) Consent of the plaintiff (*see* **13** below).
    (*b*) Default of the plaintiff (*see* **14** below).
    (*c*) Statutory authority (*see* **15** below).
    (*d*) Act of a stranger (*see* **16** below).
    (*e*) Act of God (*see* **17** below).

13. Consent of the plaintiff

(*a*) *If the plaintiff expressly or impliedly consented* to the defendant's bringing and keeping the dangerous thing on his premises, the latter will not be liable *except for negligence.* Thus, the tenants of lower floors in a building impliedly consent to damage by water which escapes, without the occupier's negligence, from the upper floors—for the water is there by the implied consent and for the *common benefit* of the various occupiers.

(b) *Extraordinary user.* The exception will *not* apply, however, to an extraordinary use, or quantity, of water, for the defendant's own purposes. See *Western Engraving Co.* v. *Film Laboratories Ltd.* (1936) where there was an escape of an excessive quantity of water accumulated by defendants for washing film.

14. Default of the plaintiff

(a) *Plaintiff causes own injury.* If the plaintiff himself caused his injury he cannot recover under the rule, *e.g.* a trespasser must take the property as he finds it.

(b) *Special sensitivity.* Furthermore, by analogy with the similar rule in nuisance, a plaintiff cannot recover for damage arising from the *special sensitivity* of his property (*see* V, 9).

> *Eastern and South African Telegraph Co. Ltd.* v. *Cape Town Tramways Co.* (1902). A very small escape of electricity disturbed operation of sensitive submarine cables. HELD: No liability in *Rylands* v. *Fletcher.*

15. Statutory authority.

(a) *Depends on construction.* The defendant may plead that he is exempt by statutory authority from *Rylands* v. *Fletcher* liability: but whether the plea succeeds will *depend on a construction of the statute* in question (*see* I, 20–27; VII, 1).

> *Green* v. *Chelsea Waterworks Co.* (1894). Defendants' water main burst, flooding plaintiff's premises. Defendants had statutory authority to lay the main and a statutory duty to supply water, and they had not been negligent. HELD: They were not liable in *Rylands* v. *Fletcher.* "That case is not to be extended beyond the legitimate principle on which the House of Lords decided it": *per* Lindley L.J.

(b) *When statutory power permissive only.* The above case should be contrasted with *Charing Cross Electricity Supply Co.* v. *Hydraulic Power Co.* (1914), in which, on similar facts, the defendants were held liable in *Rylands* v. *Fletcher.* In this case, however, the defendants, although they had statutory powers to lay mains and supply water, were under no statutory obligation actually to do so.

(c) *Effect of negligence.* A defendant with statutory exemption from *Rylands* v. *Fletcher* liability may nevertheless be liable if there was negligence.

Hardaker v. *Idle District Council* (1896). Defendants had statutory authority to supply gas. Gas escaped into plantiff's house because of negligence of Council's independent contractor. HELD: Council liable in *Rylands* v. *Fletcher*.

16. Act of a stranger.

(a) *No control by the occupier.* The occupier will not be liable in *Rylands* v. *Fletcher* where the escape of the dangerous thing arose from the act of a stranger over whom the occupier had no control.

Box v. *Jubb* (1879). A third person discharged water into defendant's reservoir, so that it overflowed and damaged plaintiff's property. HELD: No *Rylands* v. *Fletcher* liability.

(b) *Onus on the defendant.* Note carefully, however, that the onus is on the *defendant* to show (i) that the escape was due to the act of a stranger; (ii) that he had no control over that stranger: (iii) that he could not reasonably have guarded against the act.

(c) *Effect of occupier's negligence.* Note also that an occupier may be liable in *negligence* for the act of a stranger when the circumstances are such that the occupier ought to have taken reasonable steps to guard against it: *Northwest Utilities* v. *London Guarantee and Accident Co.* (1936), a Privy Council case.

(d) *Who is a "stranger"?* A "stranger" is a trespasser; or a person who causes the escape, although he did not himself come upon the land. Carefully distinguish strangers from those (*e.g.* servants) for whom the occupier is vicariously liable.

17. Act of God. Act of God is a defence to a *Rylands* v. *Fletcher* action. Indeed, *Nichols* v. *Marsland* (1876), the leading case on the matter, was such an action. Note that, because *Rylands* v. *Fletcher* liability is *strict*, inevitable accident is *not* a defence (*see* I, **30–31**).

LIABILITY FOR FIRE

18. The nature of the liability. For centuries users of fire have been under a heavy legal obligation to take care—although the common-law liability is probably not "strict" in the full technical sense of that word, *i.e.* the authorities seem to indicate that the plaintiff must show some element of negligence. However, liability for fire is often governed by the Rule in *Rylands* v. *Fletcher*, or by statutory rules; or the common-law rule is subject to certain qualifications, indicated below.

19. The Fires Prevention (Metropolis) Act, 1776, S. 86.

(*a*) *The effect of the section* is that a person on whose premises a fire "accidently begins" is not liable for damage resulting from it. *Collingwood* v. *Home & Colonial Stores Ltd.* (1936) and *Williams* v. *Owen* (1956) are modern authorities for this.

(*b*) *Effect of Rylands* v. *Fletcher*. Note carefully that fire damage which arises from a breach of the Rule in *Rylands* v. *Fletcher* is not protected by *s.* 86 of the *Fires Prevention (Metropolis) Act*, 1776. But it is often difficult to say whether the defendant "brought and kept" the cause of the fire, on his premises; and the plaintiff must prove "non-natural use" of the defendant's premises.

(*c*) *Negligence and nuisance.* Section 86 gives protection only where the fire "accidently begins," so that a defendant who was negligent will be liable. Nor does the section apply to fires which arise from or constitute a *nuisance*.

20. Liability for independent contractors. A person is liable for damage arising from fires started by the negligence of both his servants and his independent contractors (*see* XII, **8**): *Balfour* v. *Barty-King* (1957).

21. Liability for the spread of fire. A person upon whose premises a fire "accidently begins," and who is therefore protected by *s.* 86, may nevertheless be liable if he negligently allows the fire to *spread*—see *Musgrove* v. *Pandelis* (1919), where a fire started accidentally in defendant's motor car, on his premises, but his chauffeur allowed the fire to spread by negligently failing to turn off the petrol. Furthermore, apart from any liability under the *Occupiers' Liability Act* 1957, and irrespective of whether the 1776 Act applies, an occupier may be liable at *common-law* for negligently allowing a fire to spread from his premises—in *Sturge* v. *Hackett* (1962) an occupier was liable for the spread of the fire he started by igniting a bird's nest on his premises.

PROGRESS TEST 8

1. What is a rule of strict liability? **(1)**

2. State the Rule in *Rylands* v. *Fletcher* in the words of Blackburn J. **(2)**

3. What are the limits of the Rule in *Rylands* v. *Fletcher*? **(5)**

4. What was established by *Read* v. *J. Lyons & Co. Ltd.* (1947)? **(6)**

5. (*a*) Give some examples of *Rylands v. Fletcher* objects. (*b*) If a "thing" is held to be a *Rylands* v. *Fletcher* object in one case, will it always thereafter be held to be such an object? **(7)**

6. (*a*) What criteria will be adopted in deciding whether a "thing" is a *Rylands* v. *Fletcher* object? (*b*) What did *Attorney-General* v. *Corke* (1933) decide? **(8, 9)**

7. How does the Rule in *Rylands* v. *Fletcher* apply to things on the highway? **(10)**

8. (*a*) Does the Rule in *Rylands* v. *Fletcher* apply to the land itself and things naturally upon it? (*b*) What is the position of one who causes the escape of something naturally upon the land? (*c*) Explain how the rule affects one who deals with flood water upon his own land? **(11)**

9. Is *volenti non fit injuria* a defence in a *Rylands* v. *Fletcher* action? **(13)**

10. How does the Rule in *Rylands* v. *Fletcher* affect (*a*) trespassers; (*b*) specially sensitive property? **(14)**

11. Explain the extent to which (if at all) statutory authority is a defence to a *Rylands* v. *Fletcher* action. **(15)**

12. Explain the application of the defence of act of a stranger to a *Rylands* v. *Fletcher* action. **(16)**

13. Is (*a*) Act of God, (*b*) inevitable accident, a defence to *Rylands* v. *Fletcher*? **(17)**

14. Outline the nature of the liability for fire. **(18)**

15. What is the effect of the *Fires Prevention* (*Metropolis*) *Act*, 1776? How, if at all, does it affect the application of the Rule in *Rylands* v. *Fletcher*? **(19)**

16. What is the nature of the liability for fires arising from negligence and nuisance? Is an employer liable for fires negligently started by his independent contractor? **(19, 20)**

17. Explain the nature of the liability for the spread of fire. **(21)**

CHAPTER IX

LIABILITY FOR DANGEROUS PROPERTY

NATURE OF THE LIABILITY

1. The Occupiers' Liability Act, 1957. The liability of occupiers of *premises* (which include any fixed or moveable structure, including any vessel, vehicle or aircraft) in respect of their premises, is governed by the *Occupiers' Liability Act, 1957.* The Act provides that an *occupier* of premises owes *the common duty of care,* with respect to the premises, to his *visitors, i.e.* to persons lawfully on his premises, and to their property. The occupier may, in so far as he is legally free to do so, extend, restrict, modify or exclude this duty, by agreement or otherwise. The provisions and effects of the Act are considered in detail in **4–9** below.

NOTE
  (*i*) Any liability of the occupier to those (*e.g.* persons on adjoining land, or the highway) injured by his dangerous property, but not on his premises, will be in *nuisance.*
  (*ii*) There is a residual common-law duty to trespassers, who were not affected by the Act (*see* **10–12** below).
  (*iii*) Although the occupier is primarily liable, landlords not in possession and third parties on the premises may be liable in certain circumstances (*see* **14–15** below).

2. The duty at common law. An outline knowledge of the common-law rules which were replaced (although not abolished) by the *Occupiers' Liability Act, 1957,* is essential to a proper understanding of the present position. There were, at common law, three categories of persons entering premises. A person who, before the passing of the *Occupiers' Liability Act, 1957,* entered premises in the occupation or control of another, was either a licensee; an invitee; or a trespasser. The standard of care owed him by the occupier depended on which of these categories he occupied.

  (*a*) *Licensees.* At common law, a licensee is one who has the mere gratuitous permission, express or implied, of the occupier to be on the premises for a purpose in which the *occupier has no interest*. A licensee must take the premises as he finds them, subject only to the occupier's duty to warn of concealed dangers; not to set traps; and not to injure the licensee by a positive act of misfeasance.

(b) *Invitees.* At common law an invitee, sometimes called a licensee with an interest, is a person who comes onto the occupier's premises with the latter's consent, in pursuit of a *common interest with the occupier*. Thus, a customer in a shop is an invitee at common law, as shopkeeper and customer have a common interest in the customer's being there. An occupier owes his invitee, provided he remains within the terms of his invitation, a duty to take reasonable care for his safety, *i.e.* a considerably more stringent duty than that owed to a licensee. The nature of the duty was defined in *Indermaur* v. *Dames* (1866).

(c) *Trespassers.* A trespasser is a person without any kind of permission to be on the land or premises, and whose "presence is either unknown to the proprietor or, if known, is practically objected to": *Robert Addie & Sons Ltd.* v. *Dumbreck* (1929), *per* Lord Dunedin. A trespasser enters the premises entirely at his own risk, the only duty of the occupier being not to inflict damage intentionally or recklessly on a trespasser he knows to be there.

3. Reform of the law. As the law relating to dangerous property had become complex and difficult, it was referred to the Law Reform Committee. The major recommendations in the committees' report of 1954 were embodied in the *Occupiers' Liability Act*, 1957. As we have seen, this Act now governs the matter, and must therefore be considered in some detail.

THE OCCUPIERS' LIABILITY ACT, 1957

4. The common duty of care. Section 2 (2) defines the common duty of care as "a duty to take such care as in *all the circumstances of the case is reasonable* to see the visitor will be *reasonably safe* in using the premises for the purpose for which he is invited or permitted by the occupier to be there." It is clear from this, and also from the provision in *s.* 1 (2) that the Act "shall not alter the rules of common law as to the persons on whom a duty is imposed or to whom it is owed," that the obligations imposed by the Act are *not* strict. It therefore follows that:

(a) the plaintiff must prove failure to observe the common duty of care;

(b) the standard of the common duty of care may vary with the circumstances.

It is therefore necessary to consider these duties and standards under various headings.

5. The duty of care. The effect of the Act is that all persons coming onto premises subject to its provisions are either lawful visitors or trespassers. The same *duty* of care (the *common duty of care*) is owed to *all* lawful visitors, but the *standard* of the common duty of care may be different for various categories of visitors. The common-law categories of invitees and licensees are an exception to this, for the Act has the effect of abolishing the distinction between them, and imposing the common duty of care on the occupier in respect of both categories. Nevertheless, facts which would previously have been relevant in deciding whether a person was an invitee or a licensee may now be relevant in deciding whether the occupier discharged the common duty of care.

NOTE: Students who need a fuller knowledge of this somewhat complex matter are advised to consult larger works.

6. Children. Section 2 (3) (a) provides that "an occupier must be prepared for children to be less careful than adults." The standard of care owed to children is that laid down in cases preceding the Act. Briefly, an occupier is bound to take special care in respect of anything on his premises which would be especially attractive or alluring to children, and which contains dangers which children would not appreciate. Examples include derelict machinery—*Cooke* v. *Midland Great Western Railway of Ireland* (1909)—poisonous berries—*Glasgow Corporation* v. *Taylor* (1922)—and builders' vehicles—*Creed* v. *John McGeoch & Sons Ltd.* (1955).

An occupier who fails (*e.g.* by inadequate fencing or warning) to observe the appropriate standard of care may be liable to children although, in the same circumstances, he would not be liable to adults. Furthermore, the courts are more inclined to hold, in cases involving children, that the occupier has by acquiescence converted a trespasser into a visitor. On the other hand, an occupier is not liable to children injured by dangers (*e.g.* large expanses of water) which are too obviously dangerous to be "alluring"; except in the case of children so young as to be susceptible to *all* dangers: *Phipps* v. *Rochester Corporation* (1955): *see* VI, **20**, **44**.

7. Persons entering under contract. Obligations under a contract depend upon the terms of that contract. Section 5 therefore provides that *the common duty of care* shall be *implied* as a term of the contract in respect of the duty owed by the occupier "in respect of damages due to the state of the premises or to things done or omitted to be done on them," where such matters are not covered by a term forming part of the contract.

Note carefully the important exception in the case of contracts "for the hire of, or for the carriage for reward of, persons or goods in any vehicle, vessel, aircraft or other means of transport," the effects of this exception are as follows:

(*a*) It is necessary to distinguish carefully between vehicles, ships and aircraft constituting *exceptions* governed by *common-law* rules (*see* below) and vehicles, ships and aircraft which are "*premises*" governed by the Act.

(*b*) *Implied* terms in respect of carriage by vehicles, ships and aircraft, constituting exceptions under *s.* 5 are governed, not by the Act, but by the more onerous common-law rules. The effect of these is that the duty of care is not discharged unless *all* reasonable care and skill have been used to see that the vehicle, ship or aircraft is safe. The effect of this is that the "occupier" will be liable in respect of the negligence of his *independent contractor*, contrary to the general rule (*see* XII, **3**, **8**).

Note that *contracts of bailment* are also excepted from the provisions of *s.* 5.

8. Third parties entering under contract. The effect of *s.* 3 (1) is that, where an occupier is bound by contract to allow persons who are not parties to the contract (*s.* 3 (2)) to enter or use the premises, the occupier *cannot by that contract exclude the common duty of care he owes to such third parties* as lawful visitors.

Such a contract includes the occupier's duty to perform his obligations under it, "in so far as those obligations go beyond the obligations otherwise involved in that duty." Furthermore, *s.* 3 (4) provides that the same principles shall apply where a landlord or tenant is bound by the *terms of a tenancy*, though not by contract, to allow persons to enter or use premises of which he is the occupier.

9. Persons entering premises under a duty or power. Section 2 (6) provides that persons who enter premises for any purpose in the exercise of a *right conferred by law* are to be treated as permitted by the occupier to be there for that purpose, whether they have his permission or not. This means that the occupier owes the common duty of care, *e.g.*, to police officers, and to persons with certain statutory powers of entry such as Electricity and Gas Board officials. Note that the effect of the words "for that purpose" is that if such persons exceed their powers or duties they may cease to be lawful visitors and become trespassers, and lose the protection of the Act.

NOTE

(*i*) Persons entering premises occupied by public authorities (*e.g.* public libraries) have no statutory powers of entry, but are owed the common duty of care under the general provisions of the Act.

(*ii*) The *Occupiers' Liability Act*, 1957, does not apply to persons entering land under the provisions of the *National Parks and Access to the Countryside Act*, 1949.

TRESPASSERS

10. Occupier owes some duties to trespassers. The *Occupiers' Liability Act*, 1957, applies only to lawful visitors, and not to trespassers, to whom the rules of common law therefore continue to apply. Under these rules, occupiers are not entirely without duties to trespassers, nor trespassers entirely without rights. The position is as follows:

(*a*) One who entered as a trespasser may become a lawful visitor, *e.g.* by the continued acquiescence of the occupier, or by receiving the occupier's consent or permission. Note that the onus of proving acquiescence is on the plaintiff.

(*b*) Trespassers should be distinguished from those, such

as tradesmen and canvassers, who have the implied or tacit permission of the occupier to enter.

11. The duty to trespassers defined. The general rule is that a trespasser enters at his own risk, and that the occupier's only duty is that of not intentionally or recklessly inflicting damage on a trespasser he knows to be present.

This long-established rule was specifically reaffirmed by the Judicial Committee of the Privy Council in *Commissioner for Railways* v. *Quinlan* (1964). However, it was suggested both in that case and in *Videan* v. *British Transport Commission* (1963) that a person injured on premises he entered without permission might be the occupier's "neighbour" within the principle in *Donoghue* v. *Stevenson,* either additionally or alternatively to being a trespasser (*see* VI, 8).

NOTE: The two cases mentioned above are not easy to reconcile. Students are referred to the reports of the cases, and discussions in larger works.

12. The nature of the duty to trespassers.

(*a*) The occupier must not deliberately set traps or create dangers for trespassers. This goes back to cases such as *Bird* v. *Holbrook* (1828), having to do with spring guns (long since illegal). However, merely *deterrent* measures such as barbed-wire fences, spikes or glass on walls, or the keeping of a watchdog, are not made unlawful by this rule.

NOTE: Intentional harm to a trespasser may be justified as self-defence.

(*b*) Intention or recklessness, and knowledge of the trespasser's presence, are essential to liability. The occupier will not be liable to a trespasser unless the occupier knew or ought reasonably to have known of his presence; but an occupier will be liable in respect of injury arising from reckless disregard for the safety of, or deliberate intention to injure, a trespasser known to be present: *Robert Addie & Sons Ltd. (Collieries)* v. *Dumbreck* (1929).

Mourton v. *Poulter* (1930). Defendant felled a tree, thereby injuring a child who was trespassing on the land. HELD: Defendant liable, as (*i*) he failed to warn the child, whom he knew to be endangered; (*ii*) one who creates danger by doing something which *changes the condition* of the land has a duty to warn even trespassers.

Compare with the following:

Videan v. *British Transport Commission* (1963). Station-master jumped from platform in an attempt to save his small son, who had strayed on to the line, from being run down by a trolley. The father was killed and the child injured. The trolley driver was found to have been negligent. HELD: (*i*) The trolley driver owed the child trespasser no duty of care, as his presence on the line was not reasonably foreseeable; (*ii*) the presence of the father *was* reasonably foreseeable, therefore the trolley driver owed him a duty of care. His widow could recover damages under the *Fatal Accidents Acts*, 1846–1959, and the *Law Reform (Miscellaneous Provisions) Act*, 1934.

NOTE: It was held in *Davis* v. *St. Mary's Demolition & Excavation Co. Ltd.* (1954) that a duty of care was owed to the child trespasser in that case, because he was a "neighbour."

CASES WHERE THE OCCUPIER IS NOT LIABLE

13. Exclusion of Liability.

(*a*) Section 2 (1) of the *Occupiers' Liability Act*, 1957, provides that an occupier may extend, restrict, modify or exclude his duty to any visitor or visitors, insofar as he is free to do so, by agreement or otherwise.

(*b*) Section 2 (4) provides that, in determining whether the occupier of premises has discharged the common duty of care to a visitor, regard is to be had to all the circumstances. Thus:

(*i*) where damage is caused to a visitor by a danger of which he had been warned, the warning is not to be treated without more as absolving the occupier from liability unless in all the circumstances it was enough to enable the visitor to be reasonably safe;

(*ii*) where damage has been caused to a visitor through the faulty work of an independent contractor employed by the occupier, the occupier is not to be treated without more as liable for the damage if in all the circumstances he had acted reasonably in entrusting the work to an independent contractor, and in satisfying himself that the contractor was competent and the work properly done.

(*c*) Section 2 (5) provides that the common duty of care does not impose on an occupier any obligation to a visitor in respect of *risks willingly accepted* as his by the visitor, and that the question of whether a risk was so accepted is to be decided on the same principles as in other cases in which one person owes a duty of care to another.

(*d*) It seems that *contributory negligence is a defence*, although the Act itself does not say so (*see* VI, **30–39**).

14. Liability of persons other than occupiers.

(*a*) *Liability of contractors.* We have seen that the occupier is not liable under the *Occupiers' Liability Act, 1957,* for the torts of his independent contractor. However, *the contractor himself* may be liable—although not under the Act, as he is not the occupier. But he may be sued for negligence, or any other tort he may have committed, under the principle (an application of the "neighbour" principle) that one who creates a dangerous state of things on premises will be liable to those who come onto those premises and suffer damage in consequence of that dangerous state: *Billings (A.C.) & Sons Ltd.* v. *Riden* (1957).

> NOTE: Although, in fact, the above mainly concerns contractors, the principle applies to *anyone* on the premises who is under a duty to take reasonable care for the safety of lawful visitors.

(*b*) *Liability of non-occupier to trespassers.* The fact that a person who comes on to land or premises is a trespasser with regard to the occupier *will not in itself absolve a non-occupier on the premises* if, in all the circumstances, the plaintiff trespasser was one the defendant non-occupier ought reasonably to have had in contemplation: *Buckland* v. *Guildford Gas Light & Coke Co.* (1948).

15. Liability of lessors and vendors of dangerous premises. In general, lessors and vendors of premises are under no liability in *tort* with respect to the premises (they may be liable in contract), to their lessees or purchasers, or to others who come upon the premises; for, "fraud apart, there is no law against letting a tumbledown house, and the tenant's remedy is upon his contract": *Robbins* v. *Jones* (1863), *per* Erle C.J. Furthermore, the principle in *Donoghue* v. *Stevenson* does not apply to real property. However, this general rule is subject to the following qualifications.

(a) *Lessor's liability for own premises.* If a landlord, having demised premises to tenants, nevertheless retains part of the premises (*e.g.* a common hall or stairway, or the roof, chimneys or gutterings) in his own occupation, then, in respect of dangers arising from such parts of the premises, he is under a duty to take reasonable care for the safety of his lawful visitors: *Cunard* v. *Antifyre Ltd.* (1938); *Taylor* v. *Liverpool Corporation* (1939).

NOTE: The landlord, to be liable, must be the *exclusive occupier* of the defective part of the premises. Note also that, so far as concerns those parts of the premises occupied by the landlord, his lawful visitors include the tenants (as in *Cunard* v. *Antifyre*) and *their* lawful visitors.

(b) *Lessor's liability to third parties.* The *Occupiers' Liability Act,* 1957, *s.* 4, provides that a landlord who is under an obligation to maintain and repair the premises shall owe to lawful visitors, in respect of damage or injury arising from failure so to maintain and repair, the same duty of care as if he himself was the occupier. Note, however, that a *third party* cannot recover damages under this provision unless the damage he suffered would have been actionable by the *tenant* (*s.* 4. (4)).

(c) *Misfeasance of lessor.* A landlord will be liable for damage arising from a *positive act of misfeasance* committed by him, with respect to the premises, after the commencement of the lease, whereby a source of danger is created: *Billings* (*A.C.*) *& Sons Ltd.* v. *Riden* (1957).

(d) *Liability of vendors.* In accordance with the principle *caveat emptor,* the vendor has no liability in respect of damage arising from defects in the premises in the absence of an express or implied warranty of fitness. However, the *court* may *imply* such a warranty if it thinks the circumstances justify it. Note that the vendor cannot be liable for the purchaser's visitors.

(e) *Liability for fraud.* A lessor or vendor will always be liable for fraud committed by him in letting or selling the premises.

PROGRESS TEST 9

1. What are the basic provisions of the *Occupiers' Liability Act,* 1957? May any persons other than the occupier be liable under

the provisions of the Act? Are trespassers affected by the Act? **(1)**

2. Outline the position at common law before the passing of the Act. What was the significance of the difference between licensees and invitees? **(2)**

3. How does the Act define the "common duty of care"? Does the Act impose strict liability? Give reasons for your answer. **(4)**

4. Explain the differences between duty of care and standard of care under the Act. Of what significance to this is the common-law distinction between licensees and invitees? **(5)**

5. Explain, with reference to decided cases, the standard of care enjoined by the Act towards children. **(6)**

6. What are the provisions of the Act with regard to persons entering premises under a contract? Are there any exceptions—if so, what is their significance? **(7)**

7. State the duties of an occupier to a third party who enters the premises under the terms of a contract with the occupier. **(8)**

8. State the provisions of the *Occupiers' Liability Act*, 1957, with regard to persons who enter premises under a right conferred by law. **(9)**

9. Does the *Occupiers' Liability Act* apply to trespassers? By what means (if at all) may a trespasser become a lawful visitor? Is a canvasser a trespasser? **(10)**

10. What is the duty of an occupier to trespassers? Can a trespasser be the occupier's "neighbour"? **(11)**

11. Is an occupier liable to a trespasser who is injured by barbed wire when entering the premises? **(12)**

12. State, with reference to decided cases, what a trespasser must prove in order to establish that the occupier is liable to him for damage or injuries sustained on the premises. **(12)**

13. What is the effect of the *Occupiers' Liability Act*, 1957, with regard to (*a*) warnings to visitors; (*b*) visitors injured through default of an independent contractor; (*c*) *volenti non fit injuria*; (*d*) contributory negligence? **(13)**

14. State the nature of the liability (if any) of the occupier's contractors to lawful visitors to the occupier's premises. Has a non-occupier on the premises any duty to trespassers on the premises? **(14)**

15. State fully the general rule, and its qualifications, as to the liability of lessors and vendors of dangerous premises. **(15)**

CHAPTER X

LIABILITY FOR DANGEROUS THINGS

NATURE OF THE LIABILITY

1. Origins and general nature of the liability. Historically, there was no liability in *tort* for dangerous chattels, but only in contract. But the law did recognise that a duty of care existed in respect of two classes of chattels, *i.e.* those dangerous in themselves, such as firearms and explosives, and those known to the defendant to be dangerous. However, the authorities, both ancient and modern, seem to establish beyond doubt that liability for dangerous things is no more than a particular branch of the law of negligence, and that no separate *principles* of law are involved. There is equally no doubt that liability for dangerous chattels is generally recognised as a distinct and separate type of liability for negligence, having its own rules. These must therefore be considered.

NOTE: Although the term "liability for dangerous chattels" is general usage, the liability extends to other things and phenomena (such as gas, for instance) which are not chattels. Note also that liability for dangerous things may fall within the Rule in *Rylands* v. *Fletcher.*

2. The effect of Donoghue v. Stevenson (1932). Before 1932 the development of the law with regard to liability for dangerous chattels was hindered by the so-called "contract fallacy," *i.e.* the proposition that liability for things dangerous *sub modo*—as distinct from things dangerous *per se*—transferred by way of contract, loan or gift, was:

    (*a*) *very severely limited* with regard to the *immediate* recipient of the dangerous thing;

    (*b*) *non-existent* with regard to subsequent recipients, because they were not parties to the contract, and were therefore excluded by the privity rule.

Donoghue v. *Stevenson* exploded the contract fallacy, and established a considerable part of the modern law with regard to dangerous things. The consequences of *Donoghue* v. *Stevenson* are considered in detail in **6–11** below.

NOTE: In the many cases involving dangerous things in which there is liability in both tort and contract, the latter is likely to be the more stringent, *e.g.* because of the implied warranties under the *Sale of Goods Act*, 1893, or the implied conditions under the Hire Purchase Acts. Furthermore, the terms of the contract may exclude tortious liability altogether.

THE MODERN LAW OUTLINED

3. Abolition of the distinctions between things dangerous per se and sub modo. *Donoghue* v. *Stevenson* did not itself abolish the distinction; indeed, in that case the House of Lords accepted that it not only existed but was easily recognised. However, subsequent cases decided in accordance with *Donoghue* v. *Stevenson* have had the effect of abolition, and of substituting for the distinction the notion of standards of care varying with the circumstances, as in negligence generally. Thus, it was said in *Read* v. *J. Lyons & Co. Ltd.* (1946): "There is really no category of dangerous things; there are only some things which require more and some which require less care": *per* Sir H. Shawcross A.-G. The validity of this proposition is emphasised by the fact that, although a very high standard of care is demanded in the case of a very dangerous thing, this cannot amount to *strict* liability, but it is necessary for the plaintiff to prove *some* degree of negligence.

4. Liability for dangers known to the defendant. There is liability to immediate, mediate and ultimate transferees for a thing which, although not necessarily dangerous in itself, contains a danger known to the defendant, or about which he ought reasonably to have known, and about which he failed to warn transferees. Examples include the defective lid of a tin of disinfectant—*Clarke* v. *Army & Navy Co-operative Society Ltd.* (1903)—and an incorrectly fitted steam valve—*Howard* v. *Furness Houlder Ltd.* (1936). Note that warning will not by itself discharge the duty to one (*e.g.* a child) to whom a higher standard of care is owed: *Yachuk* v. *Oliver Blais Co.* (1949).

5. Liability for fraud. The defendant will be liable to both immediate and subsequent transferees for damage arising from his *fraud* with regard to a dangerous thing. So in *Langridge* v. *Levy* (1837) a gunsmith fraudulently misrepresented the make and qualities of a gun he sold for the use of a man and his sons, and was held liable in deceit for injuries to one of the sons when the gun burst in his hands.

THE CONSEQUENCES OF
DONOGHUE v. STEVENSON

6. The duty of a "manufacturer" to the ultimate consumer of his "product." Lord Atkin, in his famous leading judgment in *Donoghue* v. *Stevenson,* laid it down that: "A manufacturer of products which he sells in such a form as to show that he intends them to reach the ultimate consumer in the form in which they left him, with no reasonable possibility of intermediate examination and with the knowledge that the absence of reasonable care in the preparation or putting up of the products will result in an injury to the consumer's life or property, owes a duty to the consumer to take that reasonable care."

7. Definition of "manufacturer." Liability is not confined to "manufacturers" in the usual industrial sense of the word, but has been held to extend to: assemblers—*Howard* v. *Furness Houlder Ltd.* (1936); erectors—*Brown* v. *Cotterill* (1934); builders—*Sharp* v. *E. T. Sweeting & Son Ltd.* (1963); repairers—*Haseldine* v. *Daw & Son Ltd.* (1941). The definition is seemingly wide enough to include all who create dangerous things, or render dangerous previously harmless things, which they send, directly or indirectly, to transferees and consumers. The principle seems also to include those who hire out goods: *White* v. *Steadman* (1913).

8. Liability of suppliers. Those who sell, give, or hire out dangerous things (*e.g.* wholesalers and finance companies) are not liable under the principle *unless* they could reasonably have been expected to examine the chattel and discover the danger. Thus, a second-hand car dealer was held liable in respect of a gross and easily discoverable defect in the steering of a car: *Andrews* v. *Hopkinson* (1957). But the principle does not oblige a retailer, for example, minutely to examine each

item of his stock before selling it. *See* **10** below, on intermediate examination.

9. Definition of "product." In addition to articles of food
and drink, the principle has been held to cover, *inter alia*:
gravestones—*Brown* v. *Cotterill* (1934); underwear—*Grant* v.
Australian Knitting Mills (1936); hair dye—*Watson* v. *Buck-
ley and Osborne, Garrett & Co. Ltd.* (1940); motor vehicles—
Herschtal v. *Stewart & Ardern* (1939); and lifts—*Haseldine* v.
Daw & Son Ltd. (1941).

10. Intermediate examination. The defendant will be liable,
inter alia, if there was "no reasonable possibility of intermediate examination." We must therefore consider the extent
to which, and the circumstances in which, the defendant will
be held liable, or exonerated, if there was a reasonable possibility of intermediate examination; and if there was failure to
take advantage of it. The position may be summarised as
follows:

(*a*) The mere existence of an opportunity of intermediate
examination is not in itself enough to exonerate the defendant. The defendant must show that it was reasonable for
him to expect that the plaintiff would make the examination.

> *Herschtal* v. *Stewart & Ardern Ltd.* (1939): Defendant hired
> out a motor car to plaintiff. The next day a wheel came off
> and plaintiff was injured. HELD: Defendant liable. He could
> not rely on the fact that the plaintiff had the opportunity of
> inspecting the car, as it had never been expected or contem-
> plated that such an inspection would be made.

(*b*) The plaintiff cannot succeed if he made an examination and discovered the defect, but nevertheless used the
dangerous thing.

> *Farr* v. *Butters Bros & Co.* (1932). Defendants, manufac-
> turers, sold the constituent parts of a crane to builders, whose
> experienced employee, when assembling the crane, noticed
> defects in it. He nevertheless used the crane and was killed.
> HELD: His widow could not succeed against the manufac-
> turers because, in view of the opportunity (which was taken)
> of examining the crane, they owed the deceased no duty of
> care.

(c) The defendant is not exonerated if an intermediate examination is made, but fails to reveal the defect. Thus, in *Clay* v. *A. J. Crump & Sons Ltd.* (1963), it was held to be no defence to a firm of demolition contractors, in respect of a workman killed through the collapse of a defective wall, that the wall had been examined by an architect and a firm of builders who had failed to discover its unsafe condition.

(d) The defendant is not exonerated if he ought reasonably to have contemplated that the plaintiff, having examined the dangerous thing and realised the risk, might nevertheless reasonably incur it.

> *Denny* v. *Supplies & Transport Co. Ltd.* (1950). Defendants negligently stacked timber, thus making it dangerous to handle, whatever precautions were taken. Plaintiff, whose duty it was to unload the timber, realised the danger, but nevertheless did the work and was injured. HELD: Defendants could not rely on plaintiff's having examined the timber and his becoming aware of the danger, as he had no practical alternative to doing the work.

(e) A defendant can exonerate himself by showing that he attached to the article which caused damage a *warning* sufficient to indicate that he reasonably expected the article to be examined.

> *Kubach* v. *Hollands* (1937). The manufacturers of a chemical, intended to be used in school laboratories, attached to it a warning to distributors that the chemical was to be tested before use. The defendant distributors neither tested the chemical nor brought the warning to the notice of a school to which they sent a supply of the chemical. Plaintiff, a schoolgirl, was injured by the chemical. HELD: The distributors were liable, and could not recover indemnity from the manufacturers. Note also *Holmes* v. *Ashford* (1950): A hairdresser, not a manufacturer, was liable for hair dye which carried a warning that it was dangerous in certain circumstances.

11. The duty of care.

(a) *The duty of care and the burden of proof.* It follows from the fact that liability for dangerous things is a branch of negligence that the duty owed is that of taking reasonable

E

care in the circumstances. The consequences to this of the decision in *Donoghue* v. *Stevenson* are as follows (*see* VI, **8**).

(*b*) *The onus is on the plaintiff to prove negligence.* But he is not required to point to the particular act or omission during the process of manufacture which caused the harm—"Negligence is found as a matter of inference from the existence of the defects taken in conjunction with all the known circumstances": *Grant* v. *Australian Knitting Mills Ltd.* (1936), a Privy Council case.

(*c*) *The effect of the words* "absence of reasonable care in the preparation or putting up of the product" is that the duty of care extends to the packets and containers in which the product is packed, and to the notices, labels and instructions which accompany the product.

(*d*) The principle in *Donoghue* v. *Stevenson* is limited to injury to the consumer's life or property, and does not extend to monetary loss arising from negligent mis-statements. This does not seem to have been affected by the decision in *Hedley Byrne & Co. Ltd.* v. *Heller & Partners Ltd.* (1963): *see* VI, **10–11**.

PROGRESS TEST 10

1. Outline the origins of the liability for dangerous things. Is the liability restricted to things which are "chattels" in the strict legal sense? Is there any other head under which liability for dangerous things may fall? **(1)**

2. What was "the contract fallacy"? **(2)**

3. How did the distinction between things dangerous *per se* and things dangerous *sub modo* come to be abolished? Can there be strict liability for dangerous things? **(3)**

4. Explain, with references to decided cases, the nature of the liability for dangers known to the defendant, with respect to dangerous things. **(4)**

5. Explain the nature of the liability for fraud with respect to dangerous things. **(5)**

6. State, in the words of Lord Atkin, the duty of a manufacturer to the ultimate consumer of his product. **(6)**

7. Explain, with reference to decided cases, the definition of "manufacturerer" for the purposes of the principle in *Donoghue* v. *Stevenson*. **(7)**

8. Under what circumstances will a "supplier" be liable under the principle in *Donoghue* v. *Stevenson*? Explain the definition of "product" for the purposes of the principle. **(8, 9)**

9. Explain, with reference to decided cases, when a defendant

will, and will not, be exonerated from liability under the rules as to intermediate examination. **(10)**

10. Explain the effect of the principle in *Donoghue* v. *Stevenson* on the duty of care and the burden of proof with regard to liability for dangerous things. **(11)**

CHAPTER XI

LIABILITY FOR ANIMALS

NATURE OF THE LIABILITY

1. Two types of liability. A person may be liable for damage done by his animal(s): (*a*) under various rules applying specifically to animals; (*b*) on general principles, in trespass, nuisance and negligence: but these categories are not necessarily exclusive.

2. Four classes of animals. For the purposes of tortious liability, animals fall into four classes: (*a*) Animals *mansuetae naturae*—tame by nature; (*b*) animals *ferae naturae*—fierce by nature; (*c*) cattle; (*d*) dogs. These categories are not invariably exclusive.

3. Whether tame or fierce a question of law. Whether a species is classified as *mansuetae naturae* or *ferae naturae* is a question of *law*, and *judicially noticed*.

> *Mcquaker* v. *Goddard* (1940). Plaintiff was bitten by a camel in defendant's zoo. HELD: The action failed, it being judicially noticed that a camel is a domestic animal, *i.e. mansuetae naturae*, and there was no evidence that defendant knew of its propensity to bite. *See* **7–8** below for *scienter*.

4. Possession determines liability. Liability for animals depends primarily on *possession*, not ownership, *i.e.* liability accrues to the *keeper* of the animal at the time of the alleged damage or injury.

5. Occupiers of premises on which animals are kept. Such an occupier is not *necessarily* the person legally responsible for the animal, *i.e.* he may not be its *keeper*—even if he permits it to be on the premises and knows it to be dangerous; but he may be liable under the *Occupiers Liability Act*, 1957.

6. Liability for animals naturally on land. There is no liability in Nuisance or *Rylands* v. *Fletcher* for *wild animals not* *in possession* which go upon adjoining land and do damage, unless the defendant had deliberately and unreasonably accumulated or harboured them on his land.

Bland v. *Yates* (1914). Defendant accumulated an excessive quantity of manure adjacent to plaintiff's garden, thereby causing an extraordinary profusion of flies. HELD: Plaintiff entitled to an injunction in respect of this nuisance.

Stearn v. *Prentice Bros.* (1919). Defendants accumulated bones in their factory. This attracted rats which damaged adjacent crops. HELD: The accumulation of bones was not excessive, and plaintiff could not succeed in respect of the rats.

THE SCIENTER ACTION

7. Meaning of scienter. Liability for animals depends *prima facie* on knowledge (*scienter*) of their dangerous propensities by those in charge of them. For this purpose the significance of the classification into *ferae naturae* and *mansuetae naturae* is as follows:

(a) In the case of an animal *ferae naturae*, *scienter* is *presumed*, *i.e.* its keeper is presumed to know of its dangerous propensities.

(b) In the case of an animal *mansuetae naturae*, there is no such presumption, and the plaintiff must prove *scienter*, *i.e.* that the defendant *knew* the animal had *previously manifested behaviour of the kind now complained of*; however, the plaintiff need *not* show knowledge by the defendant that the animal had previously *inflicted the self-same harm* by which it injured the plaintiff. Previous indication of a merely general vicious tendency is sufficient.

Jackson v. *Smithson* (1846). Plaintiff was injured by defendant's ram, which defendant knew had previously attacked people. HELD: Plaintiff succeeded—"There is no distinction between the case of an animal which breaks through the tameness of its nature, and is fierce, and known by the owner to be so, and one which is *ferae naturae*": *per* Alderson B.

NOTE: The fact that liability for animals is *strict* necessarily excludes the defence of inevitable accident (*see* I, **30**).

Behrens v. *Bertram Mills Circus Ltd.* (1957). Plaintiffs, who were midgets in a circus, were injured as a result of a performing elephant's being frightened by a dog. HELD: An elephant is *ferae naturae* and it was therefore irrelevant that it was normally tame, and acted solely from fright; *volenti non fit injuria* and contributory negligence did not apply.

> NOTE: At common law, it is not unlawful *per se* to keep a wild or dangerous animal: but the keeping or importation of certain creatures (*e.g.* the Colorado beetle) is prohibited by statute.

8. Scienter compared with other actions. Proof of *scienter* is not invariably necessary. Where the defendant can be made liable in trespass, nuisance, negligence, contract or any other general head of liability, *the appropriate proof suffices*, and proof of *scienter* is unnecessary. *Scienter is essential,* however, when the defendant can be made liable *only* in the capacity of *keeper of a dangerous animal,* and not under any of the above heads.

> *Cox* v. *Burbridge* (1863). Child plaintiff injured on highway by defendant's horse, which had strayed thereon. HELD: Plaintiff (who had no proprietory interest in the highway) could not succeed in trespass, there being no liability in trespass for animals straying on the highway; nor could he succeed with *scienter,* as he could not prove that the horse (*mansuetae naturae*) had a known vicious propensity.

9. Defences to scienter. The following defences may be raised in a *scienter* action.

(*a*) *Volenti non fit injuria.* This is applicable on general principles. Plaintiff may be held to have consented to the risk: see *Cutler* v. *United Dairies Ltd.* (1933): *see* I, **16.**

(*b*) *Contributory negligence.* The *Law Reform (Contributory Negligence) Act,* 1945, applies to animal liability, and the court will apportion the loss: *see* VI, **30.**

(*c*) *Plaintiff a trespasser.* This is a good defence because an occupier owes a trespasser no duty of care in respect of the premises, except not deliberately to set traps for him: *see* IX, **10.**

(*d*) *Act of God.* Probably a good defence on general principles. There is no direct authority: *see* I, **31.**

(*e*) *Act of someone other than defendant.* It seems, on the authority of *Baker* v. *Snell* (1908), that this is *no* defence—note carefully, however, that the point is a controversial one which remains open to settlement by the House of Lords: *see*, at **7** above, *Behrens* v. *Bertram Mills Circus Ltd.* (1957).

> *Baker* v. *Snell* (1908). Defendant's servant set a dog, known to be vicious, onto the plaintiff, a fellow servant. HELD: Defendant had *scienter* of the dog, and was therefore liable; intervention of servant no defence.

CATTLE TRESPASS

10. Nature of cattle trespass. Cattle trespass has been a distinct ground of liability for hundreds of years. A person is liable *without proof of negligence or scienter* for: (*a*) the trespass of his *cattle* on the land of another; (*b*) all the ordinary and natural consequences thereof—*i.e.* he is liable for damage arising from the *natural propensities* of the animals concerned.

NOTE: "Cattle" includes all the usual farm animals, but *not* dogs and cats.

11. Scienter inapplicable to cattle trespass. Because the action is one of *trespass* and therefore actionable *per se*, proof of *scienter* is not required. Carefully distinguish between the action for cattle trespass, and the *scienter* action for damage done by an animal *mansuetae naturae* which happens to be classified as "cattle." In the *scienter* action the plaintiff must show knowledge by the defendant of the vicious propensity of the *particular animal* involved; but in *cattle trespass* it is necessary only to show that animals *of that class* have the mischievous tendency that caused the damage.

12. Damage must be direct. As the action is one of trespass, the damage suffered must be the *direct consequence* of the wrongful act—*i.e.* the plaintiff cannot succeed if the damage is too remote (*see* XVII, **15–18**).

> *Ellis* v. *Loftus Iron Co.* (1874). Defendant's horse injured plaintiff's mare by kicking it from other side of wire boundary fence. HELD: Injury direct, damage not too remote, liability in trespass.
> *Manton* v. *Brocklebank* (1923). Horse and mare in same field. Mare kicked horse, which had to be destroyed. HELD: No trespass, as both animals lawfully in field; no liability in *scienter*, as mare's owner did not know of its vicious propensity.

Note carefully that cattle trespass will lie, where appropriate, for *all* direct injuries, including personal injuries.

Wormald v. *Cole* (1954). Defendant's cattle strayed into plaintiff's garden and injured her. HELD: The injury was direct; cattle trespass will lie for personal injuries; defendant liable in trespass.

13. Defences. The following points should be noted:

(*a*) An occupier of premises adjoining the highway accepts the risks incidental to ordinary use of the highway. *Volenti non fit injuria* is therefore a good defence to one whose cattle stray from the highway, without negligence, and do damage on adjacent premises: *Tillet* v. *Ward* (1892).

(*b*) A plaintiff cannot succeed in cattle trespass if the trespass arose *from his own neglect* of a legal duty owed by him to the defendant to maintain a fence: *Singleton* v. *Williamson* (1861).

HIGHWAYS

14. Rules governing liability for animals on the highway.

(*a*) *Animals on the highway.* Persons using highways must accept the ordinary risks of so doing; therefore there is no liability, in the absence of negligence or *scienter*, for damage done by animals lawfully on the highway: *Cox* v. *Burbidge* (1863).

(*b*) *Animals straying from the highway.* Occupiers of premises adjoining the highway must accept the ordinary risks arising therefrom; therefore there is no liability, in the absence of negligence, for damage done by animals straying from the highway.

Tillet v. *Ward* (1882). A bull, without drover's negligence, entered plaintiff's shop from highway and did damage. HELD: No liability.

(*c*) Animals straying onto the highway. The general rule is that an occupier of land adjoining the highway is under no duty to fence his land so as to keep his animals off the highway; therefore he will not be liable, save in certain exceptional circumstances (*see* **15** below) for damage done by his domestic animals which stray onto the highway.

Searle v. *Wallbank* (1947). Cyclist on highway was injured by defendant's horse, which had strayed through gap in fence. There was no negligence, and the horse had no known vicious propensity. HELD: No liability. Defendant had no legal duty to fence, and owed no duty of care, in respect of his animals not known to be dangerous, to persons on the highway.

15. Exceptions. In the following instances a person will be liable for damage done by his animal on the highway.

(*a*) There is apparently a duty to prevent the escape onto the highway of an animal known to have some propensity which would endanger users of the highway.

Ellis v. *Johnstone* (1963). Defendant's dog dashed out of drive, and damaged the car of the plaintiff, who sued in negligence. HELD: No liability, as defendant under no duty to fence, and there were no special circumstances. It was said *obiter*, however, that, if the dog had been *in the habit* of turning itself "into something more like a missile than a dog," then "special circumstances would have existed . . . imposing on the defendant the duty of taking reasonable care" to cure or curb the dog's propensity: *per* Donovan L.J.

The following points, however, must be carefully noted:

- (*i*) There is no decided case in which such a "special circumstance" gave rise to liability.
- (*ii*) It cannot be a "special circumstance" that an animal merely had an extraordinary propensity to stray on to the highway.
- (*iii*) Persons who bring or drive animals on the highway incur a duty to take reasonable care to avoid damage to persons and property.

Gomberg v. *Smith* (1962). Defendant's St. Bernard ran out of a shop and damaged plaintiff's van on highway. Plaintiff sued in negligence. HELD: He could succeed. Defendant had brought the dog on the highway, and therefore had a duty to take reasonable care to control it.

NOTE: Distinguish carefully between cases in which the animal was *brought* onto the highway and those in which it *strayed* onto the highway.

(*b*) There is liability, probably in *nuisance*, for *large numbers* of animals which stray onto the highway and obstruct it, or make its use dangerous: *Cunningham* v. *Whelan* (1917).

16. Dogs. At common law, dogs are *mansuetae naturae*, with no natural propensity to attack sheep or cattle, so that proof of *scienter* was required to establish liability for such attacks. This position was altered by the following statutory rules:

(*a*) The *Dogs Act*, 1906, *s.* 1, provides that (in general terms):

(*i*) The owner of a dog shall be liable for injury done by that dog to any *cattle*, without proof of negligence or *scienter* on the part of the owner.

(*ii*) The occupier of the premises where the dog was normally kept at the time of the injury is presumed to be its owner, and shall be liable unless he can prove otherwise.

(*b*) The *Dogs* (*Amendment*) *Act*, 1928, added domestic fowls, ducks, geese, guinea fowl, pigeons and turkeys to the list of farm animals designated "cattle" in the *Dogs Act*, 1906. Note that captive rabbits are not included: *Tallents* v. *Bell & Goddard* (1944).

17. Residual liability. On general principles there can be liability in negligence, nuisance and under the rule in *Rylands* v. *Fletcher* for damage done by animals; but it has been seen that such liability is usually subsumed within the special rules relating to animals. However, the following residual liabilities also exist:

(*a*) *Negligence.* A plaintiff who can show damage consequent upon breach of a duty of care owed him by the person in charge of an animal can succeed in negligence on account of damage done by that animal, subject to the special rules and exceptions already mentioned.

(*b*) *Nuisance.* An animal which is not dangerous, or has not escaped, may nevertheless be, or cause, an actionable nuisance (*see* V), *e.g.* where it creates undue noise or smells, or runs about loose to the general public danger: *Pitcher* v. *Martin* (1937).

(*c*) *Rylands* v. *Fletcher.* Liability for animals is clearly akin to *Rylands* v. *Fletcher* liability in many ways. However, although the actions overlap, they are not co-terminous, *e.g.* a *scienter* action may succeed although there was no *escape* from defendant's premises.

PROGRESS TEST 11

1. (*a*) Classify animals for the purpose of tortious liability. For what proposition is *Mcquaker* v. *Goddard* authority? **(2, 3)**

2. What determines *prima facie* liability for animals? To what extent is the occupier of premises liable in tort for animals on such premises? **(4, 5)**

3. Explain, with reference to decided cases, liability for animals naturally on land. **(6)**

4. (*a*) Explain the difference between animals *ferae naturae* and animals *mansuetae naturae*. **(2)**

(*b*) What is the significance of this difference to a *scienter* action? **(7)**

(*c*) What must a plaintiff in a *scienter* action prove? **(7)**

(*d*) What did *Behrens* v. *Bertram Mills Circus Ltd.* decide? **(2, 3, 7)**

5. (*a*) In what circumstances (if any) is proof of *scienter* unnecessary to establish liability for an animal *mansuetae naturae*? **(7)**

(*b*) What did *Cox* v. *Burbridge* decide? **(8)**

6. (*a*) List the possible defences to a *scienter* action. **(9)**

(*b*) Does the *Law Reform (Contributory Negligence) Act*, 1945, apply to animal liability? **(9)**

(*c*) To what extent (if at all) are: (*i*) plaintiff a trespasser, (*ii*) act of a third person, good defences? **(9)**

7. (*a*) Explain the nature of the liability for cattle trespass. **(9–13)**

(*b*) Is *scienter* applicable to cattle trespass? Give reasons for your answer. **(11)**

(*c*) Will an action for cattle trespass lie for indirect damage? Illustrate by decided cases. **(10–12)**

8. (*a*) Is *volenti non fit injuria* ever a good defence to cattle trespass? **(13)**

(*b*) For what is *Singleton* v. *Williamson* authority? **(13)**

9. Outline, with reference to decided cases, the rules governing liability for animals on the highway. **(14)**

10. Explain the circumstances (if any) in which a person will be liable for damage done by his animals on the highway. **(15)**

11. Explain the effects of the *Dogs Act* 1906 and the *Dogs (Amendment) Act*, 1928. **(16)**

12. (*a*) Explain the nature of the liabilities in negligence and nuisance for damage done by animals. **(17)**

(*b*) To what extent is liability for animals co-terminous with liability under the Rule in *Rylands* v. *Fletcher*? **(17)**

CHAPTER XII

LIABILITY FOR THE TORTS OF OTHERS: MASTER AND SERVANT

VICARIOUS LIABILITY

1. Principal and agent. A principal is *jointly* and *severally* liable with his agent for torts committed by the agent which are *authorised* or *ratified* by the principal. Note the following:

(*a*) The principal must know the nature of the act done on his behalf, unless he gives the agent total authority to do any or all acts.

(*b*) The agent must have acted on the principal's behalf; but this may appear from conduct and circumstances, without specific statement by the agent.

2. Master and servant. A master is *jointly* and *severally* liable with his servant for torts committed by the servant *in the course of his employment* (*see* **11–14** below).

SERVANTS AND INDEPENDENT CONTRACTORS

3. Who is a servant? The courts have used the following criteria in deciding the often difficult question of whether a tortfeasor is a servant for the purposes of vicarious liability. If these criteria are not satisfied, the tortfeasor (if an agent at all) will not be a servant, but an *independent contractor,* for whom—with exceptions (*see* **9–10** below)—the master is not vicariously liable. When a servant is employed there is a *contract of service*; but when an independent contractor is employed there is a *contract for services*.

NOTE: The relationship of master and servant must be a voluntary one. There is no legal power to transfer an employee's services to another employer without the employee's consent: *Nokes* v. *Doncaster Amalgamated Collieries Ltd.* (1940).

The criteria mentioned above may be designated (*a*) the control test; (*b*) the integration test.

4. The control test. The main definition of a servant is that he is a person who is subject to the *control* of his master as to the manner in which the work is to be done, *i.e.* the master can tell the servant both *what to do* and *how to do it*. In modern industrial and commercial conditions, however, in which many "servants" are highly skilled and professionally qualified, this seemingly simple standard has become increasingly difficult to apply.

However, the tendency of the courts has been to extend the definition of "servant" to include persons of whom it cannot realistically be said that their employers can control how they do their work.

5. The "hospital cases." The tendency mentioned above is well exemplified by these cases. It was long held that, because of the impossibility of detailed control, a hospital authority was not vicariously liable for the negligence of its medical and nursing staffs: *Hillyer* v. *Governors of St. Bartholomew's Hospital* (1909). This is no longer so, as the following cases demonstrate.

Collins v. *Hertfordshire County Council* (1947). A junior house surgeon (who was not yet a registered practitioner) negligently caused the death of a patient through injecting cocaine when the consultant surgeon had ordered procaine. HELD: The house surgeon and the pharmacist were servants, for whom the hospital authority was vicariously liable, but the consultant surgeon was not.

Cassidy v. *Ministry of Health* (1951). Plaintiff's hand became useless because of negligent post-operative treatment in defendant's hospital. HELD: The full-time medical officer who performed the operation, and the nursing staff concerned with subsequent treatment, were servants for whom the defendants were vicariously liable.

Roe v. *Ministry of Health* (1954). In this case it was HELD that defendants would have been vicariously liable for negligence of *part-time* consultant anaesthetist (in fact, negligence was not proved). "They are responsible for the whole of their staff . . ., permanent or temporary, resident or visiting, whole-time or part-time. . . . the only exception is the case of consultants or anaesthetists . . . employed by the patient himself": *per* Denning L.J.

6. The integration test. The evidently unsatisfactory nature of the control test led Lord Denning to propose that whether or not a tortfeasor was a servant should be decided by considering whether his work was *integral* to the employer's business—in which case he would be a servant—or merely *accessory* to it—in which case he would be an independent contractor: *Stevenson, Jordan & Harrison Ltd.* v. *Macdonald & Evans Ltd.* (1952). However, although there is evidence of a move in that direction, the integration test cannot be said to have superseded the control test as the main criterion.

NOTE: Other matters which the court will take into account include: the mode of payment (*e.g.* whether wages or salary); the employer's powers of suspension or selection; the nature of the work. It is submitted, however, that these should be regarded as having *evidential* value, rather than as criteria in their own right.

7. General and special employers. Where a tort is committed by an employee whose services have been lent, for a specific purpose or a period of time, by his general employer to another (the special employer), the court must decide which (if either) of the two employers was the servant's master at the material time, so as to be vicariously liable for the tort.

Mersey Docks & Harbour Board v. *Coggins & Griffiths (Liverpool) Ltd* (1946). The Harbour Board lent a crane and driver to Coggins & Griffiths Ltd., stevedores. The Harbour Board continued to pay the driver, and had the power to dismiss him, but the contract of hire stated that he was to be the servant of the hirers. A third person having been injured by the driver's negligence, the question of vicarious liability arose. HELD: The Harbour Board remained the employer, as they retained the power to direct *how* the work was to be done.

The court will decide who was the employer on the basis of the facts, and of the criteria already mentioned. However, the rule is that the onus (which is a heavy one) lies on the *general employer* to show that vicarious responsibility passed to the special employer. In the following case, however, this onus was discharged:

Gibb v. *United Steel Companies Ltd.* (1957). A harbour authority (the second defendant) was the plaintiff's general employer, but the facts disclosed that it had lent his services to a firm of stevedores (the first defendant). Plaintiff was injured because of failure to provide a safe system of working. HELD: The special employers were liable for this negligence, as they had the power to direct the plaintiff as to both his work and the manner of doing it. The court stressed that the fact of the general employers' having continued to pay the man's wages was not conclusive.

8. Independent contractors.

(a) *Independent contractor defined.* An independent contractor may be defined as an agent whom the employer engages *to produce a given result,* the employer having *no power to direct the method of doing the work,* which is left to the discretion of the independent contractor.

(b) *Independent contractors and servants contrasted.* We have seen that a master is vicariously liable for the torts of his servants committed in the course of their employment. In general, however, a master is not liable for the torts of his independent contractor. The following cases illustrate this important difference, and the criteria adopted to delineate it:

Performing Right Society Ltd. v. *Mitchell & Booker (Palais de Danse) Ltd.* (1924). Defendants were found vicariously liable for breach of copyright by their dance band, who were HELD to have been servants in the course of their employment. "It seems . . . reasonably clear that the final test, . . . and *certainly the test to be generally applied,* lies in the nature and degree of detailed control over the person alleged to be a servant."

NOTE: A *single isolated act* by an agent may constitute a contract of service if a sufficient degree of *control* is present: *Sadler* v. *Henlock* (1855)—one was HELD to be a servant who was employed for the single transaction of cleansing a drain. Furthermore, one who gives *gratuitous* service may be held to be a servant.

Jones v. *Scullard* (1898). Defendant owned a carriage and horses, but hired a driver from a livery stable. Plaintiff's shop was damaged by driver's negligence. HELD: Driver was defendant's servant—vicarious liability.

Quarman v. *Burnett* (1840): Defendant owned a carriage but hired a driver. HELD: Driver had not become defendant's servant so as to make her vicariously liable.

The similarity of these two cases emphasises that the difference is one of *fact*, to be decided by the *jury*.

EXCEPTIONS

9. Numerous exceptions. In the following instances an employer *is* liable for the torts of his independent contractor. Note carefully, however, that the tort must arise *from the work itself*, and not merely from the manner of doing it; for there is no vicarious liability for such "collateral" negligence by an independent contractor (*see* **10** below).

The defendant is under a *strict and non-delegable duty* to avoid the damage suffered by the plaintiff. Such a duty may arise in the following ways:

(*a*) By statute, as in the case, *e.g.* of strict and absolute duties under the *Factories Act*, 1961.

(*b*) In cases of strict liability at common law, *e.g.* in carrying on certain kinds of operations, or to provide a safe system of working.

> *Hardaker* v. *Idle District Council* (1896). Plaintiff's house was damaged because defendant council's independent contractor negligently fractured a gas pipe. HELD: In these circumstances, defendants had not, by delegation to a competent contractor, discharged their duty to take reasonable care.
>
> *Wilsons & Clyde Coal Co. Ltd.* v. *English* (1937). Plaintiff sued his employers in respect of personal injuries. Defendants had delegated their duty to provide a safe system of working. HELD: This duty was one for which liability could not be avoided by delegation to a contractor or servant.

(*c*) In certain other cases of common-law liability, as follows:

(*i*) In cases where operations are on or contiguous to a highway (*see* V, **13**). *Tarry* v. *Ashton* (1876): Defendant's lamp projected over highway. Despite repair by competent contractor it fell and injured plaintiff. HELD: Defendant liable, delegation no defence.

(*ii*) In cases where there are common-law duties of masters to servants. These are *personal*, therefore liability cannot be avoided by delegation: *Wilsons & Clyde Coal Co. Ltd.* v. *English* (1937).

(*iii*) In cases of liability for fire (*see* VIII, **18**). *Balfour* v. *Barty-King* (1957): Defendant's contractor thawed pipes with blow-lamp, thus negligently setting fire to plaintiff's premises. HELD: Defendant liable for his contractor's negligence.

(*iv*) In cases of liability for "extra-hazardous" operations. *Honeywill & Stein Ltd.* v. *Larkin Bros. Ltd.* (1934): Defendant was employed by plaintiffs to take flash-light photographs in third party's cinema. Defendant negligently caused a fire therein, for which plaintiffs compensated cinema owner. HELD: Plaintiffs could recover this amount from defendants, because plaintiffs were themselves liable to the cinema owner for their independent contractor's "extra-hazardous act."

(*v*) In cases of liability under the Rule in *Rylands* v. *Fletcher*. This is because *Rylands* v. *Fletcher* liability is strict.

(*vi*) In cases where the independent contractor was engaged to do something unlawful. *Ellis* v. *Sheffield Gas Consumers' Co.* (1853): Plaintiff was injured by negligence of defendant company's contractor in excavating to lay gas pipes. The company had no legal power to lay pipes. HELD: Company liable.

(*vii*) In cases where defendant has been negligent in selecting his independent contractor.

NOTE: A defendant will also be liable if he takes control of his independent contractor's activities to such an extent as to convert him into a servant.

10. No liability for collateral negligence.

An employer is not vicariously liable for the *merely collateral* negligence of his independent contractor. For the employer to be liable, the tortiously performed act of the independent contractor must be one he was *employed to do*, and not merely an act *connected with* what he was employed to do.

Padbury v. *Holloway & Greenwood Ltd.* (1912). The defendants were main contractors, whose sub-contractor's workmen injured the plaintiff by negligently leaving a tool on a windowsill, whence it fell onto the plaintiff. HELD: Main contractors not liable, the workman's negligence being merely collateral.

Having thus differentiated servants from independent contractors, we must now proceed to further consideration of vicarious liability for *servants*.

THE COURSE OF THE
SERVANT'S EMPLOYMENT

11. Liability limited to servant's employment. The master
is always liable if he *specifically* authorises or ratifies his
servants' torts. Otherwise, a master is vicariously liable only
for torts committed by his servant *in the course of his employment.*

12. Course of employment defined. A servant will be within
the course of his employment when he does any tortious act
directly or *impliedly* authorised by his master—notwithstanding that he does it in a manner which was *not* authorised
by his master, or which is otherwise wrongful. If the unauthorised manner of performance is so closely connected with
the servants' authorised duty as to constitute a *way of doing
that duty*, then the master will be vicariously liable. This may
be so even if the servant's act was specifically forbidden by
the master, or was done entirely for the servant's own benefit,
if it nevertheless amounted to *a mode of doing that which the
servant was employed to do.* The test is: Was the servant performing a *class of act* he was employed to do, or was he doing
something he was *not* employed to do?

Ruddiman & Co. v. *Smith* (1889). Defendants provided a
lavatory for their clerks, one of whom left a tap running,
thereby damaging plaintiff's premises below. HELD: Defendants
were vicariously liable, the use of the lavatory being within the
clerks' employment. Contrast *Stevens* v. *Woodward* (1881), in
which there were similar facts, but the clerk was *forbidden* to
use lavatory; *no* vicarious liability.

Ilkiw v. *Samuels* (1963). Defendant's lorry driver, in defiance
of strict orders, allowed another to drive, whereby plaintiff was
injured. HELD: Defendant liable. Driver's negligence in allowing another to drive was within the course of driver's employment, his disobedience being immaterial. See also *Limpus* v.
London General Omnibus Co. (1862).

Lloyd v. *Grace, Smith & Co.* (1912). Defendants were solicitors
whose managing clerk, without their knowledge, deceived a
client (the appellant) into conveying certain properties to him
personally. HELD: Defendants liable, as their clerk, although he
acted for his own benefit, did so in the course of his employment.
He did a *class of act* he was employed to do.

13. No liability for servant's independent acts. The master will *not* be liable for his servant's torts where the servant acted *outside* the scope of his employment, and was on "a frolic of his own": *Joel.* v. *Morrison* (1834), *per* Parke B. This may be so even if the servant was using his master's equipment within the official hours of work.

> *Beard* v. *London General Omnibus Co.* (1900). Defendant's bus *conductor* drove bus, without driver's knowledge or consent, thereby injuring plaintiff. HELD: *No* vicarious liability, as conductor had acted beyond the scope of his employment.
>
> *Twine* v. *Bean's Express Ltd.* (1946): Defendant's van driver was forbidden, verbally and by a notice in his cab, to give lifts to unauthorised persons. An unauthorised person to whom the driver gave a lift was killed by his negligence, and the widow sued his employers. HELD: No liability, as the driver was acting beyond his employment. See also *Conway* v. *G. Wimpey & Co. Ltd.* (1951) and *Warren* v. *Henleys Ltd.* (1948).

14. Authority implied in certain circumstances. We have seen that the master is vicariously liable in respect of *authorised* acts by the servant. However, such authority need not be direct, but may be *implied from the circumstances*. This will be the case where, *e.g.*, the servant acts in an emergency to protect his master's property.

> *Poland* v. *John Parr & Sons* (1927). Defendants' carter, believing a boy was stealing from defendants' dray, struck the boy who was seriously injured when the dray ran over him. HELD: Defendants liable, their servant having acted within his implied authority to protect their property.

This case may be contrasted with the following:

> *Houghton* v. *Pilkington* (1912). Defendant's milkman placed his injured fellow servant in defendant's milk float, but in so doing injured him further. HELD: Defendant not liable. In these circumstances the milkman had gone beyond the scope of his normal duties, and had no implied authority to act as he did.

DUTIES OF MASTERS AND SERVANTS
'INTER SE'

15. Reciprocal duties. The common law enjoins upon masters certain duties to their servants, and on servants certain duties to their masters. Breach of these duties may give rise to actions in tort.

NOTE: It has been suggested in judicial *dicta* that breach of a master's duty to his servant is actionable in contract. In practice, however, it has usually resulted in tortious actions.

16. Master's duty to servant. The duty is a personal one. A master cannot by delegation to a competent agent discharge his common-law duties to his servants. "It is the obligation which is personal to him, and not the performance": *Wilsons & Clyde Coal Co.* v. *English* (1938), *per* Lord Wright.

17. Reasonable care suffices. The *common-law* duty of an employer is to take *reasonable care* for the safety of his servants, *i.e.* the ordinary standard of care in negligence. An employer's *statutory* duties, on the other hand, are normally *strict*.

Smith v. *Baker (Charles) & Sons* (1891). (For facts *see* I, **14**.) "The contract between employer and employed involves on the part of the former the duty of taking reasonable care . . . so to carry on his operations as not to subject those employed by him to unnecessary risk."

18. The nature of the duty. In order to discharge the duty mentioned above the employer must take reasonable care

    (*a*) in the selection of employees (*see* **19** below);

    (*b*) in the provision of plant, appliances, and premises (*see* **20** below);

    (*c*) in the provision of a safe system of working (*see* **21** below).

Note carefully, however, that the tendency of the courts is to stress the *unified* nature of these duties.

19. Selection of employees. The failure of an employer to discharge grossly incompetent or irresponsible workpeople will amount to actionable negligence if injury arises from it.

Hudson v. *Ridge Manufacturing Co. Ltd.* (1957). Plaintiff was injured by practical joke of fellow employee whom their employers, although they knew of the joker's dangerous proclivities, had not discharged nor adequately curbed. HELD: Defendants negligent by this failure; plaintiff could succeed.

Furthermore, the employer must adequately instruct his employees, according to their age, experience and skill.

20. Provision of adequate plant, appliances, and premises.

(a) *Plant and appliances.* The employer's duty is to use all reasonable care and skill to make his plant and equipment safe. If he requires a servant to use an appliance which is in some way inherently dangerous, the employer must take all reasonable steps to minimise the danger. Furthermore, the duty is a continuing one, and the employer must therefore do everything reasonably necessary to maintain the equipment in a safe condition; although he will not necessarily be liable for every temporary departure from complete maintenance.

Monaghan v. *Rhodes* (*W. H.*) *& Son* (1920). Plaintiff complained to his defendant employers (stevedores) about the obstruction of a permanent iron ladder, necessitating his descent into ship's hold by a rope ladder, which plaintiff considered unsafe. Plaintiff injured through using rope ladder. HELD: Defendants liable. They knew the iron ladder was unusable, and the rope ladder unsafe, but did nothing. They had broken their common-law duty to provide safe and adequate equipment.

Davie v. *New Merton Board Mills Ltd.* (1959). Appellant lost his eye solely because of a latent defect, which could not be discovered by reasonable examination, in a tool his employers had bought from a reputable supplier. HELD: Employers not liable. They had, by purchasing from a reputable supplier, discharged their common-law duty to provide adequate equipment. Furthermore, the duty to provide adequate equipment extends to all activities *normally incidental* to the employer's work.

Davidson v. *Handley Page Ltd.* (1945): Worker injured through slipping on greasy duck-board when going to sink to wash teacup for her own use. HELD: She could succeed; employer had failed to provide safe equipment.

(b) *Safe premises.* The employer must take all reasonable steps to make the premises safe, and to minimise dangers of which he is aware: *Thomas* v. *Quartermaine* (1887).

NOTE: The question of liability for injuries to servants on premises other than those occupied by their employers appears to be not finally settled; but the cases indicate that it is a matter, not of safe premises, but rather of a safe system of working (*see* below).

21. Provision of safe system of working. An employer, besides providing adequate staff and equipment, must combine them into a safe system of working. Again, the law requires no more than the provision of a *reasonably safe* system. The definition of this has presented the courts with great difficulties, but the question can be discussed here only briefly. The following are the main points to be considered:

(*a*) Whether a system is safe is a question of *fact*, which varies with the circumstances. The court will take account of, *e.g.*, the layout of the work; the sequence of operations; the provision of warnings and special instructions: *Speed* v. *Swift & Co. Ltd.* (1943), *per* Lord Greene.

(*b*) The fact that the employer followed the usual and approved practice of the trade or industry involved will have very strong evidential value on his behalf, but is not necessarily conclusive: *Cavanagh* v. *Ulster Weaving Co. Ltd.* (1960).

(*c*) The employer is entitled to expect workmen to take reasonable care for their own safety, in accordance with their skill and experience, and the extent to which the work is inherently dangerous.

Qualcast (Wolverhampton) Ltd. v. *Haynes* (1959). Experienced moulder injured because he failed to wear protective spats, which were available to him. HELD: In view of his knowledge and experience, his employers had not, by failure closely to supervise him, failed in their duty to provide a safe system of working.

Per contra the employer owes a higher standard of care in proportion to the youth, inexperience, lack of skill or disability of his servant. *Paris* v. *Stepney Borough Council* (1951).

22. Servant's duty to master. A servant owes his master a duty to take reasonable care in carrying out his (the servant's) duties, and of the master's property for which he is responsible. However, as this is an *implied contractual* duty, we need merely note it in passing.

23. The duty to indemnify and contribute. It is a rule of common law that a master can recover indemnity from a servant for whose tort the master was vicariously liable. This duty was made statutory by the *Law Reform (Married Women and Tortfeasors) Act,* 1935. Under this Act, an employer who is a joint tortfeasor with his servant or independent contractor can recover contribution from the latter; or, where the employer is vicariously liable but not a joint tortfeasor, he can recover indemnity; in either case, to the extent that the court thinks just and equitable.

Lister v. *Romford Ice & Cold Storage Co. Ltd.* (1957). The appellant and his father were employed by respondents as lorry driver and mate. The son negligently injured his father, who recovered damages from the respondent employers, as being vicariously liable for the son's negligence. HELD: the son had broken his implied contractual duty of care, and the employers were entitled to recover from him, by way of indemnity, the damages paid to the father. See also *Harvey* v. *R. G. O'Dell Ltd.* (1952).

PROGRESS TEST 12

1. Outline the nature and extent of a principal's liability for his agent. **(1)**

2. (a) Outline the vicarious liability of a master for the torts of his servant. (b) What is the effect of the decision in *Nokes* v. *Doncaster Amalgamated Collieries Ltd.* (1940)? **(2, 3)**

3. Explain the "control test." How do the "hospital cases" exemplify it? **(4, 5)**

4. What is the "integration test"? Is it more important than the "control test"? What other matters will the court consider in deciding whether a tortfeasor was a servant? **(6)**

5. Explain the respective degrees of vicarious liability of general and special employers. Illustrate by decided cases. **(7)**

6. Contrast servants and independent contractors. Illustrate by decided cases. May (a) a single isolated act, (b) a gratuitous act, constitute a contract of service? **(8)**

7. List and briefly explain the case in which an employer *is* vicariously liable for the torts of his independent contractor. For what propositions are the following cases authority: *Tarry* v. *Ashton* (1876); *Wilsons and Clyde Coal Co. Ltd.* v. *English* (1937); *Honeywill & Stein Ltd.* v. *Larkin Bros. Ltd.* (1934)? **(9)**

8. What is meant by saying that an employer is not liable for the collateral negligence of his servant or independent contractor? **(10)**

9. Explain the circumstances under which a servant will be regarded as being within the scope of his employment for the

purpose of vicarious liability. Illustrate by decided cases. (11–12)

10. Explain the circumstances under which a servant will be regarded as having gone beyond the scope of his employment. Illustrate by decided cases. (13)

11. Explain what is meant by the implied authority of a servant. (14)

12. Outline the nature and extent of a master's duty to his servant. How does this apply to plant and premises? What constitutes a safe system of working? Can a defendant employer succeed by showing that he followed the usual and approved practice? What is an employer entitled to expect from his workpeople? (16–21)

13. Outline the nature of a servant's duty to his master. (22)

14. Explain the effect of the *Law Reform (Married Women and Tortfeasors) Act*, 1935. (23)

CHAPTER XIII

DEFAMATION

DEFINITION

1. Injury to reputation. A defamatory statement is one which *injures the reputation* of the plaintiff by its tendency to "lower him in the estimation of right-thinking members of society" or to cause right-thinking members of society to "shun or avoid" him: *Sims* v. *Stretch* (1936), *per* Lord Atkin. This statement need not impute misconduct or moral turpitude, *e.g.* a statement may be defamatory which shows the plaintiff as merely ridiculous. Nor need defamation consist of connected words or sentences, but may be, *e.g.*, carving, painting, gestures.

2. "Right-thinking members of society." The meaning of this phrase was considered in *Byrne* v. *Dean*.

Byrne v. *Dean* (1937). It was alleged that a lampoon was defamatory because it accused plaintiff of "sneaking" to the police about unlawful gambling in his club. HELD: The action of the club committee in allowing the lampoon to remain on the notice board did not constitute defamation, as members of society would not be right-thinking if they thought it defamatory to say that a man had discharged his public duty to help suppress crime.

3. Defamation objective. The test of defamation is objective, *i.e.* would an ordinary right-thinking member of society have thought the statement defamatory *in the circumstances*?

TWO FORMS OF DEFAMATION

4. Division into libel and slander. A defamatory statement is either a libel or a slander. The difference between the two forms are as follows:

(*a*) *Libel.*

(*i*) The defamation is in a *permanent* form.

(*ii*) It is actionable *per se*, *i.e.* without proof of damage.

(*iii*) It may be a *crime*, *e.g.* seditious or obscene libel.

(*b*) *Slander*.

(*i*) The defamation is in a *non-permanent* form.

(*ii*) It is actionable only on proof of special damage, *i.e.* damage capable of being expressed in terms of *money*. (There are four exceptions: *see* 6 below.)

(*iii*) It cannot be a crime.

NOTE: The distinction between libel and slander is *not necessarily* that between written and spoken defamation—although usually so in fact.

5. Films and broadcasting.

(*a*) *Films*. Defamation in a film is *libel*.

> *Yousoupoff* v. *M.G.M. Pictures Ltd*. (1934). The defendants implied, in a film, that the Princess Y had been raped by Rasputin. HELD: A libel. To say a woman had been raped would tend to make her shunned and avoided, even though she was morally blameless.

(*b*) *Broadcasting*. The *Defamation Act*, 1952, *s.* 1, provides that, "for the purposes of the law of libel and slander, the broadcasting of words by means of wireless telegraphy shall be treated as publication in permanent form."

NOTE: There is no direct authority as to whether defamation on a gramophone record is libel or slander, but the better opinion seems to be that it is libel.

6. Slander sometimes actionable per se. In the following four instances slander is (contrary to the general rule) actionable without proof of special damage.

(*a*) Imputing that the plaintiff has committed a crime *not punishable by fine alone*. The essential feature is the tendency to make others *shun* the plaintiff, *not* his being exposed to criminal prosecution.

(*b*) Imputing that the plaintiff has an *existing* contagious or infectious disease which would cause others to *shun* him.

(*c*) Imputing that a female has committed adultery or is not chaste: *Slander of Women Act*, 1891. This includes an imputation of lesbianism: *Kerr* v. *Kennedy* (1942).

(*d*) Making statements about the plaintiff "calculated to

disparage" him "in any office, profession, calling, trade or business held or carried on by him at the time of the publication": the *Defamation Act, 1952, s. 2.*

7. The effect of the Defamation Act, s. 2. The section (exception **6**(*d*) above) altered the common-law rule that such a statement was not actionable unless it amounted to a *charge against* the plaintiff in respect of his profession, etc. It is now sufficient to show that the words were "calculated to disparage," whether or not spoken of the plaintiff "in the way of" his profession, etc. Thus before the Act it would not have been actionable to say a solicitor was dishonest *except* in respect to a client; now the mere imputation of dishonesty would suffice in itself.

8. The limits of defamation. Defamation should be distinguished from the following:

(*a*) *Mere vulgar abuse*—which injures a man's *dignity only, not* his reputation.

> *Penfold* v. *Westcote* (1806). "You blackguard, rascal, scoundrel, Penfold, you are a thief." HELD: "Blackguard," etc., was mere abuse, but was defamatory in conjunction with "thief."

(*b*) *Injurious falsehood.* A statement is not defamatory unless it injures the plaintiff's *reputation*; *e.g.* a statement which injures his business but not his personal reputation is actionable (if at all) as *injurious falsehood* (*see* XIV, **21**).

STANDARD OF PROOF

9. What the plaintiff must prove. Proof must be given of the following:

(*a*) That the statement was *defamatory* (*see* **10–13** below).
(*b*) That the statement *referred* to the plaintiff (*see* **14–15** below).
(*c*) That the statement was *published* (*see* **16–19** below).

10. That the statement was defamatory. The test is *not* the nature of the defendant's intention but *the meaning which would be imputed by reasonable persons.* Innocent intention is no defence (although it may mitigate damages); conversely, defamatory intention is of no significance if others did not reasonably understand the statement to be defamatory.

11. Functions of judge and jury.

(a) The judge's function is to decide *as a matter of law* whether the statement is *reasonably capable* of bearing the defamatory meaning alleged by the plaintiff. If not so satisfied, he withholds the case from the jury.

(b) The jury's function is to decide *as a matter of fact* whether the statement complained of *is* defamatory.

> *Capital & Counties Bank Ltd.* v. *George Henty & Sons* (1882). It was alleged that an imputation of the bank's insolvency was defamatory. HELD: The statement was not reasonably capable of such a construction, and the case should not have been put to the jury.

(c) If the statement is clearly and necessarily defamatory, *i.e.* such as to bring the plaintiff into hatred or contempt, the judge should so direct the jury at the outset. This can rarely be so in slander, however, for the meaning of spoken words can rarely be obvious when recited out of their original context.

12. Innuendo.

(a) *Effect of innuendo.* An apparently innocent statement may nevertheless be defamatory if it contains an *innuendo* ("an oblique hint, allusive remark, usually depreciatory": *O.E.D.*).

(b) *Special pleading necessary.* An innuendo must be *specially pleaded, i.e.* the plaintiff must state and prove the grounds (with supporting evidence, *e.g.* his special knowledge) on which he alleges that the apparently innocent remark is defamatory, *i.e.* he must prove the meaning he himself attributes to the words.

(c) *Surrounding circumstances.* An innuendo may arise, not from the words, but from the facts and circumstances surrounding the publication.

> *Tolley* v. *Fry* (1931). It was imputed in a cartoon forming part of an advertisement that a famous amateur golfer had, by consenting to the use of his name, compromised his

amateur status. In fact, he had not consented, and knew nothing of the advertisement until it appeared. HELD: Libel by innuendo.

(d) *Objective test of innuendo.* It is no defence that the defendant did not know of the facts or circumstances turning the seemingly innocent statement into an innuendo if the innuendo would have been inferred by reasonable persons.

NOTE

    (i) Damages for "unintentional defamation" may be avoided by reliance on *s.* 4 of the *Defamation Act,* 1952 (*see* **37** below).

    (ii) Innuendo can be pleaded *additionally* to a plea that the statement is defamatory in its ordinary meaning.

13. Physical relationship. Defamation (direct or by innuendo) may take the form of the mere physical relationship of objects.

Monson v. *Tussauds Ltd.* (1894). Defendants placed an effigy of plaintiff, against whom a charge of murder was "not proven," close to those of convicted murderers. HELD: A libel *prima facie,* although an interlocutory injunction was not granted.

14. That the statement referred to the plaintiff.

(a) *Reference may be express or latent.* The reference need not be express but may be *latent.* It is sufficient if it is understood as defamatory by one person only.

Le Fanu v. *Malcolmson* (1848). There was an imputation in a newspaper of cruelty in certain Irish factories. HELD: A libel, on the jury finding that the statement was understood to refer to a particular factory.

(b) *Objective test.* It is not necessary to show that the defendant intended to refer to the plaintiff, or even that the defendant knew of the plaintiff's existence. The test is: Would a person to whom the statement was published *reasonably think* it referred to the plaintiff?

(c) *Standard of proof.* It is not necessary to show that reasonable persons *did* understand the statement as referring to the plaintiff—but only that it was *capable of being so understood* by reasonable persons.

Hulton & Co. v. *Jones* (1910). A newspaper article named a supposedly fictitious "Artemus Jones" as having a mistress in France. The real Artemus Jones proved that persons reasonably believed that the reference was to him. HELD: A libel.

Newstead v. *London Express Newspapers Ltd.* (1939). Defendant newspaper reported the trial for bigamy of "Harold Newstead, 30-year-old Camberwell man." HELD: Defamatory, as reasonable persons would have understood the words to apply to another Harold Newstead (the plaintiff) also of Camberwell.

15. Defamation of a class.

(*a*) *A class cannot be defamed as such,* but it may be *so small and well defined* that what is said of the class necessarily refers to any or every member of it.

(*b*) *The class must be clearly defined.* The plaintiff may be defamed, although not specifically identified, if the *class* to which he belongs—and which is defamed—is so *small and clearly defined* that reasonable persons would take the words complained of as referring to the plaintiff; but, the *larger and more ill defined* the class, the greater the difficulty of showing the plaintiff was referred to.

Knupffer v. *London Express Newspapers Ltd.* (1944). Allegedly defamatory imputations were made against a group of twenty-four foreign refugees. There was evidence that the reference was thought to be to their leader. HELD: No libel, as reasonable persons would not have thought so.

16. That the statement was published. To be published, a statement must be made known to *at least one person other than the person defamed.* Publication need not be to the public at large.

NOTE: Publication only to the party defamed suffices in *criminal* (but not *civil*) libel, because of the tendency to cause a breach of the peace.

The following are examples of published and unpublished statements:

(*a*) Communications of husbands and wives *inter se* do not constitute publication: *Wennhak* v. *Morgan* (1888). But a statement *by a third person* to one spouse about the other *is* publication: *Wenman* v. *Ash* (1853).

(b) A defamation may be published by dictation, *e.g.* to a secretary, but this is probably slander only. If the communication is privileged (*see* **29–36** below) the dictation, or other attendant circumstance, is also privileged.

(c) It is not publication when a printer returns the printed version of a manuscript to its author: *Eglantine Inn Ltd.* v. *Smith* (1948).

(d) Failure to remove defamatory matter from one's premises may amount to publication, unless removal would be very difficult or impossible: *Byrne* v. *Deane* (1937).

(e) A statement is not published unless understood. A person to whom an allegedly defamatory statement is published must understand:

   (*i*) its meaning; and
   (*ii*) that it refers to the plaintiff: *Sadgrove* v. *Hole* (1901).

17. Publication sometimes presumed. Publication is presumed, and the burden of disproof thrown on the defendant, in the following cases:

   (a) When a letter or postcard is posted.
   (b) When a document is printed.
   (c) When a telegram is despatched.

18. Dissemination.

(a) *Repetition.* Every repetition is a separate and distinct publication which creates a new cause of action. Thus the proprietor, editor, publisher and printer may all be sued for libel in a newspaper: and in some circumstances a person (*e.g.* a newsagent) may be liable who does no more than offer the offending publication for sale.

(b) *Originator jointly liable.* The originator of defamatory matter who authorises others to repeat it remains liable, jointly and severally, with those others.

(c) *Originator's liability strict.* Furthermore, the liability of the originator remains strict, *i.e.* innocent intention or lack of negligence is no defence. However, the defence provided by the *Defamation Act*, 1952, *s.* 4 (*see* **37** below), may be available if the defamation was unintentional, *e.g.* publication to the wrong person by mistake. In *Hebditch* v. *MacIlwaine* (1894) a communication would have been privileged if sent to intended addressee, but was defamatory when mistakenly sent to another.

(d) *Effect of negligence.* An unintentional publication may be defamatory if made negligently, *e.g.* where dissemination is unnecessarily widespread: *White* v. *Stone* (1939)—defamatory matter spoken by a man to his wife overheard by third person; *Sadgrove* v. *Hole* (1901)—defamatory statement sent in privileged circumstances, but written on a postcard. However, unintentional dissemination to a third person will not be negligent if the disseminator had no reason to anticipate the third person's receiving it: *Powell* v. *Gelston* (1916).

(e) *Dissemination to employees.* Publication to the defendant's own employees in the ordinary course of business is *prima facie* sufficient to create liability; *but* "if a business communication is privileged . . . the privilege covers all . . . treatment of the communication . . . in accordance with the usual and reasonable course of business": *Edmonson* v. *Birch & Co. Ltd.* (1907). Dictation to a shorthand typist is "reasonable and usual": *Osborn* v. *Boulter* (1930).

19. Innocent dissemination.

(a) *Absence of knowledge.* Dissemination will not amount to actionable publication if the defendant (i) did not know, and (ii) was not negligent in failing to discover, that the matter in question was defamatory.

> *Emmens* v. *Pottle* (1885). Defendant newsvendor widely disseminated defamatory matter. HELD: No publication, as there was neither knowledge nor negligence in the defendant.
> *Bottomley* v. *Woolworth & Co. Ltd.* (1932): Innocent dissemination by sale of magazines in Woolworth stores.

(b) *Presence of negligence.* The cases above should be contrasted with *Vizettelly* v. *Mudie's Select Library Ltd.* (1900) and *Sun Life Assurance* v. *W. H. Smith & Son Ltd.* (1934), in which the defendants were held to have published libels through negligence in failing to discover defamatory matter in publications which they circulated.

DEFENCES

20. Defendant may traverse. A defendant in a defamation action may:

  (a) deny that the matter is defamatory;
  (b) deny publication.

21. Other defences. The following defences are also available.

  (a) Justification (*see* **22–23** below).
  (b) Fair comment (*see* **24–28** below).
  (c) Privilege—absolute and qualified (*see* **29–36** below).
  (d) Offer of amends: *Defamation Act*, 1952 (*see* **37–40** below).
  (e) Apology: *Libel Act*, 1843 (*see* **41** below).
  (f) Consent (*see* **42** below).

22. Justification. Justification consists of proof that the allegedly defamatory matter was *true*. Justification is a dangerous defence, because if it fails heavier damages will probably be awarded.

  (a) *Onus of proof.* The defendant must prove the statement was true, not the plaintiff its falsity. Justification must be specially pleaded.

  (b) *Substantial truth suffices.* It is sufficient to prove the substantial truth of the statement, *i.e.* a minor inaccuracy will not vitiate the defence. Whether the inaccuracy *was* minor is a matter of fact for the jury—which is almost always actually present at a defamation action.

> *Alexander* v. *North Eastern Railway Co.* (1865). "Fine or fourteen days" reported as "five or three weeks." HELD: Not sufficiently inaccurate to defeat justification. Conversely however, "the justification must be as broad as the charge."
> *Bishop* v. *Latimer* (1861): "How lawyer Bishop treats his clients." HELD: One example insufficient to establish justification.

  (c) *Effect of Defamation Act*, 1952. Section 5 provides that justification will not fail merely because the truth of *one* of several charges is not established—if, having regard

F

to the other charges, it did no material injury to the plaintiff's reputation.

(d) *Defendant's motive irrelevant.* The defence of justification, if otherwise good, will not fail because the defendant acted from a malicious or improper motive. However, an honest and reasonable but mistaken belief in the truth of the statement will not suffice to support justification.

(e) *Justification in criminal libel.* In criminal libel justification is a good defence *if* publication was for the public good—*Libel Act*, 1843, *s.* 6. At common law, truth was no defence.

23. Rumour, suspicion, innuendo and abuse.

(a) Truth is essential. Proof of the *existence* of a rumour or suspicion is insufficient; its *truth* must be proved.

(b) One who *repeats* a statement must prove its truth; proof of accurate repetition is insufficient.

(c) Mere abuse or invective incidental to the main charge need not be justified.

(d) If the words are held capable of bearing an innuendo, *the truth of the innuendo* must be proved.

(e) The defendant may justify *part* of the alleged defamation, provided it is *severable* from the rest of the statement.

24. Fair comment.

(a) *Definition.* Fair comment is comment *honestly made* on a matter of *public interest.*

(b) *Comment means opinion.* The defendant must prove that the statement was comment, *i.e.* one of *opinion*, not fact. If the statement consists of facts, *justification* is the appropriate defence.

(c) *Good faith is essential.* The defendant must have made the comment in good faith, *i.e.* believing in its truth and without malicious distortion.

> *Merivale* v. *Carson* (1887). A *false* statement was made that a play contained an incident of adultery. HELD: Fair comment excluded.

(d) *Public interest is essential.* The defendant must prove that the matter commented on was one of public interest.

(e) *Fairness is not synonymous with moderation.* Although

the comment must be fair, *i.e.* the *honestly held opinion* of the defendant, "fair comment does not mean moderate comment." The opinion of the court or the jury must not be substituted for that of the defendant: *McQuire* v. *Western Morning News* (1903). The test is: "Was this an opinion, however exaggerated, obstinate or prejudiced, which was honestly held by the writer?": *Silkin* v. *Beaverbrook Newspapers Ltd.* (1958), *per* Diplock J.

25. Effect of malice.

(*a*) *Malice may defeat fair comment.* *Express* malice excludes fair comment, *i.e.* malice on the part of the defendant does not *necessarily* vitiate the defence, but it does so where the malice *distorts* the comment.

Thomas v. *Bradbury Agnew & Co. Ltd.* (1906). The writer of a review made untrue allegations of fact, and harboured personal spite against the author. HELD: The comment was distorted by malice, and therefore not fair.

(*b*) An attack on the plaintiff's *moral character*, because it consists essentially of *allegations of fact* about the plaintiff's character, cannot be fair comment. *Justification* is the appropriate defence.

Campbell v. *Spottiswoode* (1863). It was alleged that the plaintiff's statement that he wished to spread the gospel in China was a hypocritical pretence to increase the sales of his newspaper. HELD: Not fair comment, but an attack on character—"A writer in a public paper may comment on the conduct of public men in the strongest terms; but, if he imputes dishonesty, he must be prepared to justify": *per* Cockburn C.J.

26. The "rolled-up" plea.

(*a*) Fact and comment are difficult to separate. Because of this, the plea is sometimes couched in the form: "In so far as the words complained of are statements of fact they are true in substance and in fact; and in so far as they consist of comment they are fair comment on a matter of public interest." This—the "rolled-up" plea—*is a plea of fair comment, not justification*. The facts are proved merely to lay a foundation for the defence of fair comment. Furthermore, the Rules of Court provide that the plaintiff is entitled to be informed of the facts on which the defendant intends to rely.

(b) The *Defamation Act*, 1952, *s.* 6, altered the position. Formerly, the slightest inaccuracy in the facts stated defeated fair comment; but *s.* 6 provides that, where a statement consists partly of fact and partly of comment, the defence of fair comment "shall not fail by reason only that the truth of every allegation of fact is not proved" if the expression of opinion is nevertheless fair, having regard to the facts which *are* proved.

27. Functions of judge and jury.

(a) The *judge* decides the following as matters of *law*:

    (i) Whether the words used are capable of being statements of fact.

    (ii) Whether the subject, in law, is open to comment.

    (iii) Whether there is reasonable evidence to go to the jury that the comment was not fair.

(b) If the judge decides these in the affirmative, the *issue of unfairness* goes to the jury. Note that, contrary to the general modern practice in civil actions, a jury is almost always present in defamation cases.

28. Public interest. The basis of the defence of fair comment is the necessity for free and fair comment on matters of public interest.

(a) *Comment on private matters excluded.* The defence is not available where the comment was on purely private matters. However, "public interest" is widely defined. It includes: the conduct of public men; the administration of public institutions; and even the affairs of private businesses which effect the public at large, or a section of it.

(b) *Voluntary submission to comment.* The defence applies to activities which are *voluntarily submitted* to comment, *e.g.* acting, writing, painting, sculpture, music, works of criticism; also advertisements, circulars and public speeches.

    South Hetton Coal Co. Ltd. v. *North-Eastern News Association Ltd.* (1894). The defendants, in their newspaper, alleged failure by the company to provide its employees with proper and hygienic housing. The defendants pleaded fair comment.

HELD: (a) The defence of fair comment can be raised only on a matter of public interest; (b) the public interest may be involved although only a small section of the public is affected; (c) a limited company can bring an action for libel in respect of the conduct of its business.

Purcell v. *Sowler* (1877). "Public interest" may be confined to a locality—what is primarily of public interest in Manchester is only indirectly so to the country.

NOTE: *Salmond* proposed that fair comment was merely a species of qualified privilege. It has been pointed out, however, that when privilege is pleaded the defamation is *admitted*; but where fair comment is pleaded the defamation is *denied*.

29. Privilege.

(a) A privileged communication may be defined as one in respect of which the law holds that the public interest in free speech overrides, wholly or conditionally, the private right to an untarnished reputation.

(b) Privilege is of two kinds. It may be:

- (i) absolute—not actionable under any circumstances (*see* **30** below) or
- (ii) qualified—actionable only on proof of *express* malice (*see* **31** below).

30. Absolute privilege. The following classes of statements are absolutely privileged.

(a) *Those made in either House of Parliament.* This stems from the *Bill of Rights*, 1689, which stated: "The freedom of speech and debates or proceedings in Parliament ought not to be impeached or questioned in any court or place out of Parliament."

NOTE: It is seemingly undecided whether a letter from an MP to a Minister enjoys absolute privilege as a "proceeding in Parliament."

(b) *Reports of parliamentary proceedings* published by order of either House, or their *re-publication in full*: *Parliamentary Papers Act*, 1840.

NOTE: Such re-publications were not privileged at common law: *Stockdale* v. *Hansard* (1839).

(c) *Judicial proceedings.* Statements made by judges, advocates, jurors, witnesses or parties:

(i) *in the course of* judicial proceedings, civil or military; or

(ii) *with reference to* such proceedings.

Addis v. *Crocker* (1961). This extends to tribunals exercising *judicial* (as distinct from merely administrative) functions. An order of the Disciplinary Committee of the Law Society *sitting in private* was held absolutely privileged.

Contrast with the following case:

Royal Aquarium Society Ltd. v. *Parkinson* (1892). London County Council is *not* a court when hearing certain licensing applications, therefore statements by its members are not privileged.

Watson v. *McEwen* (1905): The privilege extends to statements made by a witness to a party or his solicitor *before* (but with reference to) the trial.

NOTE: A statement *inadmissible as evidence* may nevertheless be privileged, if made *with reference* to the proceedings.

(d) *Officers of state.* A statement is absolutely privileged if made by one officer of state to another in the course of official duty.

Chatterton v. *Secretary of State for India* (1895). This involved a communication by a Minister to the Under-Secretary of State for India, to enable him to answer a parliamentary question. HELD: Privileged.

NOTE

(i) The following have been held to be "officers of state": a Military officer reporting to his superiors; a Minister communicating with an official; a High Commissioner reporting to Prime Minister: But *not* a police officer to his superior.

(ii) Statements made in Great Britain by officials of foreign governments are probably protected by *diplomatic* privilege.

(iii) A purely commercial communication may enjoy absolute privilege under this head: *Isaac & Sons Ltd.* v. *Cook* (1925). This case is also authority for saying that, if a statement is absolutely privileged, all *consequential statements* enjoy the same privilege.

(e) *Husband and wife.* Statements made by one spouse *to* the other are absolutely privileged; but not statements by one spouse to a third party *about* the other.

31. Qualified privilege.

(*a*) *Definition.* For a statement to enjoy qualified privilege there must be:

   (*i*) a legal, moral or social *duty* to make it on one side;
   (*ii*) a *corresponding interest* to receive it on the other.

Both these conditions must be satisfied.

   Adam v. *Ward* (1917): "This reciprocity is essential," *per* Lord Atkinson.

   Watt v. *Longsdon* (1930). This case established that the reciprocal duty and interest are essential in *all* cases of qualified privilege, not only those in which the allegedly defamatory statement was made in discharge of a duty. In this case, W and L were members of the same firm. A (also a member of the firm) wrote to L, making defamatory statements about W's morals and behaviour. L showed the letter (*a*) to the chairman of the firm; (*b*) to W's wife. HELD: The publication to the chairman was privileged, as there was a reciprocal duty to make it and a reciprocal interest to receive it; but publication to W's wife was *not* privileged; she had an interest to receive the information but L had *no duty* to show her the letter.

   NOTE: The *judge* decides whether the duty exists. The test of what constitutes a moral or social duty seems to be an objective one—"Would the great mass of right-minded men . . . have considered it their duty . . . to make the communication?": *Watt* v. *Longsdon, per* Green L.J.

(*b*) *Extent of the privilege.* The following statements enjoy qualified privilege.

   (*i*) Those made in *discharging a duty* (*see* **32** below).
   (*ii*) Those made in *protecting an interest* (*see* **33** below).
   (*iii*) Those made in *reports* of parliamentary, judicial and certain other public proceedings (*see* **34** below).

   NOTE: It is not absolutely settled whether professional communications between solicitor and client enjoy qualified or absolute privilege, but the better opinion seems to be that the privilege is qualified only.

32. Discharging a duty.
A purely voluntary or gratuitous defamatory statement will *not* be privileged *unless* the relationship of the maker and recipient was such as to *create a duty* in

the maker to speak on his own initiative. Examples include: communication from servant to master about the master's interests—*Lawless* v. *Anglo-Egyptian Cotton Co.* (1869); communications from host to guest about a servant's dishonesty—*Stuart* v. *Bell* (1891); statements in good faith by members of public bodies in pursuance of their duties—*Andrew* v. *Nott-Bower* (1895).

It is a necessary extension of the duty/interest relationship that a statement may enjoy qualified privilege if the maker and recipient have a *common interest* in its being made about the plaintiff.

Nevill v. *Fine Art & General Insurance Co.* (1897). This involved a communication by an insurance company to its policy holders about one of its agents. HELD: Privileged because of common interest in the finance of the company.

Winstanley v. *Bampton* (1943): This concerned a complaint by tradesman to a commanding officer about an officer's unpaid bills. HELD: Privileged because of common interest in the financial probity of H.M. officers.

Contrast with the following case:

Botterill v. *Whytehead* (1879). A general interest in church architecture did not constitute a common interest between a clergyman and the parishioners of a church with which he had no connection.

NOTE: The existence of the common interest is a matter of law for the judge. A mere honest belief in its existence is not enough. There is no established test, but the interest must be common, *e.g.* there is no common interest between X and Y in the case of mere gratuitous meddling by one in the affairs of the other.

33. Protecting an interest.

(*a*) *Nature of the privilege.* A statement enjoys qualified privilege, even if there is *no duty* to make it, if made to protect a *lawful interest*, *e.g.* the person, property or reputation of its maker.

(*b*) *Reciprocity.* Again, reciprocity is essential: there must be an *interest* to be protected and a *duty* to protect it.

Somerville v. *Hawkins* (1851). Master warned his servants about the character of a fellow servant. HELD: Privilege;

master and servants had a common interest in the matter, and there was a duty to protect the servants.

Quartz Hill Gold Mining Co. v. *Beall* (1882). Publications *inter se* of members or shareholders of an enterprise have qualified privilege if made in defence or furtherance of their common interest.

(*c*) *Public interest.* The interest to be protected may be that of the public at large in the honest and efficient discharge of public duties; and the reciprocal duty of an individual may be to disclose breaches of such duty. Thus, charges of misconduct against public officials will be privileged only if made to one, *e.g.* a Member of Parliament, or the official's superior, with a corresponding interest to receive them. The privilege would be exceeded and lost, *e.g.*, by publication of the complaint to a newspaper.

NOTE: The *Defamation Act, 1952, s.* 10, provides that a defamatory statement made by or on behalf of a candidate at an election is not privileged merely because it refers to an issue in the election.

34. Reports of parliamentary, judicial and public proceedings.

(*a*) *Reports* of statements should not be confused with the *statements themselves, e.g.* by a judge in court or an MP in the House—which are *absolutely* privileged.

(*b*) Fair and accurate reports of *public* proceedings in *any* court of justice enjoy qualified privilege at common law. This extends to foreign courts if the matter is of legitimate interest to the British public.

(*c*) This privilege does *not* extend to:

    (*i*) Tribunals to which the public is not admitted;
    (*ii*) domestic tribunals;
    (*iii*) cases of which the subject-matter is obscene or blasphemous.

(*d*) Fair and accurate reports of parliamentary debates are also conditionally privileged at common law. This extends to certain other bodies, such as statutory commissions, where it is in the public interest that their proceedings should be published. NOTE: Fairness and accuracy are questions of *fact*.

35. Qualified privilege: Defamation Act, 1952, s. 7.

(a) *Public meetings.* Reports of public meetings are not privileged at common law; but the *Defamation Act*, 1952, *s.* 7, extending the protection given by the *Law of Libel Amendment Act*, 1888, *s.* 4—gives qualified privilege to the publication, in a newspaper or by broadcasting, of certain reports and other material. In some of these instances, the defence of qualified privilege cannot be raised if the defendant had failed to accede, or had inadequately acceded, to a request by the plaintiff to publish a reasonable explanation or contradiction.

(b) *National and public bodies.* In general, fair and accurate reports of the proceedings of national and public bodies (*e.g.* Parliament, the courts, royal and statutory commissions, and international bodies) enjoy qualified privilege under *s.* 7, *without* explanation or contradiction; whereas reports of *private or local bodies* (*e.g.* trade and professional associations or local government authorities) possess such qualified privilege *subject to* explanation or contradiction. The two categories are set out fully in the schedule to the Act.

(c) *Limits of s.* 7. The section does *not* protect the following: publications prohibited by law; publications not of public concern; the publication of matter not in the public interest, *i.e.* a defamatory statement made at a meeting but irrelevant to its purpose.

36. Solicitor and client.
Professional communications between solicitor and client possess qualified privilege on the grounds that the interests of justice demand it. The communication must be made by or to the solicitor in his *professional capacity, e.g.* not merely as a personal friend, and must be relevant to the relationship of solicitor and client, having regard to the business in hand.

NOTE: It seems now to be generally agreed that this privilege is *qualified*: but the point is not absolutely settled as the Court of Appeal has treated it (on separate occasions) as both absolute and qualified: and in *Minter* v. *Priest* (1930) the House of Lords expressly reserved its opinion.

37. Offer of amends: Defamation Act, 1952, s. 4.
Section 4 may be invoked by a defendant who claims that the alleged

defamation was made *innocently* with regard to the plaintiff. Such a defendant may make an *offer of amends*.

38. Innocent defamation defined.

For words to be treated as innocent, the following conditions must be satisfied:

(*a*) That the publisher did not intend to publish the offending words of the plaintiff, and did not know of circumstances whereby they might be taken to refer to him.

(*b*) That the publisher did not know of circumstances by which apparently innocent words might be understood as defaming the plaintiff.

(*c*) That the publisher exercised reasonable care with respect to the publication.

NOTE: The publisher, in adducing evidence that the publication was innocent, is restricted to the facts contained in the affidavit accompanying his offer of amends.

38. What the defendant must do.

A defendant who relies on *s*. 4 must:

(*a*) plead that his offer of amends is made pursuant to *s*. 4;

(*b*) submit with his offer an affidavit of the facts he relies on to establish the innocence of the defamation;

(*c*) offer to publish a suitable correction of the offending matter, and a sufficient apology;

(*d*) take reasonable steps to notify persons to whom he sent copies of the offending matter that it is alleged to be defamatory of the plaintiff.

39. The offer may be accepted or rejected.

(*a*) If the offer is accepted:

(*i*) the person aggrieved may take no further proceedings for defamation against the maker of the offer;

(*ii*) the High Court has power to grant an application by the aggrieved party that his costs and expenses be paid by the maker of the offer "on an indemnity basis."

NOTE: The acceptance of an offer of amends does not prejudice action against anyone alleged to be jointly responsible for the offending publication.

(*b*) If the offer is rejected, then, in the case of any further proceedings, it shall be a defence to the person making the offer that:

    (*i*) the publication was made innocently with regard to the plaintiff;

    (*ii*) the offer was made without unreasonable delay, and has not been withdrawn.

40. Publication other than by the author. The above does not apply to a person other than the author (*e.g.* an editor), who cannot rely on this defence unless he proves that the words were written by the author *without malice*.

41. Apology: Libel Act, 1843. Apology was no defence at common law. The *Libel Act*, 1843, provides that:

(*a*) In the case of a libel in a newspaper, it is a defence that the defendant apologised at the earliest opportunity, and paid monies into court by way of amends;

(*b*) The defendant's having offered an apology at the earliest opportunity may be pleaded in mitigation of damages.

The Act is seldom invoked, as failure increases the damages by the amount paid into court.

42. Consent. It is a defence that the plaintiff gave *express or implied* consent to the allegedly defamatory publication.

PROGRESS TEST 13

1. Define defamation. **(1–3)**
2. Differentiate libel and slander. **(4)**
3. Is defamation by films, broadcasting and recordings libel or slander? **(5)**
4. Explain the circumstances in which slander is actionable *per se*. **(6)**
5. What is the difference between defamation and injurious falsehood? **(8)**
6. What must a plaintiff in defamation prove? **(9)**
7. Explain the functions of judge and jury in a defamation action. **(11)**
8. Explain defamation by innuendo. **(12)**
9. Outline the criteria a plaintiff must meet in proving that the allegedly defamatory statement referred to him. **(14)**

10. Can a *class* be defamed? **(15)**

11. What is meant by "publication"? Are there any circumstances in which publication will be presumed? **(16, 17)**

12. What is the effect of dissemination on liability for defamation? How (if at all) does negligence effect the matter? **(18)**

13. Explain "innocent dissemination." **(19)**

14. List the possible defences to an action for defamation. **(20–21)**

15. Explain the defence of justification. What is the position with regard to criminal libel? What are the effects of rumour, suspicion, innuendo and abuse? **(22, 23)**

16. Define "fair comment." What must a defendant prove to make good this defence? **(24)**

17. What is the "rolled-up" plea? What are the respective functions of judge and jury with respect to it? **(26, 27)**

18. Define and explain "public interest" with respect to the defence of fair comment. **(28)**

19. Explain absolute privilege. What statements, made by what persons, enjoy this privilege? **(30)**

20. Explain qualified privilege. What classes of statements enjoy this privilege? **(31)**

21. Under what circumstances will a voluntary statement enjoy qualified privilege? **(32)**

22. How may qualified privilege be invoked in protecting an interest? **(33)**

23. To what extent, (if at all), and how, can the defence of qualified privilege be invoked, with respect to: (a) reports of public meetings, (b) reports of parliamentary, judicial and public proceedings? Are communications between solicitor and client privileged in any way? **(35, 36)**

24. Explain the defence of offer of amends. What is the effect of (a) acceptance of the offer; (b) rejection of the offer? **(37, 38, 39)**

25. What is the effect of the *Libel Act*, 1843? Can consent be an effective defence in defamation? **(41, 42)**

CHAPTER XIV

CONSPIRACY; DECEIT OR FRAUD; INJURIOUS FALSEHOOD

CONSPIRACY

1. Conspiracy defined. The tort of conspiracy is committed when:

    (*a*) two or more persons (2).

    (*b*) wilfully and without lawful justification (3–5).

    (*c*) combine to cause actual injury or damage to a legitimate interest of the plaintiff (6).

NOTE: Such a combination may be either the tort of conspiracy *per se*, or a conspiracy to commit *some other tort, e.g.* inducement of breach of contract. In either case, however, the essence of the wrong is the *wilful and unjustified combination to injure* and the *consequential injury*.

It is clear from the above that conspiracy is primarily concerned with the *purposes* of the defendants, *not* the consequences of their actions. Conspiracy is unique among torts in the extent to which this is so.

2. Two or more persons. Historically, the tort of conspiracy derives from the crime of conspiracy, which is defined as "the agreement of two or more to do an unlawful act, or to do a lawful act by unlawful means": *Mulcahy* v. *R.* (1868), *per* Willes J. This applies also to the tort, as far as the element of combination is concerned. Note carefully that a *combination* may be unlawful even though it results in acts which would be lawful if done by one person.

3. Wilfully and without lawful justification. The *presence* of the will to injure the plaintiff and the *absence* of lawful justification for the defendants' acts are both necessary. This was laid down by Viscount Cave L.C. in *Sorrell* v. *Smith* (1925) in the following two propositions:

(*a*) A combination of two or more persons wilfully to injure a man is unlawful and, if it results in damage to him, is actionable.

(*b*) If the real purpose of the combination is, not to injure another, but to forward or defend the trade of those who enter into it, then no wrong is committed and no action will lie, although damage to another ensues.

These propositions were adopted and expanded by the House of Lords in *Crofter Hand Woven Harris Tweed Co. Ltd.* v. *Veitch* (1942), which is now the leading case on tortious conspiracy.

> *Crofter Hand Woven Harris Tweed Co. Ltd.* v. *Veitch* (1942). Certain crofters in the Hebrides, weavers of Harris Tweed, began to use cheaper yarn from the mainland in preference to that spun on the islands. The Transport and General Workers' Union, whose members in the Hebridean spinning mills were adversely affected by this trend, refused to load tweed made from mainland yarn. The crofters therefore sued the officials of the union. HELD: The primary object of the union's action was to benefit their members, not to inflict damage on the plaintiffs, and it was therefore not an actionable conspiracy. See also *Thorne* v. *Motor Trade Association* (1937) and *Thomson (D.C.) and Co. Ltd.* v. *Deakin* (1952).

4. Lawful justification defined. A combination will be lawfully justified if its purpose is to further the legitimate economic or other interests of the defendants. This may include interests incapable of being estimated in money terms: *Scala Ballroom (Wolverhampton) Ltd.* v. *Ratcliffe* (1958). Justification as defined above is no defence if the defendants, although predominantly concerned to protect their interests, nevertheless act unlawfully.

5. Effect of diverse motives. A combination which protects the defendant's interests will nevertheless *not* be lawful if its *predominant* motive was hatred or ill will, or a desire to dominate, or mere prejudice. Conversely, the presence of these motives will not make the combination unlawful if the *predominant* motive of the defendants was to protect their interests. This is a matter of fact for the jury, and is to be viewed broadly.

> NOTE: The motives of the several combiners need not be identical; and one or more of them may lack justification without necessarily invalidating that of the others.

6. Overt acts necessary. We have seen that, for a combination to amount to an actionable conspiracy, not only must the combiners *intend* to injure the plaintiff, they must *actually do so*, *i.e.* the plaintiff must prove overt acts to his detriment, and not merely agreement by the defendants: *Marrinan* v. *Vibart* (1962).

DECEIT OR FRAUD

7. Deceit defined. The tort of deceit is committed when:

- (a) the defendant fraudulently makes a false statement of fact (**12**; but *see* also **9** for the effect of the *Misrepresentation Act*, 1967)
- (b) intending that the plaintiff shall act upon it (**16**), and when
- (c) the plaintiff does act upon it (**15–16**) and
- (d) suffers damage in consequence (**17**).

NOTE: "Deceit" is the tort often designated "fraud." It is submitted, however, that "deceit" is preferable so as to avoid possible confusion with criminal and equitable frauds.

8. The statement must be fraudulent. The *common-law* definition of fraud is enshrined in the classic but narrow Rule in *Derry* v. *Peek* (1889), *i.e.* "Fraud is proved when it is shown that a false representation has been made (1) knowingly, or (2) without belief in its truth, or (3) recklessly, careless whether it be true or false." Because of the narrowness of this definition, and the consequently heavy burden falling on the plaintiff, the following points should be carefully noted, together with the qualifications of the rule set out in the next paragraph (*see* also **11** below on the effect of the *Misrepresentation Act*, 1967).

(a) *Negligence cannot constitute fraud.* The following case serves as an example.

> *Le Lievre* v. *Gould* (1893). Plaintiff advanced an unduly large sum of money to a builder on the strength of negligent but not fraudulent mis-statements by the defendant, a surveyor. HELD: Because of the absence of fraud, these misrepresentations were not actionable.

Note carefully that although careless mis-statements are now, in general, actionable in *negligence—Hedley Byrne* v. *Heller* (1964)—they still cannot amount to *fraud*.

(b) *An honest belief in the truth of the statement excludes fraud.* A statement in the truth of which the defendant honestly believed—however mistakenly—cannot be fraudulent.

(c) *The defendant's motive is immaterial.* If the defendant intended to deceive he will have behaved fraudulently, even though his motives were not those of self-interest: *Smith* v. *Chadwick* (1884).

9. The Misrepresentation Act, 1967. This Act makes basic alterations to the law of misrepresentation. However, as far as the tort of deceit or fraud is concerned, *s.* 2 (1) is of immediate importance. The effect of the subsection is that where a person, in order to induce the formation of a contract, makes a false statement *innocently*, and would have been liable in damages if it had been made *fraudulently*, he will be liable to pay common-law damages despite the innocence of the misrepresentation *unless* he can prove that he believed, on reasonable grounds, and up to the time of formation of the contract, that the facts he represented were true.

10. Effect on the Rule in Derry v. Peek. The Rule in *Derry* v. *Peek* (1889) is abrogated by the *Misrepresentation Act, 1967,* to the extent that damages at common law can now be claimed in respect of an *innocent* misrepresentation which *induces the formation of a contract.* It is as yet too early to assess the effects of the Act on the exceptions to the Rule in *Derry* v. *Peek* set out in **11** below.

11. The Rule in Derry v. Peek qualified. Apart from the *Misrepresentation Act,* 1967, the operation of the rule is also excluded or restricted in the following instances.

(a) *By statute.* The *Companies Act*, 1948, *s.* 43, which repealed and re-enacted the *Directors Liability Act*, 1890, makes directors liable for damage arising from negligent statements in prospectuses, even though the statements were not fraudulent.

(b) *By contract.* The Rule in *Derry* v. *Peek* does not affect liability under a contract to take care in making statements. Note that this protects only parties to such a contract, not third persons adversely affected by its breach.

(c) Special relationships. Where there is a fiduciary or other special relationship between the parties (*e.g.* solicitor and client—*Nocton* v. *Ashburton* (1914); banker and customer—*Woods* v. *Martins Bank Ltd.* (1959)), there will be liability in *Equity* for its breach, despite the absence of fraud. Note that there is a "special relationship" between the maker of a negligent mis-statement and the person relying on it. Thus, liability for negligent mis-statements under *Hedley Byrne* v. *Heller* is not affected by *Derry* v. *Peek*.

(d) Dangerous premises. A plaintiff who sues pursuant to the *Occupiers' Liability Act*, 1957, in consequence of damage arising from a negligent mis-statement that the property was safe, is unaffected by *Derry* v. *Peek*, *i.e.* he need not show that the statement was fraudulent.

12. The statement must be one of fact. The statement must be not merely an opinion or promise (which is actionable, if at all, in contract), but one of *fact*. Note, however, that a promise will be an actionable misrepresentation if it amounts to a *false* statement of intention: see *Edgington* v. *Fitzmaurice* (1885), in which a false statement was made by directors about proposed use of a loan.

13. Various kinds of false statements. False statements of fact may be made in various ways, apart from the obvious one of telling deliberate lies. Note the following.

(a) Concealment of the truth. Active steps to conceal the truth constitute mis-statement of the facts concealed: see *Scheinder* v. *Heath* (1813), in which vendors of ship deliberately put her in the water to conceal defective bottom.

(b) Conduct. A false statement of fact may be made by conduct: see *R.* v. *Barnard* (1837), in which the accused wore academic dress so as to deceive tradesmen into thinking him an undergraduate.

(c) Silence. It is a false statement of fact to leave uncorrected a statement which was true when made, but subsequently, to the defendant's knowledge, became false. Note that a statement false when made but true when acted upon is *not* a false statement of fact.

(d) Non-disclosure. Suppression or concealment of *part* of the truth may make the part revealed, even though true in

itself, a false statement of fact. Furthermore, there may be a *statutory duty to disclose* (*e.g.* under the *Companies Act*, 1948), breach of which constitutes an actionable false statement.

14. Defendant must have meant plaintiff to act on statement. Only persons who were intended to act on the false statement can sue for the deceit; others are precluded, even though they suffered because of the false statement.

Peek v. *Gurney* (1873). The plaintiff, acting upon wilfully false statements in a prospectus, bought shares on the market, which had been placed there by an allottee. HELD: Plaintiff could not recover, as only the *original allottees* of the shares were intended to act on the false statements in the prospectus.

15. The plaintiff must have acted on the false statement. If the plaintiff would have acted in the same way had there been no deceit, or he never knew of the deceit, he cannot be said to have acted on the false statement.

Horsfall v. *Thomas* (1863). Plaintiff sued defendant for the price of making a gun. Defendant alleged gun was useless because of a defect which plaintiff had concealed with intent to deceive. HELD: As defendant had not examined the gun, he had not been deceived.

16. Plaintiff's negligence no defence. It is no defence that the plaintiff was careless or stupid in acting on the false statement, or that a reasonable man would not have done so. If the statement induced the plaintiff to act, he can sue.

17. Plaintiff must have been harmed by the deceit. No action will lie unless the damage to the plaintiff was the *direct consequence* of the deceit; but it is not essential that the deceit was the *only* inducement to the plaintiff to act as he did.

18. False statements as to credit of third persons. The effect of *Lord Tenterden's Act*, 1828, is that false representations as to the credit, conduct, abilities or trade of a third person are not actionable unless made in writing and personally signed by the defendant. The object of this was to prevent evasions of *s.* 4 of the *Statute of Frauds*, 1667.

19. Principal and agent. A principal is liable for the frauds of his agent in the following cases:

(a) Where the principal expressly authorised the agent's fraudulent statements, whether or not the agent believed them to be true.

(b) Where the agent deliberately makes a statement he knows to be false.

(c) Where the principal deliberately, with intent to deceive, employs an agent ignorant of the truth.

(d) Where the principal keeps silent, knowing that his agent has innocently made false statements.

20. When principal not liable. The principal will *not* be liable where an agent innocently makes false statements which the principal knows to be untrue, but where the principal is not a party to the agent's making them: *Armstrong* v. *Strain* (1952).

INJURIOUS FALSEHOOD

21. Injurious falsehood defined. An injurious falsehood is:

(a) a *false* statement
(b) made *maliciously*
(c) about a *person* or his *property* or *goods*
(d) so that *other persons* are deceived
(e) with *consequential damage* to the plaintiff.

22. Injurious falsehood contrasted with deceit and defamation (XIII, **9**). In deceit and defamation the *plaintiff himself* is the direct object of the deceitful or defamatory statement, but in injurious falsehood the plaintiff suffers because of false statements made to *others* about the plaintiff.

23. Injurious falsehoods classified. Injurious falsehoods are of four types:

(a) Slander of title (*see* **24–26** below).
(b) Slander of goods (*see* **24–26** below).
(c) False statements which damage the plaintiff's trade or business (*see* **27** below).
(d) Passing off (*see* **28–30** below).

24. Slander of title and goods. These two types of injurious falsehood are appropriately conjoined because they are of common origin. The action originally lay for damage to the plaintiff arising from aspersions cast upon his title to *land*. It was later extended to cover similar cases involving:

(*a*) The plaintiff's personal and incorporeal property (*e.g.* patents and copyrights);

(*b*) the quality of his goods, stock-in-trade or products.

Note carefully, however, that at common law the action will not succeed unless the plaintiff can prove *actual damage*.

White v. *Mellin* (1895). Defendant, a retail chemist, without plaintiff's permission, labelled plaintiff's baby food to the effect that defendant's baby food was superior to all other such products. HELD: Plaintiff not entitled to an injunction as the statement neither injured nor was calculated to injure him.

25. Effect of Defamation Act, 1952, s. 3. This section alters the common-law rule by providing that, in an action for malicious falsehood, the plaintiff need not prove special damage if:

(*a*) the statement was published in writing or other permanent form, and was calculated to cause pecuniary damage to the plaintiff;

(*b*) the statement was calculated to cause pecuniary damage to the plaintiff in respect of any office, profession, calling, trade or business held or carried on by him at the time of the publication: see *Calvet* v. *Tomkies* (1963).

26. Mere puffing not actionable. It is not an injurious falsehood merely to say, in general terms, that one's goods are superior to those of one's competitors, even if it is untrue and maliciously motivated. This is to prevent the courts being used "in trying the relative merits of rival productions": *White* v. *Mellin* (1895), *per* Lord Herschell L.C.

27. False statements which damage the plaintiff's trade or business. Such a statement is actionable even though it does not fall within the purview of slander of title, slander of goods, or passing off.

Ratcliffe v. *Evans* (1892). Defendant, proprietor of a newspaper, maliciously and falsely implied in a published article that plaintiffs had gone out of business. Their trade suffered in consequence. HELD: The action for malicious falsehood would succeed.

28. Passing off defined. Passing off consists essentially in deliberately acting so as to mislead persons generally into believing that one's goods are those of another, so as to take illicit and unfair advantage of the reputation of that other, thus infringing his right of property in the goodwill of his trade or business. It is not necessary for the plaintiff to prove damage.

29. Modes of passing off. The following constitute passing off:

(a) *Marketing goods under the plaintiff's trade name*, or one so like it as to be mistaken for it. If goods have been marketed under a particular name for so long that it has become generally recognised that such goods are those of the plaintiff, it is actionable if another markets goods under the same or a closely similar name.

NOTE:

(i) the public must have been misled;
(ii) the name must be a *trade name*, i.e. not a mere general description of a class of goods;
(iii) the protection is not confined to business stock-in-trade, e.g. a performer may bring a passing-off action in respect of his stage name: *Hines* v. *Winnick* (1948).

Reddaway v. *Banham* (1896). Machine belting called "camel-hair belting" was generally acknowledged in the trade to be that manufactured by the plaintiff. Defendant marked his goods "camel-hair belting." HELD: Injunction granted to prevent this practice unless defendant clearly differentiated his belting from that of plaintiff. Note also *Bollinger* (*J*) v. *Costa Brava Wine Co. Ltd.* (1961), where an injunction was granted to forbid use of misleading description "Spanish Champagne."

NOTE

(i) The onus is on the *plaintiff* to prove that ordinary descriptive words have become exclusively associated with his goods.
(ii) Conversely, a trade name may, by usage, become merely descriptive, e.g. Liebig's "Extract of Meat" ceased exclusively to mean the product of a particu-

lar company and became a general description of meat extract: *Liebig's Extract of Meat Co.* v. *Hanbury* (1867). In such a case, the onus is on the *defendant* to show that he was using a general description which would not deceive the public.

(b) *Illicitly using the plaintiff's trade mark,* or an imitation of it, with intent to deceive the public. Registered trade marks are protected by the *Trade Marks Act,* 1938; unregistered trade marks by a common-law action for passing off.

(c) *Imitating the appearance or presentation of the plaintiff's goods,* with intent to deceive. Apart from the obvious forms of imitation, this species of passing off may also be committed through:

(i) using processes or materials which, by usage, have become exclusively associated with the plaintiff:—*Sales Affiliates Ltd.* v. *Le Jean Ltd.* (1949)—"Jamal Hairwave";

(ii) marketing second hand goods as new: *Morris Motors Ltd.* v. *Lilley* (1959).

30. Similar names. There are certain restrictions on the use of one's own name. The rules may be summarised as follows:

(a) It is not passing off for a person to trade under his own name *honestly,* even though confusion is thereby caused with the trade or business of another, with detriment to the older-established trader and benefit to the newer. It is otherwise if dishonest or fraudulent intention can be shown.

(b) It is not passing off for a person to trade under an assumed name by which he has become generally known.

Jay's Ltd. v. *Jacobi* (1933): Injunction sought to restrain plaintiff's ex-manageress, Mrs. Jacobi, from trading under the name "Miss Jay," by which she had become generally known. HELD: She was entitled so to describe herself, and the claim failed.

(c) It is passing off for a person to use either his own or a licitly assumed name deliberately to pass off his *goods* as those of another, *e.g.* by taking advantage of the fact that his name happens also to be that of a well-known product.

(d) At common-law a *company* must not choose a deceptive name, and cannot avoid this prohibition by using the name of a shareholder, which he would be entitled to use in his personal capacity. Furthermore, the *Companies Act,* 1948, *s.* 17, gives the Board of Trade powers to forbid companies to use "undesirable" names: but neither rule operates to prevent a person passing on the name under which he has acquired goodwill to a company which is taking over his business.

PROGRESS TEST 14

1. (*a*) Define conspiracy. (*b*) What factors are common to conspiracy *per se* and conspiracy to commit some other tort? **(1)**

2. What feature is unique to the tort of conspiracy? **(1)**

3. What were the two propositions laid down in *Sorrel* v. *Smith* (1925)? What is the *ratio decidendi* of *Crofter Hand Woven Harris Tweed Co. Ltd.* v. *Veitch* (1942)? **(3)**

4. Under what circumstances will a combination be lawfully justified? To what extent (if at all) will this be affected by the motives of the defendants? **(4, 5)**

5. What will be the effect of the use of unlawful means by the defendants? Is it sufficient for the plaintiff to prove agreement by the defendants to injure him? **(4, 6)**

6. Define the tort of deceit. **(7)**

7. State The Rule in *Derry* v. *Peek.* Is it in any way affected by later statutory rules? Can negligence constitute fraud? **(8)**

8. What is the effect of the *Misrepresentation Act,* 1967, *s.* 2 (1)? **(9–10)**

9. Apart from the *Misrepresentation Act,* 1967, what other qualifications are there of the Rule in *Derry* v. *Peek*? **(11)**

10. Under what circumstances (if at all) can a promise amount to an actionable misrepresentation? **(12)**

11. Of what can false statements consist? Can silence amount to a false statement? **(13)**

12. For what proposition is *Peek* v. *Gurney* authority? **(14)**

13. For the false statement to be actionable, must the plaintiff have acted on it? In what circumstances will he not be held to have acted on it? Does the plaintiff's negligence furnish a defence? **(15, 16)**

14. Will a false statement be actionable if the plaintiff was indirectly harmed by it? **(17)**

15. What were the intention and effect of *Lord Tenterden's Act,* 828? **(18)**

16. Under what circumstances will a principal be (*a*) liable, (*b*) not liable, for the frauds of his agent? **(19–20)**

17. Define injurious falsehood. How does it differ from (*a*) deceit, (*b*) defamation? **(21–22)**

18. Classify injurious falsehoods. What are the essentials of slander of title and slander of goods? **(23–24)**

19. What is the effect of the *Defamation Act*, 1952, *s.* 3? **(27)**

20. Are the following actionable: (*a*) advertising "puffs," (*b*) false statements which damage the plaintiff's trade or business? **(26–27)**

21. Give a general definition of passing off. **(28)**

22. (*a*) Must a plaintiff in passing off prove damage? (*b*) What three conditions must be met in order to maintain an action for passing off by misuse of the plaintiff's trade name? **(29)**

23. (*a*) For what proposition is *Liebig's Extract of Meat Co.* v. *Hanbury* (1867) authority? (*b*) How are registered and unregistered trade marks protected? **(29)**

24. What restrictions are there on the use of a person's own name for trading purposes? **(30)**

25. (*a*) Is it always passing off for a person to use an assumed name? (*b*) Outline the rules governing passing off by a company. Can an individual give his name to the company which is acquiring his business? **(30)**

CHAPTER XV

INJURIES TO DOMESTIC AND CONTRACTURAL RELATIONSHIPS

1. Definition. In certain circumstances it is an actionable tort to interfere with the following relationships.

    (*a*) Husband and wife (*see* **2–3** below).

    (*b*) Parent and child (*see* **4–5** below).

    (*c*) Master and servant (*see* **6–11** below).

The wrongful interference may involve the torts of enticement (*see* **2–4, 7** below); harbouring (*see* **2–4, 7** below); loss of consortium (*see* **2–3** below); seduction (*see* **5** below).

NOTE: A considerable part of this branch of the law has become archaic, and the *Eleventh Report of the Law Reform Committee*, published in 1963, recommended far-reaching reforms.

HUSBAND AND WIFE

2. Actions by the husband. A husband can sue a third party for the following:

    (*a*) *Enticement.* It is a wrong actionable at the suit of the husband for a third party to entice his wife to leave him. The enticement must consist of *persuasion*, not merely advice; but the plaintiff need not show that his wife's will was overborne by that of the defendant: *Place* v. *Searle* (1932).

NOTE

    (*i*) the action will not lie against a mother-in-law: *Gottlieb* v. *Gleiser* (1957);

    (*ii*) it is a good defence that the defendant honestly believed that the wife was justified in leaving her husband because of his conduct: *Philp* v. *Squire* (1791).

    (*b*) *Harbouring.* It is actionable to harbour the wife of another after a request by the husband to cease doing so. The husband must prove loss of *consortium*, but not that the defendant enticed his wife, or even knew that she was his wife. The decision in *Philp* v. *Squire* (above) also applies to habouring.

(*c*) *Loss of services.* A husband may recover damages from another who wrongfully deprives him of the *consortium et servitium* of his wife. Any tort against the wife which has this effect will ground the action. The husband must prove: (*i*) the tort against the wife; (*ii*) the *consequential* loss to him of her society or services.

3. Actions by the wife. A wife may sue for enticement; but *not* for harbouring or loss of consortium.

(*a*) *Enticement.* A wife may recover damages from one who entices her husband, or dissuades him from consorting with her. Note that the action is recognised by the *Law Reform* (*Miscellaneous Provisions*) *Act, 1934, s.* 1 (1).

(*b*) A wife cannot sue for harbouring or loss of *consortium*. The effect of the decisions in *Winchester* v. *Fleming* (1957) and *Best* v. *Samuel Fox & Co. Ltd.* (1952) is that, as these actions by a husband are anomalous, there is no justification for extending the anomaly to actions by a wife.

PARENT AND CHILD

4. Enticement and harbouring. A parent may sue, in respect of his child, for enticement and harbouring. It is an actionable tort unjustifiably to abduct a child capable of service, or to induce such a child to leave or remain away from its parents against their will. In *Lough* v. *Ward* (1945) a father succeeded against a religious order for enticement of his 16-year-old daughter, with consequent loss of her services.

5. Loss of service and seduction.

(*a*) *A father or a person in loco parentis* can recover damages from one who, by a tort against the child, deprives the father of the child's services. The relationship of *master and servant* must exist between parent and child so that, *e.g.*, the action will not lie if the child is too young to give service, or was in the service of another at the material time.

(*b*) *A parent or employer* can recover damages for the seduction of a female child or servant. The basis of the action is the loss of service to the parent or master. In the case of a master, "service" bears its usual meaning; but in the case of a parent any service, paid or unpaid, however temporary or trivial, will suffice, provided the child was old enough to give service and was resident in the parent's house—"residence" includes temporary absence with the intention of returning. A parent need not prove actual service, as "constructive" service is presumed to follow from the fact of the daughter's residence at home.

Hedges v. *Tagg* (1872). This case shows that loss of service is essential. A girl employed elsewhere as a governess was seduced while at home on a holiday which was not given as part of her contract of service. HELD: The mother's action for seduction failed, as the daughter was not in the mother's service, either at the time of seduction or during the subsequent confinement.

Beetham v. *James* (1937). Plaintiff's adult daughter was seduced. She had a full-time job, but also did domestic work at home. HELD: The father's action for seduction could succeed, as he had lost his daughter's services.

MASTER AND SERVANT

6. The nature of the wrong. A master may recover damages from one who, by a wrong against a servant, deprives the master of that servant's services. It is essential to prove the tort against the servant, and the consequent loss of service to the master. Note also the following.

(*a*) The service need not be contractual.

(*b*) The action is seemingly restricted to cases involving 'menial" servants; certainly it does not extend to public servants. See *Inland Revenue Commissioners* v. *Hambrook* (1956) and *Monmouthshire County Council* v. *Smith* (1957), which involved the failure of actions for loss of services of tax official and police officer respectively. In the former case the Court of Appeal held that the plaintiff failed because the action *per quod servitium amisit* applied only to domestic services rendered within the plaintiff's household. On the other hand, the action has succeeded in respect of an apprentice—*Hodsoll* v. *Stallebrass* (1840)—and a theatrical performer—*Mankin* v. *Scala Theodrome Co. Ltd.* (1947).

(*c*) The action will lie whether the injury to the servant was intentional or negligent. Nor is it a defence that the tortfeasor did not know his victim was the plaintiff's servant.

(*d*) The servant's contributory negligence is no defence in respect of the master's action for loss of services.

(*e*) Damages are normally assessed by reference to the wages of the incapacitated servant. Note that damages cannot be recovered in respect of *voluntary* payments to the injured servant.

(*f*) The action does not lie with respect to torts causing the death of the servant.

NOTE: The *Law Reform Committee* (*Eleventh Report*, 1963) recommended that the action for loss of services be abolished, and replaced by a claim by the employer for reimbursement of all payments made to the incapacitated employee. For details see the Report.

7. Enticement and harbouring of servants.

(*a*) *Enticement*. It is an actionable tort *wrongfully* (*e.g.* by fraud or coercion) to induce a servant to leave the employ of his master; or by any means to induce a servant to leave his master's employ *in a wrongful manner* (*e.g.* without giving due notice). Note that the action is not confined to menial service: *Lumley* v. *Gye* (1853).

(*b*) *Harbouring*. It is an actionable wrong to employ a servant, knowing that he is legally the servant of another. The defendant master need not have procured the servant's defection. Damage must be proved.

Jones Bros. (*Hunstanton*) *Ltd.* v. *Stevens* (1954). Plaintiff's servant left his employ without notice, and immediately began to work for defendant, who continued to employ him despite his knowledge of the true facts, and plaintiff's protests. HELD: Plaintiff could not succeed in an action for harbouring, as he had suffered no damage in view of the fact that the servant would not have returned to him in any case.

In harbouring, as in enticement, the *strict relationship* of master and servant *need not have existed*: *Lumley* v. *Gye* (1853).

8. Inducing breach of contract.
It is a tort, actionable by one damaged thereby, to induce or procure a breach of contract to which he is a party. The rules are as follows:

(*a*) The interference must be intentional and without lawful justification: but the plaintiff need not prove malice by the defendant.

(b) Proof of damage to the plaintiff is essential.

(c) The action is available in respect of *any* type of contract: *Temperton* v. *Russell* (1893). It is not confined (as was once thought) to contracts involving the strict common-law relationship of master and servant. This was established by *Lumley* v. *Gye* (1853), from which the modern form of the tort stems.

> *Lumley* v. *Gye* (1853). The plaintiff engaged a singer to perform exclusively at his theatre. The defendant induced her to break her contract by refusing to perform. HELD: The action for inducing the breach succeeded.

(d) The action protects only *existing* contracts. It does not lie for inducement not to enter into contracts: *Allen* v. *Flood* (1898), confirmed in *Rookes* v. *Barnard* (1964).

(e) The defendant must have known of the existence of the contract; but *constructive* knowledge probably suffices.

9. Inducing and procuring defined. Apart from direct persuasion to break the contract, the following, if done with knowledge of the contract and intent to procure its breach, also constitute inducing or procuring.

(a) *Physical interference* with a party or his equipment, rendering performance of the contract impossible.

(b) *Inducing or procuring a third party* to do some wrongful act *necessarily* making performance of the contract impossible. Examples would be persuading or inducing a customer to break a contract of service, or of sale or hire. Note that mere exhortation or advice is not enough (*see* **10** below). See also *Thompson D.C. Ltd.* v. *Deakin* (1952) and note carefully the protection given by *s.* 3 of the *Trade Disputes Act*, 1906, to persons who induce a breach of contract in contemplation or furtherance of a trade dispute.

> NOTE: For the law on interferences with competition, and the effect of the *Trade Disputes Act*, 1906, and subsequent legislation on the legality of acts done in the course of strikes and other industrial disputes, see textbooks on industrial law.

(c) *Wrongful interferences with the contract by a third party*, against the will and without the knowledge of the parties to the contract, of a kind which would have constituted a breach if done by one of the parties: *G.W.K. Ltd.* v. *Dunlop Rubber Co. Ltd.* (1926).

(*d*) *Action by a third party, with knowledge of the contract,* which is inconsistent with the performance of the contract; as where the interferer contracts with a party who is in breach of *his* contract with the plaintiff, in a manner inconsistent with the performance of *that* contract: *B.M.T.A.* v. *Salvadori* (1949).

10. Actions not amounting to inducing or procuring. The following activities do *not* constitute the tort:

(*a*) *A third party* does not induce or procure a breach merely by doing an act, *lawful in itself*, which has that effect, even if he was activated by spite and intended to procure the breach.

(*b*) The procurement or inducement may be *justified*.

Brimelow v. *Casson* (1924). Defendants induced theatre proprietors to break their contracts with plaintiff because he paid his chorus girls so little they were forced into prostitution. HELD: The interference was justified.

NOTE carefully, however, that:

(*i*) justification cannot be precisely defined;
(*ii*) justification is a question of *law*, to be decided in the circumstances of each case. Possible examples are: father inducing his daughter to break her engagement to an undesirable young man; doctor persuading his patient to break his contract of service on health grounds.

(*c*) Mere *advice* does not constitute procurement, for the advisor merely points out *existing* reasons for breaking the contract: but inducement involves the *creation* of a reason for the breach.

11. Intimidation. The case of *Rookes* v. *Barnard* (1964) established that intimidation is a distinct tort. It consists of:

(*a*) *coercing the plaintiff* by unlawful deeds or threats, so as to make him do or refrain from some act or course of conduct, to his damage;

(*b*) *coercing a third person* by unlawful deeds or threats, so as to make him do or refrain from some act or course of conduct, to the damage of the plaintiff.

Rookes v. *Barnard* (1964). Plaintiff, a draughtsman employed by B.O.A.C., resigned from his trade union. Defendants, officers of the union, threatened B.O.A.C. with a strike by their members unless plaintiff was dismissed. B.O.A.C. therefore dismissed him. He sued the union officials in consequence. HELD: Although the union officials had acted in furtherance of a trade dispute, they were not protected by *s.* 3. of the *Trade Disputes Act*, 1906, in respect of an unlawful threat to procure a breach of contract, *i.e.* the tort of intimidation. Plaintiff could succeed.

NOTE: The widespread fears that *Rookes* v. *Barnard* would nullify the protection given to trade unions by the *Trade Disputes Act*, 1906, were quieted by the decision in *Stratford* (*J.T.*) *& Son Ltd.* v. *Lindley* and by *s.* 1 of the *Trade Disputes Act*, 1965.

NOTE

  (*i*) A threat, to constitute intimidation, must be a threat to do an *unlawful* act.
 (*ii*) The plaintiff must have been damaged, *i.e.* he must have responded to the threat.
(*iii*) It is not necessary to prove any element of violence or threatened violence.
 (*iv*) Intimidation does not necessarily involve any other *tortious* act. A breach of contract, or the threat of such a breach, can in itself constitute intimidation.

PROGRESS TEST 15

1. Which domestic and contractual relationships are involved? What torts may be committed by way of interference with them? **(1)**

2. What must a husband prove who alleges that his wife has been enticed? Can he maintain the action against his mother-in-law? What is established by *Philp* v. *Squire* (1791)? **(2)**

3. What constitutes the harbouring of a wife, and what must a husband prove to establish it? **(2)**

4. What must a husband prove who sues for loss of his wife's services? **(2)**

5. Can a wife sue for harbouring and loss of *consortium*? Is there any, and if so what, statutory recognition of a wife's action for enticement? **(3)**

6. For which torts may a parent sue in respect of his child? **(4, 5)**

7. Define the torts of enticing and harbouring a child. **(4)**

8. What must be proved to establish the loss of a child's services? **(5)**

9. Outline the essentials of the tort of seduction as it applies to a child. **(5)**

10. Define the tort of deprivation of a servant's services. Is the action restricted to any particular classes of servants? Does it apply to deprivation through negligence? Would it make any difference if the defendant did not know that the person he had injured was the plaintiff's servant? **(6)**

11. Is the contributory negligence of the injured servant a defence? On what basis are damages assessed? Does the action lie for causing the death of a servant? What did the Law Reform Committee recommend? **(6)**

12. Define the torts of enticement of a servant and harbouring a servant. Must the strict relationship of master and servant exist for the action to lie? **(7)**

13. Explain the rules governing the action for inducing or procuring a breach of contract. **(8)**

14. Explain the various actions which can constitute inducing or procuring. **(9)**

15. Explain what activities do *not* amount to inducing or procuring. **(10)**

16. Define intimidation. **(11)**

17. Briefly outline the facts, and the relevant part of the judgment, in *Rookes* v. *Barnard* (1964). **(11)**

18. Of what must a threat consist to constitute intimidation? **(11)**

19. Is it necessary to prove violence or threatened violence? **(11)**

20. Does intimidation necessarily involve any other tortious act? **(11)**

CHAPTER XVI

PARTIES

SOVEREIGNS AND DIPLOMATS

1. The Crown.

(a) The *Crown Proceedings Act*, 1947, abolished the former immunity of the Crown from suits in tort, so that generally the Crown is now in the same position with regard to tortious liability as a private person. Section 2 (1) of the Act provides as follows:

"Subject to the provisions of this Act, the Crown shall be subject to all those liabilities in tort to which, if it were a private person of full age and capacity, it would be subject:

(a) in respect of torts committed by its servants or agents;

(b) in respect of any breach of those duties which a person owes to his servants or agents at common law by reason of being their employer;

(c) in respect of any breach of the duties attaching at common law to the ownership, possession or control of property."

Note that the Occupiers Liability Act, 1957, binds the Crown.

(b) *Breach of statutory duty*. Section 2 (2) provides that the Crown shall be liable for breach of statutory duties, provided they are "binding also upon persons other than the Crown and its officers." Note that the Crown is *not* bound by statute in the absence of express words or necessary implications.

2. Servants or agents of the Crown. Note the following points:

(a) Ministers of state and their subordinates, *i.e.* government departments, are servants of the Crown. Action lies against the appropriate Minister or, if none, the Attorney-General.

(b) The Crown will *not* be liable for the tort of its servant or agent, unless his act or omission would have made him *personally* liable: *s.* 2 (1) (*c*).

(*c*) A tortfeasor will *not* be a servant or agent of the Crown unless:

(*i*) he was directly or indirectly appointed by the Crown;

(*ii*) he was, at the time of the alleged tort, paid wholly from the Consolidated Fund, or from funds provided by Parliament, or from a source certified by the Treasury as equivalent thereto.

(*d*) There is no liability for the police. The police are not paid as above, nor is a police officer the servant of the local authority which employs him: *Fisher* v. *Oldham Corporation* (1930). But the *Police Act*, 1964, *s.* 48, provides that the chief officer of police for the area shall be vicariously liable, on general principles, for the torts of his officers committed in the course of their employment, and that damages and costs shall be paid from the police fund.

(*e*) *Public corporations.* It seems that these are not Crown servants, although the point cannot be regarded as absolutely settled. A corporation will not be a Crown servant unless the Act which created it provides that it acts on behalf of the Crown; otherwise "it acts on its own behalf, even though it is controlled by a government department": *Tamlin* v. *Hannaford* (1950). Thus *whether it acts on its own behalf* is the test of whether or not it is a Crown servant.

NOTE: Hospital authorities are probably not Crown servants.

3. Foreign sovereigns and ambassadors.

(*a*) *Foreign sovereigns are completely immune.* A foreign sovereign is not liable, civilly or criminally, in any British court, either for an act of state or for a personal act, unless he waives his immunity. This applies also to acts done in his personal capacity: *Mighell* v. *Sultan of Johore* (1894). The privilege ceases with the sovereign status.

(*b*) *Diplomatic immunity.* The *Diplomatic Privileges Act*, 1964, confers varying degrees of immunity on members of diplomatic missions, by dividing them into three categories, as follows:

(*i*) *Members of the diplomatic staff.* Complete civil and criminal immunity, except from certain actions relating to real property, succession and *personal* commercial activities.

(*ii*) *Technical and administrative staff.* Civil—but *not* criminal—liability for acts outside the course of their duties.

(*iii*) *Service staff.* Civil *and* criminal liability for acts outside the course of their duties.

Categories (*ii*) and (*iii*) are fully immune in respect of their *official* acts. The court determines whether the act was official.

(*c*) The *Visiting Forces Act*, 1952, *s.* 9, lays down procedure for the settlement of claims in tort against Commonwealth and NATO military personnel in this country in respect of their *official* acts. They have no personal immunity.

ASSOCIATED BODIES

4. Corporations.

(*a*) In general, a corporation is liable for all torts except those (*e.g.* assault) it would be impossible for it to commit. Furthermore, the intention or malice of its servants or agents will be imputed to a corporation, in respect of torts requiring proof of malice or intention.

Cornford v. *Carlton Bank Ltd.* (1899). The corporation, maliciously and without reasonable or probable cause, prosecuted the plaintiff. HELD: She could succeed for malicious prosecution.

(*b*) There is no liability for *ultra vires* acts. A corporation cannot authorise acts which are beyond its legal powers.

Poulton v. *London & South Western Rly Co.* (1867): Defendants' station master detained plaintiff for alleged non-payment of certain charges. HELD: The company had no power of detention, and therefore could not authorise its servant to detain. No vicarious liability for false imprisonment.

Note, however, that a corporation is probably liable for *ultra vires* torts which the *corporation itself* expressly authorised. See *Campbell* v. *Paddington Corporation* (1911) and consult larger works for details on this difficult point.

(*c*) A corporation can sue for any tort it would be possible to commit against a corporation. To succeed in defamation, however, a corporation must prove a tendency to cause actual damage to its business or property.

5. Unincorporated associations. Although unincorporated bodies are in general not liable in tort, the following rules and exceptions may enable a plaintiff to obtain satisfaction.

(*a*) Friendly Societies have been expressly held liable: *Longdon-Griffiths* v. *Smith* (1950); as have Trustee Savings Banks—*Knight & Searle* v. *Dove* (1964).

(*b*) It may be possible to bring a *representative action* under R.S.C. Ord. 15 if:

(*i*) the persons named in the writ may reasonably be taken to represent the unincorporated body;

(*ii*) all the members of the unincorporated body have a *common interest* in the action.

Campbell v. *Thompson* (1953): In this case a representation order was brought against two officers of an unincorporated members' club.

(*c*) The committee members may be *personally* liable. *Brown* v. *Lewis* (1896): in this case the committee of a football club were personally liable in respect of injuries caused by defective stand.

6. Trade unions. The *Trade Disputes Act*, 1906, *s.* 4, provides that no action in tort can be brought against a trade union, whether of workpeople or employers, even in cases of torts not connected with a trade dispute. It is possible, however, for a *quia timet* injunction to be obtained: *Boulting* v. *Association of Cinematograph Television and Allied Technicians* (1963).

NOTE: The Act does not remove the *personal* liability of members of trades unions for torts they may commit during a trade dispute.

INDIVIDUALS

7. Infants.

(*a*) *Liability of infants.* In general, infancy is no defence, and a minor is therefore liable for his torts. Note the following qualifications:

(*i*) In the case of torts in which the plaintiff must prove *malice or intention,* an infant defendant may be held too young to have evinced them.

(*ii*) *Where lack of reasonable care must be shown,* the standard of care expected of a minor will be that commensurate with his age and understanding. Note, however, that the authority for this consists of cases involving the *contributory* negligence of minors.

(*b*) *Contract and tort.* An infant cannot be made liable in tort for what is essentially a breach of contract, *i.e.* the court will not allow a plaintiff to circumvent an infant's contractual immunity by framing the action against him in tort. However, although an infant cannot be made liable in tort for what is merely a wrongful way of performing a contract, he *can* be made liable in tort for an act which, although it constitutes a breach of a contract, also goes beyond the bounds of that contract. The following cases illustrate the difference.

Jennings v. *Rundall* (1798). An infant hired a horse for *riding* and injured it by *excessive riding.* HELD: No liability in tort for what was fundamentally a breach of contract.

Burnard v. *Haggis* (1863). Infant defendant hired a mare for *riding* and, in breach of a term of the contract of hire, killed the mare by *jumping* her. HELD: Liability for the tort, which went beyond the bounds of the contract, although also a breach of one of its terms.

(*c*) *No tortious liability for fraud in procuring a contract.* An infant cannot be made liable in fraud or deceit for procuring a contract by pretending to be of full age, as that would amount to enforcing the contract.

However, such an infant is under an *equitable* obligation to restore any material gain thus obtained: *R. Leslie Ltd.* v. *Shiell* (1914).

(*d*) *Parents not liable.* A parent is not liable *as such* for his child's tort, but note the following:

(*i*) The parent may be liable in *negligence* for *affording the opportunity* for the child's tort.

Bebee v. *Sales* (1916). Father, although he knew the boy had previously done damage with it, allowed his son to retain an air gun, with which he injured the plaintiff. HELD: The father was negligent.

(*ii*) The infant may be the *servant* of his parent, so as to give rise to vicarious liability by the parent in his capacity of *employer*.

(e) *An infant can sue.* An infant sues by his *next friend* (usually his parent). An infant may sue his parent: *Deziel* v. *Deziel* (1953).

(f) *Pre-natal injuries.* There is no English authority as to whether damages can be recovered by a living person for injuries suffered before birth. In *Walker* v. *Great Northern Rly. Co. of Ireland* (1891), the Queen's Bench Division of Ireland held that no such action lay; but damages were awarded by the Supreme Court of Canada in 1933: *Montreal Tramways* v. *Leveille* (1933).

8. Insane persons. Insanity is *in itself* no defence in tort, but may operate as a defence in the following circumstances.

(a) *In negligence,* the defendant's mental deficiency may be evidence that he lacks the necessary knowledge, actual or constructive.

(b) *Where the defendant's malice or intention* must be proved (*e.g.* in deceit, malicious prosecution) his mental ill health may be held to have prevented his conceiving such malice or intention.

(c) *Insanity will operate as a defence if so extreme* as to make the defendant's act *involuntary.* This will not be so if he knew the nature and quality of his act, even if he did not know it was wrong.

> *Morris* v. *Marsden* (1952). Defendant violently attacked plaintiff, but was found unfit to plead to a criminal charge of assault. HELD: Plaintiff could succeed in civil action for personal injuries, as defendant knew the nature and quality of his act.

9. Convicts. Conviction is no bar to action. By the *Criminal Justice Act*, 1948, a prisoner can bring an action in tort.

10. Aliens. There are two categories, friendly and enemy aliens.

(a) *Friendly aliens* may bring or defend actions as if they were British subjects.

(b) *Enemy aliens* cannot sue, but may defend, and appeal if they lose.

11. Bankrupts. These have no general disability. A bankrupt may sue or be sued in tort.

(a) *A bankrupt may sue.* Rights of action for injuries to the bankrupt's *person*—as distinct from his estate—do not pass to the trustee in bankruptcy. For injuries affecting *both* person and estate, the bankrupt and trustee may sue severally or jointly. In the latter case, the damages will be assessed separately.

(b) *A bankrupt may be sued.* A bankrupt remains *personally* liable for his torts committed before or during his bankruptcy. Nevertheless, a breach of contract may be proved against the trustee although the action might also have been framed in tort; and unliquidated damages for tort may be recovered from the estate of a deceased and insolvent tortfeasor.

12. Spouses. Before the *Law Reform (Married Women and Tortfeasors) Act*, 1935, a husband was liable for his wife's torts, but the Act amended the law as follows:

(a) Section 1 provides that a wife is now liable for her torts exactly as if she were a *femme sole*.

(b) Section 3 provides that a husband is not, *by reason of his being her husband*, liable for his wife's torts. Note carefully that he may nevertheless be liable as *e.g.* her employer.

(c) Section 4 provides that nothing in the Act shall prevent husband and wife from being *jointly* liable in tort.

Section 1 of the *Husband and Wife Act*, 1963, provides that each spouse can sue the other in tort as if they were not married: but by *s.* 2 the court may stay the action if it is satisfied

(a) that no substantial benefit would accrue to either party;

(b) that the question could more conveniently be settled by recourse to the *Married Women's Property Act*, 1882, *s.* 17.

13. Deceased persons. Before the *Law Reform (Miscellaneous Provisions) Act*, 1934, an action in tort could be brought only if plaintiff and defendant were *both* alive; so that, if either died before judgment, the action abated—*actio personalis moritur cum persona*. However, the Act provides that all causes of action vested in or subsisting against a deceased person shall survive for or against his estate; *except that* actions for seduction, defamation, inducement of spouses, or for damages for adultery, do *not* survive.

The Act does not abolish the common-law rule that it is not a tort to cause another's death, but merely provides that the deceased's rights of action pass to his personal representative. Thus, because the cause of action is *not the death but the tort which caused it*, it follows that the deceased's right to claim damages for loss of expectation of life arising from that tort survive to his personal representative.

Rose v. *Ford* (1937). The plaintiff was the father of the deceased, whose death was caused by defendant's negligent driving. HELD: The deceased's right to recover damages for loss of expectation of life passed to her personal representative under the *Law Reform (Miscellaneous Provisions) Act*, 1934. £1000 was awarded under that head.

NOTE: Section 1 applies even if the interval of time between the tort and the death was so small that the death was practically instantaneous: *Morgan* v. *Scoulding* (1938).

JOINT TORTFEASORS

14. Partners. Partners are jointly and severally liable for their own and each other's torts committed in the course of the firm's business, both at common-law and by the *Partnership Act*, 1890, *ss.* 10 and 12.

15. Joint and several tortfeasors. Joint and several tortfeasors should be distinguished.

(*a*) *Persons are joint tortfeasors* if they commit the *same* tort. This is so in cases of vicarious liability and agency, and also in that of *common action* by two or more tortfeasors.

Brooke v. *Boole* (1928). Boole and Morris investigated gas leak in plaintiff's shop, thus causing explosion. HELD: B and M were joint tortfeasors. "The act . . . was their joint act done in pursuance of a concerted purpose."

(*b*) *Several tortfeasors.* Distinguish carefully between *joint* torts and *separate but coincidental* torts which cause the same damage. These give rise to separate actions against the *several* tortfeasors.

The "Koursk" (1924). The *Koursk* collided with the *Clan Chisholm*, causing her to sink the *Itria*. The owners of the

Itria, having succeeded against those of the *Clan Chisholm*, then sued the owners of the *Koursk*. HELD: The plaintiffs could bring the latter action, as the defendants were not joint, but several, tortfeasors as they had no concerted purpose.

(*c*) *Liability*. Joint tortfeasors are *jointly and severally* liable for the damages, *i.e.* the full amount can be recovered from *one* of them, even if they were sued in the same action, and even from a tortfeasor who inflicted a minor proportion of the damage suffered by the plaintiff.

(*d*) *Tortfeasors not sued ab initio*. At common law, when the plaintiff had enforced judgment against one or more tortfeasors, he was thereby debarred from action against any tortfeasors not sued in the first action: but *s*. 6 of the *Law Reform (Married Women and Tortfeasors) Act*, 1935, provides that "judgment recovered against any tortfeasor liable in respect of that damage shall not be a bar to an action against any other person who would, if sued, have been liable as a joint tortfeasor in respect of the same damage."

16. Contribution.

(*a*) *The Law Reform (Married Women and Tortfeasors) Act*, 1935, *s*. 6. At common-law there was no contribution between tortfeasors; but *s*. 6 provides that: "where damage is suffered by any person as a result of a tort (whether a crime or not) any tortfeasor . . . may recover contribution from any other tortfeasor who is, or would if sued have been, liable in respect of the same damage, whether as a joint tortfeasor or otherwise, so, however, that no person shall be entitled to recover under this section from any person entitled to be indemnified by him in respect of the liability in respect of which the contribution is sought."

NOTE particularly the following:

   (*i*) *The fact that the tort was also a crime* is no bar to contribution. This is an exception to the principle *ex turpi causa non oritur actio*.
   (*ii*) *Contribution may be recovered* from tortfeasors who were not sued, if they would have been liable.
   (*iii*) *Contribution may be recovered* from one who was not a *joint* tortfeasor, *i.e.* between *separate* tortfeasors contributing to the same damage.

(*iv*) *A tortfeasor cannot recover contribution* from a person who is entitled to be indemnified by that tortfeasor.

(*b*) *Amount of contribution: the effect of s.* 6 (2). The amount of contribution shall be such as is found by the court to be just and equitable, having regard to each tortfeasor's responsibility for the damage. The court has power to exempt any person from liability to contribute.

(*c*) *Different periods of limitation.* It has not been finally decided whether, when the various tortfeasors are subject to differing periods of limitation, all rights to claim contribution expire at the end of the first of such periods of limitation. The better opinion seems to be that it does not, and that the tortfeasor enjoying the longest period of limitation can sue for contribution at any time within that period, notwithstanding that the party from whom contribution is claimed was subject to a period of limitation that has already expired (*see* XIX).

17. Indemnity.

(*a*) The *Law Reform (Married Women and Tortfeasors) Act*, 1935, *s.* 6 (2), provides that "the court shall have power to direct that the contribution to be recovered from any person shall amount to a complete indemnity."

(*b*) At common-law. This governs the case of master and servant, so that a master may recover contribution from a servant for whom the master is vicariously liable: see *Lister* v. *Romford Ice & Cold Storage Co. Ltd.* (1957). Also, a servant who, in the course of his employment, innocently commits a tort at his master's behest can claim contribution from the master: *Adamson* v. *Jarvis* (1827).

PROGRESS TEST 16

1. Summarise the provisions of the *Crown Proceedings Act*, 1947, *s.* 2. Under what circumstances will the Crown be liable for breach of statutory duty? **(1)**

2. Is the Crown liable for the torts of its servants or agents who would not have been personally liable? What conditions as to appointment and payment must be met for a tortfeasor to be a servant or agent of the Crown? **(2)**

3. To what extent (if at all) are the following servants of the Crown for the purposes of tortious liability: the police; public

corporations; hospital authorities; the Post Office; members of H.M. forces? **(2)**

4. Is a foreign sovereign liable in tort for acts done in his personal capacity? When does the immunity of a foreign sovereign cease? **(3)**

5. Summarise the main provisions of the *Diplomatic Privileges Act,* 1964, as to the immunity from actions in tort of members of diplomatic missions in this country. **(3)**

6. What is the effect of *s.* 9 of the *Visiting Forces Act,* 1952? Have members of visiting forces any personal immunity? **(3)**

7. Can a corporation be made liable for a tort involving proof of intention or negligence? What is an *ultra vires* act? Is a corporation ever liable for its *ultra vires* acts? **(4)**

8. Can a corporation succeed in an action for defamation? **(4)**

9. Summarise the tortious liability (if any) of unincorporated associations? **(5)**

10. What Act governs the liability of trade unions in tort? Can *any* remedy be obtained against a trade union? **(6)**

11. To what extent (if at all) is an infant liable in tort? **(7)**

12. Explain the effects of the following decisions: *Jennings* v. *Rundall* (1798); *Burnard* v. *Harris* (1863); *R. Leslie Ltd.* v. *Shiell* (1914). **(7)**

13. Explain the liability (if any) of a parent for the torts of his child. **(7)**

14. Can a minor sue his own parent? Can damages be recovered in respect of pre-natal injuries? **(7)**

15. Explain the extent to which (if at all) insanity can furnish a defence to an action in tort. **(8)**

16. Can a convict bring an action in tort? **(9)**

17. What rights (if any) have (*a*) friendly, (*b*) enemy, aliens with regard to actions in tort? **(10)**

18. Explain the capacity (if any) of a bankrupt to sue and be sued. **(11)**

19. What statute governs the tortious liability of spouses? Are there any circumstances in which a husband is liable for his wife's torts? Can a husband and wife be jointly liable in tort? Can one spouse sue the other in tort? Are there any circumstances in which the court will not hear such an action? **(12)**

20. To what extent (if at all) does the maxim *actio personalis moritur cum persona* apply to actions in tort? **(13)**

21. Is the infliction of death a tort? What authority (if any) is there for saying that the rights in tort of a deceased person pass to his personal representative? What is the position if death was instantaneous? **(13)**

22. Outline the tortious liability of partners. **(14)**

23. Distinguish between joint and several tortfeasors. Explain the liability of joint tortfeasors. **(15)**

24. When a plaintiff has enforced judgment against one tortfeasor, is he thereby debarred from action against another tortfeasor not sued in the same action? **(15)**

25. What statute governs the question of contribution between tortfeasors? Did it alter the common-law position? Does the maxim *ex turpi causa non oritur actio* apply to the question of contribution? Is contribution restricted to joint tortfeasors? Can a tortfeasor recover contribution from one whom he must indemnify? What is the effect of *s.* 6 (2) of the statute on the amount of contribution? **(16)**

26. When various tortfeasors are subject to differing periods of limitation, does the right of all of them to claim contribution expire at the end of the first of such periods of limitation? **(16)**

27. Is it possible to recover a complete indemnity (*a*) by statute; (*b*) at common law? Can a servant who innocently commits a tort at the master's behest recover contribution from the master? **(17)**

CHAPTER XVII

REMEDIES

1. Judicial and extra-judicial remedies. Remedies are often classified as *judicial* and *extra-judicial*. However, as the extra-judicial—*e.g.* abating nuisances, ejecting trespassers—are discussed in the chapters dealing with the torts to which these remedies apply, this chapter will deal only with the judicial remedies of damages, injunction and restitution of property.

DAMAGES GENERALLY

2. Damages classified. Damages may be classified in two groups: (*a*) general and special; (*b*) nominal, real or substantial, exemplary, contemptuous, aggravated.

3. General and special damages differentiated.

(*a*) *General damages* are damages awarded because a tort has been committed from which the law *presumes* loss or injury to follow. General damages are *unliquidated*, *i.e.* the amount is at the discretion of the court.

(*b*) *Special damages* are awarded for injury or loss *arising from* the tort which is of a kind that the law does *not presume to follow from it*: *e.g.* loss of earnings; pain and suffering; hospital expenses. Special damages must be specially pleaded, and quantified in the pleadings.

Note carefully, however, that the definitions of general and special damages are not entirely self-contained and mutually exclusive, *e.g.* damages for pain and suffering in personal injury claims are "general."

4. Nominal damages. Nominal damages are a small sum of money awarded, not as compensation, but solely because the plaintiff has proved that a tort has been committed against him, *e.g.* in a case of trespass to land involving no physical damage to the land or other loss to the plaintiff. It follows that nominal damages are confined to torts actionable *per se*.

Constantine v. *Imperial London Hotels Ltd.* (1944). The famous West Indian cricketer was refused admittance to defendants' hotel without reasonable cause. He suffered no special damage. HELD: The exclusion was tortious, and he could recover nominal damages of five guineas.

5. Real, substantial or ordinary damages. These are the general, unliquidated, damages awarded to compensate the successful plaintiff for the loss, injury or damage he has suffered, and, as far as possible, to restore him to the condition he was in before the tort—*restitutio in integrum.* The *quantum* of damages is a question of *fact*, but the methods of assessment used by the courts are outside the scope of this book.

6. Exemplary damages. Exemplary damages (sometimes called vindicative or punitive damages) represent an *addition* to what is awarded as real damages, to compensate the plaintiff for what the court considers deplorable or outrageous conduct by the defendant, and (in effect) by way of punishment for it. Exemplary damages are sometimes criticised on the grounds that a civil court should have no concern with punishment. In *Rookes* v. *Barnard* (1964), the House of Lords laid it down that exemplary damages should be awarded only in the following types of cases:

(*a*) Where there is oppressive, arbitrary or unconstitutional action by the servants of the government (but *not* by private persons or corporations).

(*b*) Where the defendant's conduct (*e.g.* by deliberately and tortiously interfering with the plaintiff's trade) was calculated to gain him a profit which might exceed the compensation payable to the plaintiff.

(*c*) Where a statute expressly provides for exemplary damages.

7. Contemptuous damages. These are awarded to unmeritorious plaintiffs who are nevertheless entitled to succeed. They are the court's expression of its displeasure at a frivolous, vexatious or vindictive action. A plaintiff awarded contemptuous damages is unlikely to be awarded costs.

8. Aggravated damages. These are the reciprocal of contemptuous damages, in that they represent an additional sum awarded to the plaintiff because the defendant's conduct was, *e.g.*, wilful or malicious. Aggravated damages differ from exemplary damages in that aggravated damages represent merely additional compensation, whereas exemplary damages contain a punitive and deterrent element.

9. Measure of damages. The function of damages is that, theoretically, they should restore the successful plaintiff to his original condition—*restitutio in integrum*. In practice, however, this is often impossible, *e.g.* where the plaintiff has lost a limb. It is therefore better to regard damages merely as monetary compensation (in so far as, in any given case, money can compensate) for the loss or injury suffered by the plaintiff.

For the purposes of assessment, damages may be classified under the headings (*a*) damage to property; (*b*) injuries to the person. Bear in mind, however, that the actual sum arrived at will be a question of *fact* in each case.

10. Damage to property.

(*a*) *Trespass to land.* The damages awarded represent *the loss actually suffered by the plaintiff*, as represented by the decrease in the value of the land, *not* the cost of restoring the land to its original condition. Note, however, that damages can be recovered where the defendant derived benefit from *wrongfully using* the plaintiff's land, *thereby depriving him of its use*, even though the land was not damaged: *Whitwham* v. *Westminster Brymbo Coal & Coke Co.* (1896).

(*b*) *Mesne profits.* A plaintiff wrongfully excluded from his land can recover, in an action for mesne profits, the losses he suffered as a result of the exclusion. The action for mesne profits is usually joined with one for ejectment; but a plaintiff may also sue for mesne profits:

(*i*) after regaining possession;

(*ii*) without ejectment or repossession, if his interest in the land has already ended.

(*c*) *Damage to chattels.* A plaintiff is entitled to the market value of a chattel of which he has been *permanently* deprived; for a damaged chattel he can recover the full cost of restoring the damage; except that he cannot recover from the *defendant* the cost of restoring damage done *by someone else* to a chattel which was *also damaged by the defendant*.

Performance Cars Ltd. v. *Abraham* (1961). Plaintiff's car, damaged by someone other than defendant, was subsequently damaged by defendant before repairs to the first damage had been done. HELD: Plaintiff could not recover from defendant for repairs arising from the first accident.

(*d*) *Temporary deprivation of chattel.* A plaintiff thus deprived can recover:

(*i*) for the loss of use of the chattel;

(*ii*) by way of special damages, for its repair and the cost of hiring a replacement (even if no replacement was, in fact, hired), and for other expenses arising from the deprivation.

11. Conversion. (*See* III, 7–17.)

(*a*) *Damages for conversion.* The *quantum* of damages for conversion and its assessment raise some special points, the more important of which may be summarised as follows:

(*i*) A person with *less than full legal ownership* of a chattel (*e.g.* an agent or bailee) who had *actual possession* of a chattel may recover in an action for conversion the *entire value* of the chattel, and not merely the value of his interest.

(*ii*) The amount the plaintiff recovers over and above his own interest he holds on trust for those entitled to it, and will be liable to them in an action for money had and received to their use. Clearly, however, if the *defendant himself,* or a *third party to whom the defendant was responsible,* is among those entitled to the surplus value, then the plaintiff's claim will be reduced by the amounts of such interests.

(*b*) *Assessment of damages for conversion.* The plaintiff may be entitled to recover:

(*i*) the chattel itself—either in lieu of monetary damages, or merely by way of reduction of them;

(*ii*) the market value of the chattel *at the time of the conversion;*

(*iii*) if the chattel had no market value, the cost of its replacement;

(*iv*) damages for any other losses consequent on the conversion, which are not too remote.

(*c*) *No double satisfaction.* A plaintiff who obtains judgment for the *value* of property nevertheless retains his title to it, and may therefore, *before satisfaction of the judgment,* seize it or bring action (where appropriate) for its specific restitution. But he cannot exercise these rights in such a way as to obtain both the property *and* its value: for satisfaction of a judgment, *either* by return of the property *or* by paying its value, extinguishes all further rights of action in respect of the same conversion of the same property.

DAMAGES FOR PERSONAL INJURY

This is a difficult and complex matter, of which only the main points can be indicated in a book of this nature.

12. General and special damages. The assessment of the actual amount of damages is a question of fact in each case. We have seen, however, that general damages are intended to effect *restitutio in integrum*, whereas special damages are awarded to compensate for injuries not presumed to follow from the tort.

13. General damages. General damages for personal injuries may be awarded for: loss of expectation of life; loss of amenities of life; pain and suffering.

(*a*) *Loss of expectation of life.* This as an independent head of damages was established in the following cases.

Flint v. *Lovell* (1935). The expectation of life of the elderly but active plaintiff was reduced to one year through defendant's negligent driving. HELD: Plaintiff could recover, *inter alia*, for loss of expectation of life.

Rose v. *Ford* (1937). A girl died four days after being injured through defendant's negligent driving. The Court of Appeal declined to award damages for loss of expectation of life for the benefit of the estate under the *Law Reform (Miscellaneous Provisions) Act*, 1934. Plaintiffs appealed to the House of Lords. HELD: £1000 awarded as of right, under the *Law Reform (Miscellaneous Provisions) Act*, 1934, *s.* 1, for loss of expectation of life.

In 1941, in the case of *Benham* v. *Gambling*, the House of Lords laid down the following rules for assessing damages for loss of expectation of life. They apply both to claims on behalf of the deceased's estate under the *Law Reform (Miscellaneous Provisions) Act*, 1934, and to actions by living plaintiffs:

(*i*) The award should be moderate in amount, as the

hypothetical prospective happiness of an injured or deceased person's life cannot be computed.

NOTE: This part of the Rule in *Benham* v. *Gambling* was reiterated by the House of Lords in *Yorkshire Electricity Board* v. *Naylor* (1967).

(*ii*) Since happiness of life and not its length is the criterion, "expectation" is not to be determined actuarially or statistically. It follows from this that presumed unhappiness may justify a lower award.

(*iii*) The test of future or hypothetical happiness is *objective*, *i.e.* not that of the plaintiff or victim. It is therefore irrelevant that he was rendered mentally incapable of realising the extent of his loss.

(*iv*) The plaintiff's social and financial standing and expectations are to be disregarded.

(*v*) A reduced sum should be awarded in the case of a very young child.

NOTE: Any sum awarded under the *Law Reform (Miscellaneous Provisions) Act*, 1934, will be deducted from an award under the *Fatal Accidents Acts*.

(*b*) *Loss of amenities of life.* The extent of the loss is a question of *fact*, *e.g.* a young and active person suffers more under this head than an elderly and infirm one. It is immaterial:

(*i*) that the plaintiff is mentally incapable of realising his loss;

(*ii*) that he himself will not be able to use the money: *West & Son Ltd.* v. *Sheppard* (1963).

(*c*) *Pain and suffering.* We have already noted that damages under this head are *general* in personal injury claims. Where there is reasonable apprehension of prolonged suffering, even a large sum may be awarded in respect of the plaintiff's knowledge of his diminished expectation of life.

14. Special damages. Special damages for personal injuries are awarded for loss of earnings and for expenses.

(*a*) *Loss of earnings.* The plaintiff is entitled to claim his earnings, *less* income tax and national-insurance contributions for the period between the start of his incapacity and the actual or estimated date of his recovery or death. However, in the case of a deceased person whose estate sues under the *Law Reform (Miscellaneous Provisions) Act*, 1934, damages for loss of earnings are subsumed within those for loss of expectation of life.

British Transport Commission v. *Gourley* (1955). The respondent, a person of high earnings, was incapacitated by appellant's negligence, and had been awarded £37,720 for loss of earnings. HELD: He was entitled only to recover his earnings after tax, and the award would therefore be reduced to £6695.

NOTE

    (*i*) In assessing damages, account is taken of any benefits received under the *National Insurance (Industrial Injuries) Act*, 1946.

    (*ii*) Although income tax and national-insurance contributions are deductible from damages, the proceeds of insurance policies are not, nor are pensions payable at *discretion*; but pensions *payable as of right* are deductible.

(*b*) *Expenses*. The plaintiff may recover by way of special damages all expenses actually and reasonably incurred before the trial. These include, *e.g.*, those for lost or damaged clothing, loss of no-claims bonus, and for medical and nursing expenses. Note that, for the purpose of assessing expenses, no account is taken of benefits under the welfare-state legislation.

REMOTENESS OF DAMAGE

15. Remoteness and intention mutually exclusive. Damages in tort cannot be recovered if the wrong complained of is *too remote*, *i.e.* not sufficiently closely connected with the harm suffered by the plaintiff. However, damage is never too remote if it was *intended* by the defendant; and a person is *presumed to intend* the *natural and inevitable consequences* of his acts and omissions.

16. Remoteness of damage in negligence: effect of The Wagon Mound.

(*a*) The position before *The "Wagon Mound."* (*Overseas Tankship (U.K.) Ltd.* v. *Morts Dock & Engineering Co. Ltd.* (1961).) Before 1961 the rule was that a defendant in negligence was liable for all the *direct* consequences of his act, *notwithstanding* that he could not reasonably foresee them.

This was the effect of the decision in the case usually referred to as *Re Polemis*.

> *Re Polemis & Furness, Withy & Co. Ltd.* (1921). Through the negligence of the charterer's servants a plank fell into the hold of a ship, striking a spark, and igniting petrol vapour escaping from defective tins. The resultant fire destroyed the ship. HELD: The loss of the ship was the *direct consequence* of the negligence of servants of the charterers, and the latter were therefore liable for it, although they could not reasonably have foreseen it.

(b) *The "Wagon Mound."* As a result of this case, *reasonable foreseeability* was re-established as the test of remoteness of damage in *negligence* cases, and *Re Polemis* ceased to be good law. This seems to have been accepted by the House of Lords—*Hughes* v. *Lord Advocate* (1963)—and was specifically accepted by the Court of Appeal—*Doughty* v. *Turner Manufacturing Co. Ltd.* (1964)—despite the fact that *The "Wagon Mound"* was decided by the Judicial Committee of the Privy Council, and is therefore of persuasive authority only. Nor does it appear to be finally decided whether the decision applies only to negligence—but the better opinion seems to be that such is the case.

> *Overseas Tankship (U.K.) Ltd.* v. *Morts Dock & Engineering Co. Ltd.* (1961), a Privy Council case. Appellants, charterers of the *Wagon Mound*, allowed oil to escape from her in Sydney harbour. The appellants could not reasonably have discovered that the oil might ignite when floating on water; in fact, it was ignited by sparks from welding operations on respondent's wharf, to which considerable damage was caused. HELD: Appellants were not liable for this damage *because they could not reasonably have foreseen it.* "[*Re Polemis*] should no longer be regarded as good law. . . . Thus foreseeability becomes the effective test": *per* Lord Simonds.

17. Remoteness of damage in torts other than negligence. Whether the damage was the direct consequence of the defendant's act or omission remains the test of whether or not it was too remote in the following classes of cases, which are unaffected by *The "Wagon Mound."*

(a) Torts of strict liability, *e.g. Rylands* v. *Fletcher*.

(b) Breaches of strict statutory duties, *e.g.* those imposed by the *Factories Acts*.

(c) Claims under, *e.g.*, the *Fatal Accidents Acts*, where the question is simply whether the plaintiff is entitled to the compensation for which the Act provides.

18. Extent and amount of damage irrelevant. The test of reasonable foreseeability applies to the *type* of damage caused, but not to its *amount*. Thus, provided the damage caused was of a *type* the defendant ought reasonably to have foreseen, he will be liable for it notwithstanding that its *amount* is larger than he could reasonably have foreseen. The following cases illustrate these points.

Smith v. *Leech Brain & Co. Ltd.* (1961). An employee of the defendants was, through the latter's negligence, splashed by molten metal, as a result of which he subsequently contracted cancer, from which he died. HELD: The widow could recover damages under the Fatal Accidents Acts and the *Law Reform (Miscellaneous Provisions) Act*, 1934, as the injury suffered by the deceased was reasonably foreseeable—although its consequences were not.

Hughes v. *Lord Advocate* (1963). Post Office workmen, having opened a manhole, left it covered by a tent, but with a gap between the bottom of the tent and the ground. Paraffin warning lamps were also left. Two young boys took a lamp and entered the tent, subsequently dropping the lamp into the manhole, causing an explosion through which one of the boys was badly burned. HELD: The workmen were negligent in thus leaving the manhole, as children were known to play near by. The boy could recover damages because the accident was of a type reasonably foreseeable in the circumstances—the fact that it happened in an unforeseeable way being irrelevant.

Doughty v. *Turner Manufacturing Co. Ltd.* (1964). The plaintiff, an employee in defendant's factory, unintentionally knocked an asbestos cement cover into molten liquid at high temperature, thus causing an explosion, in consequence of which metal was thrown from the vat, injuring the plaintiff. HELD: Plaintiff could not succeed because, in the state of knowledge at the time, the explosion was not reasonably foreseeable. The explosion (which was the sole cause of the accident) was a phenomenon entirely different from the foreseeable splash caused by the cover entering the liquid.

CAUSATION; NOVUS ACTUS INTERVENIENS

19. Causation essential for liability. We have seen that a man is responsible for the natural and probable consequences of his acts or omissions: but he will *not* be so liable unless his act or omission *caused* the plaintiff's injury; and there will be no such causation if an *independent act*, or an *act of a third party*—*Weld Blundell* v. *Stephens* (1920)—or an *act of the plaintiff himself*—*Cumming* (or *McWilliams*) v. *Sir Wm. Arrol & Co. Ltd.* (1962)—intervened *so as to break the chain of causation* and become an independent cause of the harm suffered by the plaintiff.

Note carefully, however, that not every such action breaks the chain of causation—for it may be a "mere conduit pipe" through which injury is transmitted from defendant to plaintiff.

20. Intervening act defined. An intervening act, to break the chain of causation, must be "extraneous" or "extrinsic" to the extent that it so *"disturbs the sequence of events"* as to divorce the tort of the defendant from the consequences suffered by the plaintiff: *Lord* v. *Pacific Steam Navigation Co. Ltd. The Orepesa* (1943), *per* Lord Wright.

> *Owners of S.S. Temple Bar* v. *Owners of M.V. Guildford. The "Guildford"* (1956). The *Guildford* and the *Temple Bar* collided. The *Guildford* refused the *Temple Bar's* offer of a tow, and waited several hours for a tug. However, she sank before she could be towed into harbour. HELD: The *Guildford* could recover damages in respect of the *Temple Bar's* negligence, the decision of the *Guildford's* Master to await the tug being reasonable in the circumstances, and therefore not a *novus actus interveniens.*
>
> Contrast with:
>
> *Harnett* v. *Bond* (1925). The plaintiff was on leave from a mental hospital, the superintendent of which had a discretionary power to take the plaintiff back into confinement if his condition warranted it. The plaintiff called upon a commissioner in lunacy, who, mistakenly believing him to be wrongly at large, detained him for some hours while the superintendent was summoned to take him back to the hospital, where he was detained a further nine years. Eventually, when free, the plaintiff sued the commissioner for false imprisonment. HELD: He could succeed in respect of the time he was detained in the commissioner's house, but not for the subsequent nine years, the superintendent's exercise of his discretion being a *novus actus interveniens.*

21. The intervening act may be inoperative. A *novus actus interveniens* does not necessarily absolve the defendant. In the following instances, the defendant remains liable despite the *novus actus interveniens*. The basis of this liability is that the *novus actus interveniens* was *reasonably foreseeable* by the defendant, and therefore *inoperative*.

(a) Where the intervening act is *the natural and probable consequence of the tort*. If the injury to the plaintiff was "the very kind of thing which is likely to happen if the want of care which is alleged takes place"—*Haynes* v. *Harwood* (1935), *per* Green L.J.—then the intervening act will not absolve the defendant, who will remain liable.

> *Clay* v. *A. J. Crump & Sons Ltd.* (1963). The plaintiff was injured by the collapse of an unsafe wall, which an architect and demolition contractors had negligently allowed to remain standing. Plaintiff's employers, building contractors, in reliance on their two co-defendants, did not carefully inspect the wall, which any reasonably careful expert would have seen was unsafe. HELD: The demolition contractor's negligence was not a *novus actus interveniens* absolving the architect and building contractors; and the plaintiff's employers were in breach of their duty to provide a safe system of work. All three were liable to the plaintiff.

(b) Where the intervening act was *that of the defendant himself*. The defendant remains liable if: (*i*) he himself committed the intervening act; (*ii*) he authorised or instigated another to commit it.

(c) Where the intervener *lacked full tortious responsibility*. If the intervening act was that of, *e.g.*, a child—*Bebee* v. *Sales* (1916)—or a person whom the defendant had thrown into a state of sudden alarm, the chain of causation is not broken and the defendant remains liable.

> *Scott* v. *Shepherd* (1773). Defendant threw a lighted squib onto Yates's stall. Willis, a bystander, threw it onto Ryal's stall. Ryal threw it away, so that it struck plaintiff and put out his eye. HELD: Defendant liable: Willis and Ryal did not break the chain of causation, as they acted instinctively for their own safety.

(d) Where the intervening act was a *legal or moral duty*. In such a case, the chain of causation is unbroken, and the defendant remains liable: *Baker* v. *T. E. Hopkins & Son Ltd.* (1959).

(e) Where the intervener is *asserting or defending his*

rights. Again, there is no *novus actus interveniens,* and the defendant remains liable: *Clayards* v. *Dethick* (1948).

(*f*) Where *the plaintiff acts to minimise danger.* We have seen that the intervening act may be that of the plaintiff himself, but this will not be so where he was doing no more than discharge his duty to minimise the danger. This does not break the chain of causation and the defendant remains liable.

(*g*) Where the alleged intervention was *contemporaneous with the tort.* The *novus actus interveniens* must *follow* the tort it is alleged to nullify. If two contemporaneous but independent acts cause the same damage, one cannot be an intervening act so as to absolve from liability for the other.

INJUNCTIONS AND RESTITUTION

22. Injunction a discretionary remedy. An injunction is an *equitable* remedy given at the *discretion of the court.* However, since the *Supreme Court of Judicature (Consolidation) Act, 1925,* it can be granted by any division of the High Court, and may be given in addition to damages. Injunctions may also be granted by county courts.

23. Injunctions of four kinds. Note carefully, however, that they are *not exclusive, i.e.* prohibitory and mandatory injunctions may each be either interlocutory or perpetual.

(*a*) *Prohibitory* injunctions are granted to prohibit the doing of an act, *e.g.* closing a right of way.

(*b*) *Mandatory* injunctions are granted to compel the defendant to perform some act, *e.g.* to abate a nuisance.

(*c*) *Interlocutory* injunctions are granted summarily on the plaintiff's affidavit to prohibit the commission or continuance of some activity by the defendant, pending the hearing of the action. The plaintiff must satisfy the court: (*i*) that he has a triable case, and is probably entitled to relief; (*ii*) that a just settlement would be difficult or impossible unless the interlocutory injunction was granted. The *quia timet* action is a variant of that for an interlocutory injunction. It is granted to restrain the threatened commission of a tort, and is not necessarily followed by any further action.

(d) *Perpetual* injunctions are granted permanently to compel the defendant to, or prohibit him from, some action.

24. Damages in lieu of injunction. The *Supreme Court of Judicature (Consolidation) Act,* 1925, *s.* 37, preserves the power of the High Court, originally given by *Lord Cairn's Act,* 1858, to award *damages in lieu of an injunction.* However, as the courts are generally unwilling to allow a defendant, in effect, to purchase a licence to continue his tortious activity, they will grant damages in lieu of an injunction only if the following conditions, laid down in *Shelfer* v. *London Electric Lighting Co.* (1895), *per* A. L. Smith L.J., are fulfilled:

(a) If the injury to the plaintiff's legal rights is small.
(b) If it is capable of being estimated in money.
(c) If it would be oppressive to the defendant to grant an injunction.

25. An injunction may be suspended. The courts may *suspend* the operation of an injunction, *e.g.* to allow the defendant time to adjust his affairs so as to be able to comply with the injunction when it is reimposed.

26. Restitution of property. The court has a discretionary jurisdiction under the *Judicature Act,* 1873, to order the specific restitution of property of which the plaintiff was tortiously dispossessed by the defendant. The following rules apply:

(a) Specific restitution will normally be ordered where the value of the chattel exceeds the damages recoverable by the plaintiff.
(b) The court will not order restitution of a chattel of no special interest or value to the plaintiff where damages would be adequate compensation.
(c) If the defendant, while tortiously in possession of the plaintiff's property, *increased its value,* the plaintiff can recover only its *original value.*

PROGRESS TEST 17

1. Give examples of (a) judicial remedies; (b) extra-judicial remedies. **(1)**
2. (a) Suggest some classifications of damages. (b) Differentiate general and special damages. **(2, 3)**

3. What are nominal damages? To what (if any) class of torts are they confined? **(4)**

4. What is meant by *restitutio in integrum*? **(5)**

5. (*a*) What are exemplary damages? (*b*) Are there any—and if so what—limits on the award of exemplary damages? **(6)**

6. What are (*a*) contemptuous, (*b*) aggravated, damages? **(7, 8)**

7. Are damages for trespass to land based on the restoration of the land to its original condition? Are there any (and if so what) circumstances in which damages for trespass to land can be recovered although the land was not damaged? **(9)**

8. What is an action for mesne profits? Must it be joined with an action for ejectment? **(10)**

9. What damages can a successful plaintiff recover (*a*) for permanent deprivation of a chattel; (*b*) for temporary deprivation of a chattel; (*c*) for damage to a chattel? **(10)**

10. Can an agent or bailee recover damages for conversion? If a plaintiff in conversion recovers more than his own interest, how must he deal with the surplus? What is the position if the defendant is entitled to the surplus value? **(11)**

11. In what ways are damages for conversion assessed? What is meant by saying that a plaintiff in conversion cannot obtain double satisfaction? **(11)**

12. On what grounds may general damages for personal injuries be awarded? What are the rules governing damages for loss of expectation of life? **(13)**

13. What may a successful plaintiff in a personal-injuries claim recover (*a*) for loss of earnings; (*b*) for expenses? **(14)**

14. What is meant by damage that is too remote? Can intentional damage ever be too remote? **(15)**

15. Explain the effect of the decision in *The "Wagon Mound"* on remoteness of damage in negligence. **(16)**

16. Did *The "Wagon Mound"* have any effect on torts other than negligence? **(17)**

17. To what extent is the *amount* of damage inflicted on the plaintiff relevant to the question of whether the damage was too remote? Illustrate by decided cases. **(18)**

18. What is a *novus actus interveniens*? Outline the relationship of causation with liability. **(19, 20)**

19. In what circumstances (if any) will a *novus actus interveniens* be inoperative? Illustrate by decided cases. **(21)**

20. (*a*) What is an injunction? (*b*) How may injunctions be classified? (*c*) Under what circumstances may damages be awarded in lieu of injunction? (*d*) May an injunction be suspended? **(22–25)**

21. Outline the rules governing the remedy of specific restitution of property. **(26)**

CHAPTER XVIII

ABUSE OF LEGAL PROCESS

1. Four types of abuse. Abuse of legal process may take the following forms.

(a) Malicious prosecution (*see* 2–7 below).

(b) Maliciously instituting certain civil proceedings (*see* 8–9 below).

(c) Maintenance and champerty now abolished—see note to Para. 9 (*see* 10–13 below).

MALICIOUS PROSECUTION

2. Definition. To establish malicious prosecution the plaintiff must prove that the defendant:

(a) instituted a criminal prosecution of the plaintiff **(3)**,

(b) maliciously **(4)**,

(c) without reasonable or probable cause **(5)**, and

(d) unsuccessfully **(6)**,

(e) resulting in damage to the plaintiff **(7)**.

3. Instituted criminal proceedings. The defendant must have instituted the proceedings *personally* and *actively*. It is not enough that the defendant merely stated what he believed to be the facts to the police or a magistrate, leaving them to initiate the prosecution. On the other hand, if the plaintiff suffered damage, he need not prove that the stage of actual prosecution was reached; although it must be shown that legal proceedings were commenced: *Mohammed Amin* v. *Bannerjee* (1947), a Privy Council case.

Danby v. *Beardsley* (1880). The defendant told the police that property had been stolen from him, and had been seen in the possession of the plaintiff, who had been defendant's gardener. The police therefore arrested the plaintiff. HELD: Defendant had not actively instigated the proceedings, and no action would lie for malicious prosecution.

Fitzjohn v. *Mackinder* (1861). In the course of civil litigation between the parties, Fitzjohn alleged, on oath, that his signa-

194

ture to a certain document produced by Mackinder was a forgery. The judge committed Fitzjohn for trial for perjury, and Mackinder was bound over to prosecute. The prosecution failed, and Fitzjohn sued Mackinder for malicious prosecution. HELD: Fitzjohn could succeed, Mackinder having wrongfully and maliciously procured the prosecution.

NOTE: The fact that Mackinder had been bound over to bring the prosecution did not prevent its being found malicious.

4. Defendant must have acted maliciously.

(a) The defendant must have acted from a motive *other than that of bringing a criminal to justice*—this is the definition of a malicious motive in this context. Thus, *e.g.*, the prosecution will be malicious if defendant's main motive was to deter others—*Stevens* v. *Midland Counties Railway Co.* (1854). Conversely, the fact that defendant was actuated by personal spite against the plaintiff will not make the prosecution malicious if the plaintiff's *major* motive was to see justice done.

(b) The judge decides as a matter of *law* whether there is reasonable evidence of malice; the jury whether, as a matter of *fact*, the defendant acted maliciously.

(c) The *plaintiff* must show, not only malice by the defendant, but *also* absence of reasonable and probable cause. Both are essential.

5. Absence of reasonable or probable cause. The criteria for deciding whether such cause existed may be summarised as follows:

(a) The defendant must have had an *honest and reasonable belief* in the plaintiff's guilt, *i.e.* a belief such as would lead an ordinarily cautious and prudent man to believe the plaintiff was *probably* guilty of the crime charged: *Hicks* v. *Faulkner* (1881).

(b) The *judge* decides as to the existence of reasonable and probable cause; but he does so on the basis of the jury's findings as to the facts known to the allegedly malicious prosecutor: *Tempest* v. *Snowdon* (1952). Note carefully, however, that, although this is the general rule, the issue of whether the defendant had an *honest belief* in the charge made may be put to the jury as one of fact, *provided that* the plaintiff had adduced facts tending to prove that the defendant did not believe in the plaintiff's guilt.

(c) The *jury* must be asked specific questions. When the issue of whether the defendant had an honest belief in the charge made is put to the jury, they must be asked either (i) whether the defendant honestly believed in the plaintiff's guilt, or (ii) whether the defendant honestly believed in the charges he made: but the jury should *not* be asked to decide the whole issue of reasonable and probable cause: *Glinski* v. *McIver* (1962).

6. The criminal charge must have ended in the plaintiff's favour. Note the following:

(a) The basis of the rule is the general principle that criminal charges should not be retried as civil issues.

(b) A *convicted* person cannot sue for malicious prosecution in respect of the charge on which he was convicted, even though he can prove that he was innocent and that the charge was malicious. Further, it makes no difference that he could not appeal.

Basebe v. *Mathews* (1867). Plaintiff alleged that defendant, by making false and malicious statements, procured plaintiff's wrongful conviction by magistrates. HELD: The action must fail, as the criminal proceedings had not ended in accused's favour; her lack of right of appeal was immaterial. BUT NOTE also the following case.

Boaler v. *Holder* (1887). Plaintiff, on defendant's information, was convicted of one charge, but acquitted on a more serious one. HELD: Plaintiff was not barred from action for malicious prosecution in respect of the latter charge.

(c) *Acquittal on* any *grounds suffices.* Action for malicious prosecution is not barred because, *e.g.*, the acquittal was on a technicality, or the prosecution offered no evidence. There need not have been an acquittal on the merits.

(d) *The action is not barred* if it was impossible for the criminal charge to end in the accused's favour.

7. The prosecution must have damaged the plaintiff.

(a) The damage must have been *the consequence of the criminal prosecution. Wiffen* v. *Bailey and Romford U.D.C.* (1915). Defendant, a local-government officer, officially complained before justices of plaintiff's failure to cleanse rooms. The justices dismissed the complaint and awarded costs to the plaintiff. HELD: Although defendant had acted maliciously and without reasonable or probable cause, the action would fail because there was no necessary or natural damage to the plaintiff arising from the complaint.

(b) The prosecution may have damaged the plaintiff in three ways:

> (i) It may have caused him financial loss, e.g. the cost of his successful defence.
> (ii) It may have endangered his liberty.
> (iii) It may have damaged his good name and reputation.

MALICIOUSLY INSTITUTING CIVIL PROCEEDINGS

8. Examples of the action. (*See* **9** below.) If done maliciously and without reasonable and probable cause, the following are actionable:

(a) The institution of proceedings in *bankruptcy*: possibly an individual—as distinct from a company—must prove special damage.

(b) The institution of proceedings to have a company wound up as insolvent.

The basis of the action is the adverse effect on the plaintiff's credit. The requirements are the same as for malicious prosecution.

9. No action in respect of other malicious civil proceedings. It seems, though the point is not absolutely settled, that no action will lie in respect of malicious and unfounded *civil* actions other than those above. Note that the *Supreme Court of Judicature* (*Consolidation*) *Act*, 1925, *s.* 51, gives the courts power to circumscribe the activities of persistently vexatious litigants.

> *The Criminal Law Act, 1967, s. 14, has abolished maintenance and champerty as crimes and torts. Note carefully, however, that this abolition does not effect "any rule of that law as to the cases in which a contract is to be treated as contrary to public policy or otherwise illegal." This means, e.g., that champertous contracts are unenforceable.*

*The sections which follow have been allowed to stand as
a matter of interest. They can be read lightly.*

10. Maintenance defined. The tort of maintenance consisted
of aiding another, financially or otherwise, to bring, carry on
or defend a civil action, without lawful justification. The
right of action lay in the party who opposed the aided litigant,
provided the former *suffered damage, i.e.* maintenance was not
actionable *per se.*

> *Bradelaugh* v. *Newdegate* (1883). The defendant maintained
> Clarke, by promising to pay his costs and expenses, in sueing
> Bradelaugh for a statutory penalty of £500 for sitting and voting
> in the House of Commons without having taken the oath.
> HELD: Bradelaugh could succeed in an action for maintenance,
> as the defendant could not legally justify his aiding Clarke, as
> they had no common interest (*see* below).

11. Lawful justification. Aiding another's action was
legally justified if the maintainer had a *common interest* with
the aided litigant, or if the maintainer acted from *charitable
motives.*

(a) *Common interest.* This was fairly widely defined
and include, *e.g.*, the common interests of master and servant, landlord and tenant, relations (including in-laws),
trades unions and their members, members of professional
associations, and many common economic and business
interests. Widespread insurance had extended the ambit of
common interest, as had legal aid also.

> *Martel* v. *Consett Iron Co. Ltd.* (1955). The Anglers' Co-
> operative Association undertook to assist a local angling
> association in an action against the respondents for an in-
> junction and damages in respect of the pollution of a fishery.
> HELD: This did not constitute maintenance, as the two as-
> sociations had a legitimate common interest in the matter.

(b) *Charitable motives.* One who aided the action of another did not commit maintenance if he was motivated *solely*
by charitable feelings as, *e.g.*, where a rich man helped a poor
person to obtain a remedy to which he was entitled, but
which he would otherwise have been obliged to forego.

12. Further aspects of maintenance. The following two
points should be noted:

(*a*) Proof of special damage to the plaintiff was essential to the success of an action for maintenance.

(*b*) It was no defence that the aided action was successful.

Neville v. *London Express Newspapers Ltd.* (1919). The defendants, by instituting actions of which they paid the costs and expenses, recovered monies on behalf of persons whom the plaintiff had swindled. He alleged, *inter alia*, maintenance by the defendants. HELD: (*a*) His claim in maintenance failed, as he had not suffered special damage, but had merely been obliged to fulfil his legal obligations; (*b*) the fact that the aided litigation was successful does not bar a claim in maintenance.

13. Champerty defined. Champerty was that species of maintenance in which the person aiding another's action did so for the promise of part of any proceeds of its success. It was the crime and tort of champerty for a solicitor to conduct an action on a "contingency-fee" basis. Note also that charitable motives were no defence in champerty.

PROGRESS TEST 18

1. What forms may misuse of legal process take? **(1)**

2. What must a plaintiff prove to establish malicious prosecution? Can a person institute a malicious prosecution by a report to the police? **(2-3)**

3. What is the definition of malice for the purpose of malicious prosecution? Does personal spite by the defendant necessarily constitute malice? **(4)**

4. What are the criteria for deciding whether the defendant had reasonable or probable cause for instituting the prosecution? Can a convicted person sue for malicious prosecution? Illustrate by decided cases. **(5, 6)**

5. What forms may damage to the plaintiff take to ground an action for malicious prosecution? **(7)**

6. What forms of maliciously instituted civil proceedings will give rise to an action? What is the basis of such an action? What must the plaintiff prove? What is the effect of the *Supreme Court of Judicature (Consolidation) Act*, 1925, *s.* 51? **(8-9)**

H

CHAPTER XIX

LIMITATION OF ACTIONS

STATUTES

1. Various statutory periods. The various periods of limitation of actions in tort are governed by the following statutes: *Limitation Act*, 1939; *Law Reform* (*Limitation of Actions*) *Act*, 1954; *Limitation Act*, 1963; *Fatal Accidents Acts*, 1846–1959; *Maritime Conventions Act*, 1911; *Carriage by Air Act*, 1932; *Carriage by Air Act*, 1961; *Law Reform* (*Miscellaneous Provisions*) *Act*, 1934.

2. The general rule. The *Limitation Act*, 1939, provides that an action in tort must be brought within *six years* of the date on which the right of action accrued. This general rule is subject to a number of exceptions, which are considered in **3–8** below.

3. Personal-injury claims. The *Law Reform* (*Limitation of Actions*) *Act*, 1954, lays down a limitation period of *three years* from the date of accrual of the cause of action, in respect of claims for damages for *personal injuries* arising from nuisance, negligence or breach of duty—whether the duty was statutory, contractual or independent of statute or contract.

4. Effect of the Limitation Act, 1963. The case of *Cartledge* v. *E. Jopling & Sons Ltd.* (1963) revealed a weakness in the *Law Reform* (*Limitation of Actions*) *Act*, 1954, in that it would debar from action a person who suffered, as a result of negligence or breach of duty, personal injury (in this case pneumonocosis) of which he did not know, or could not reasonably have discovered, until *after* the expiry of the three-year limitation period laid down by the 1954 Act. The *Limitation Act*, 1963, *s.* 1, obviates this source of injustice; its effect may be summarised as follows. A person who discovers an injury or disease of which he had no actual or constructive previous knowledge may, *by leave of the court*, bring an action *within a* *year* after the expiry of the three-year limitation period laid down by the 1954 Act, provided that he did not make the discovery *more than a year before* the end of the three-year period.

NOTE: This summary, whilst accurate within its limits, is also very elliptical. Students who require a more extensive knowledge of this matter should study the full text of the Act.

5. The accrual of the cause of action. We have seen that, in all cases, time begins to run against the plaintiff when the cause of action accrues. It is therefore necessary in any given case to determine this time, which varies according to the type of action and the statute which governs it. The rules are as follows.

(*a*) In torts actionable *per se*, time runs from *the day after the date of commission of the wrong*.

(*b*) In torts actionable only on proof of damage, time runs from *the moment of commencement of the damage*. *See* 4 above for the effect on this of *s*. 1 of the *Limitation Act*, 1963, in certain kinds of personal injury claims.

(*c*) In the case of a *continuing tort, e.g.* nuisance, time begins to run *in respect of every fresh accrual of the tort from day to day*, but is subject to the *Limitation Act*, 1939. Thus, *e.g.*, if a nuisance has continued for eight years when the action is brought, damages can be recovered only in respect of the previous six years, the two years before that being statute barred.

(*d*) *Conversion and detinue.* Time begins to run *only from the date of the wrong*, and a person may be in possession of another's chattel *without having converted it*. Note the following:

(*i*) Time runs *either* from the day the rightful owner demanded the chattel and was refused, *or* from any date during the time in which the chattel was in the possession of the defendant and he committed an act of conversion in respect of it.

(*ii*) In the case of *successive* conversions, time begins to run against the rightful owner from the date of the *first* conversion: *Limitation Act*, 1939, *s*. 3 (1).

(*iii*) The *Limitation Act*, 1939, *s*. 3 (2), provides that the owner's title to a chattel is extinguished when he has been *wrongfully deprived of it for six years*.

6. Disability. Where the cause of action accrues to a person who is under a disability, because he is of unsound mind or an infant, time begins to run against him from the date *either* of the cessation of the disability *or* of his death, whichever occurs first: *Limitation Act*, 1939, *s.* 22. Note further that subsequent disability does not interrupt the running of time, whether in respect of the original potential plaintiff or one claiming through him: *Limitation Act*, 1939, *s.* 22 (*a*). Time does not begin to run against a person under *successive* disabilities until the *last* of them has ended; but, when a right of action belonging to a person under a disability passes on his death to another person *also* under a disability, time begins to run against him from the date of death of the *first* person: *Limitation Act*, 1939, *s.* 22 (*b*).

7. Fraud. The *Limitation Act*, 1939, *s.* 26, provides for postponement of the beginning of the period of limitation in the following cases:

(*a*) Where the right of action is *based on the fraud* of the defendant.

(*b*) Where the right of action was *concealed by the fraud* of the defendant.

(*c*) Where the action is for relief from the *consequences of a mistake*.

In these cases, time does not begin to run against the plaintiff until he has discovered the fraud or mistake, or could have done so with reasonable diligence.

NOTE:

(*i*) The rights of a purchaser of property in good faith and for valuable consideration are protected from the effects of these provisions: *Limitation Act*, 1939, *s.* 26, proviso 1.

(*ii*) The expression "concealed fraud" is defined widely, to include any wilful wrongdoing or unconscionable conduct, and may mean no more than that the fraud was unknown to the plaintiff when it was committed; *i.e.* he need not show any active concealment by the defendant: *Beaman* v. *A.R.T.S. Ltd.* (1949).

8. Other statutory limitations.

(*a*) *Fatal Accidents Acts*, 1846–1959. Three years.

(*b*) *Maritime Conventions Act*, 1911, *s.* 8. Two years, in respect of damage to a vessel or her cargo, or loss of life or

personal injury to persons on board a vessel, caused by the
fault of any other vessel.

(c) *Carriage by Air Act*, 1961. Two years in respect of
proceedings against carriers by air subject to the Act. Note
carefully that the *Carriage by Air Act*, 1932, is still in force,
and provides for a *three-year* limitation period in respect of
some carriers by air.

(d) *Limitation Act*, 1963, *s.* 4. Two years in respect of
actions for contribution between tortfeasors.

(e) *Law Reform (Miscellaneous Provisions) Act*, 1934, as
amended by the *Law Reform (Limitation of Actions) Act*,
1954. In actions against the estate of a deceased tortfeasor,
proceedings (unless pending at deceased's death) must be
brought within *six months of the assumption of legal responsibility* by his estate; and in any case in accordance with
the provisions of the *Limitation Act*, 1939, and the *Law
Reform (Limitation of Actions) Act*, 1954.

MISCELLANEOUS MATTERS

The following matters are not strictly concerned with
limitation, but as they have some affinity with it they are
dealt with here for convenience.

9. Waiver of tort. Some historical explanation is necessary.
Before the abolition of the Forms of Action, where the defendant had wrongfully gained possession of the plaintiff's money
by committing a tort against him, the plaintiff could *either*
bring an action for damages in respect of the tort *or* "waive the
tort" and bring a contractual or quasi-contractual action in
the nature of *assumpsit*. This was clearly a crucial decision
when the plaintiff was restricted to one form of action, and the
wrong choice might cause him to be non-suited. However,
despite the fact that since the *Judicature Act*, 1873, alternative
actions may be pursued concurrently on the same facts,
waiver has not altogether lost its importance. The modern
position is outlined below.

(a) *Election at the point of judgment.* If the plaintiff has
pursued alternative remedies, *i.e.* pleaded in contract and
also in quasi-contract and tort, he is not put to his election
until the stage of *judgment* is reached—at which point

judgment for the plaintiff in the one cause of action extinguishes his claim in the others. Thus, if he elects for judgment on the contractual action, he does not waive the *tort*, but merely *the right to recover damages for it.*

(*b*) *Two or more defendants.* If a plaintiff has a right of action against two or more defendants who have *independently* caused him harm in a matter arising out of the same facts (*i.e.* they are *several*, not joint, tortfeasors) then his having taken—*but not obtained judgment in*—an action for money had and received against *one* tortfeasor is no bar to his pursuing an action in *tort* against the *other*: *United Australia Ltd.* v. *Barclays Bank Ltd.* (1941).

(*c*) *Joint tortfeasors.* Although the point has not been tested in the courts, it seems apparent that the effect of the *Law Reform (Married Women and Tortfeasors) Act*, 1935, is that the above applies also to *joint* tortfeasors.

(*d*) *Waiver restricted.* The doctrine of waiver applies only to the torts of trespass to land, trespass to goods, deceit, and extortion of money by threats. In the case of other torts, such as defamation, the doctrine clearly cannot apply, as no question arises of the defendant's wrongfully gaining possession of the plaintiff's money.

10. Assignment generally forbidden. The general rule is that a right of action in tort is *not* assignable. It is obviously undesirable that choses in action should become commercial properties. There are the following exceptions.

(*a*) *Bankruptcy of potential plaintiff.* The assets of a bankrupt, including his choses in action, pass to the trustee in bankruptcy, who has the statutory power to sell such assets.

(*b*) *Judgment debts.* One to whom a judgment debt is owing, arising from a tort, may assign that judgment debt. This is because what is assigned does not arise directly from the tort, but is conferred by the court.

(*c*) *Assignment on death of plaintiff.* As we have seen, by the *Law Reform (Miscellaneous Provisions) Act*, 1934, *s.* 1, causes of action by or against the deceased survive, with certain exceptions.

(*d*) *Insurance.* When an insurer pays an insured person for injury or damage arising from a tort, the insured's rights are subrogated to the insurer, who can sue the tortfeasor.

(e) *Future damages.* Damages yet to be recovered in a contemplated or uncompleted action may be assigned, as the assignment is not of the cause of action, but merely of a property identified by reference to the action.

The Criminal Law Act, 1967, s. 1, has abolished the distinction between felonies and misdemeanours. The effect of this is to abolish the Rule in Smith v. Selwyn (1914) (11 below) that a civil action on a felonious tort could not be brought until after prosecution for the felony. In 11 is set out the position as it existed before 1 January 1968, when the Act came into force.

11. Civil action postponed to prosecution. In the case of a tort which was also a *felony* (the rule did not apply to misdemeanours or summary offences), a civil action could not be brought until the felon had been prosecuted, or reasonable cause shown for his not being prosecuted: *Smith* v. *Selwyn* (1914). Note the following:

(a) The rule did *not* apply to the *Fatal Accidents Acts*, 1846–1959, actions under which were not postponed by the deceased's death having been caused feloniously.

(b) The rule did *not* prevent action against a person civilly responsible for the felonious tort but innocent of the felony; *e.g.* a master might be vicariously liable for the felonious tort of his servant, and the action was not postponed to the prosecution of the servant.

(c) Only the person *injured* by the felony was affected by the rule; *e.g.* if his right of action passed to his trustee in bankruptcy, the latter might sue in advance of the prosecution.

(d) The prosecution had to be *concluded* (not merely instigated) before the feloniously injured person may sue.

PROGRESS TEST 19

1. Enumerate the various statutes which govern limitation. What is the general rule as to limitation? By which statute is it provided? **(1–2)**

2. What is the nature and source of the rule as to personal-injury claims? What was the effect of *Cartledge* v. *E. Jopling & Sons Ltd.* (1963), and what amendment of the law resulted? **(3–4)**

3. When does time begin to run against the plaintiff in (a) torts

actionable *per se*; (*b*) torts actionable on proof of damage, continuing torts, conversion and detinue? What is the effect of the *Limitation Act*, 1939, *s.* 3 (2)? **(5)**

4. Outline the rules as to the limitation of an action which accrues to a person under a disability. **(6)**

5. State the rules laid down by the *Limitation Act*, 1939, *s.* 26, in cases in which the plaintiff's right of action is based upon the fraud of the defendant. What is meant, in this context, by the expression "concealed fraud"? **(7)**

6. State the periods of limitation enjoined by the following statutes: (*a*) the *Fatal Accidents Acts*, 1846–1959; (*b*) the *Maritime Conventions Act*, 1911; the *Carriage by Air Acts*, 1932 and 1961; The *Law Reform (Miscellaneous Provisions) Act*, 1934. **(8)**

7. What is the historical explanation of the rule as to waiver of tort? **(9)**

8. At what point must a plaintiff who has pursued alternative remedies decide as to waiver? What does he waive? What is the position as to waiver (*a*) where there are two or more defendants; (*b*) where there are joint tortfeasors? To which torts (if any) is the doctrine of waiver restricted? **(9)**

9. Why is it undesirable that actions in tort should not be assignable? Is an unlawful assignment itself a tort? State the exceptions to the rule that actions in tort cannot be assigned. **(10)**

BIBLIOGRAPHY

TEXTBOOKS

James, *General principles of the law of torts*, (Butterworth).
Salmond, *Law of torts*, (Sweet & Maxwell).
Street, *The law of torts* (Butterworth).
Winfield, *Tort* (Sweet & Maxwell).

CASE BOOKS

Fridman, *Modern tort cases* (Butterworth, 1968).
Weir, *A casebook on tort* (Sweet & Maxwell, 1967).
Wright, *Cases on the law of torts*, fourth edition (Butterworth, 1967).

Students should be very careful to use only the latest editions of books.

There are a number of works on particular topics, but they are intended mainly as practitioners' reference books. Students would be better advised to postpone reference to them until the fundamentals of the subject have been mastered.

Students should take every opportunity of reading cases in their original reports. The potted versions in textbooks cannot show the process of judicial reasoning by which the decision was arrived at.

EXAMINATION TECHNIQUE

1. On study generally. There is no need to wait until you are qualified to take a professional attitude to your work. As a student you are a professional learner and examinee, so resolve to master the expertise of those arts. A professional is one who does his work with optimum efficiency, at the time it has to be done, whether he feels like it or not. You will find the simple determination to be professional much more effective than self-administered moral exhortation and condemnation.

Psychologists and others have done much work on the processes of memory and learning. The following is a necessarily incomplete and over-simplified summary of their main findings, as they concern students.

(*a*) *Strong motivation* is of the first importance. This means that —particularly towards those parts of your work you find least attractive—you should not think, negatively and dolefully, "Now I must do several hours' work on a boring and difficult subject," but, positively and cheerfully, "Now I will do some of the work which will enable me to achieve my ambition." If you have no ambition, get some quickly; you will get nowhere without it. If you like, it can be idealistic rather than materialistic, but a combination of both is the better idea.

(*b*) *Regular attempts to recall* what you have learned are absolutely essential to retaining it. In one experiment subjects who practised regular recall were more than 50 per cent more efficient in retaining the material learned than a control group who did not, the two groups being otherwise equal. Remember that there is a crucial difference between *reading something with a view to recalling it and actually recalling it*. A successful examinee is not merely an efficient learner, but an efficient *recaller*. Therefore constantly practise recalling what you have learned. You will find that both the amount retained and subsequent improvements in ease and efficiency of learning are progressively more than proportional to the effort involved.

(*c*) *Intensity and efficiency* of periods of study are much more important than their length. Thus, concentrated spells of as little as twenty minutes' intensive study, interspersed by rests, have been found to be significantly more effective than a similar total period of continuous study. It is very common for a student to say

209

"I worked for four hours" when for the last three and a half hours of that period he merely continued in the working posture with very low efficiency. You will find it well worth while to discover by trial and error what is the period of optimum efficiency for *you* (it varies with temperament) and base your work on that period: of course, you must not use the knowledge in this paragraph as a mere rationalisation for doing very little work. Whatever your optimum period, you will have to do a great deal of work in *total*: but concentrate on *efficiency*, and do not crudely equate it merely with hours spent at the desk. It is perhaps worth mentioning that the more efficient you are as a student, *i.e.* the greater the amount learned *and retained* per unit of time spent in study, the more time you will have for other things, without detriment to your academic prospects.

(*d*) *Regular and frequent information about your progress* is essential to efficiency of study. You can get this essential feedback by constantly practising recall, as recommended above, and by regular self-testing by working through past examination questions. In universities, at any rate, this is properly regarded as mainly your responsibility. Class examinations will not be held more than once a term, probably less. For full efficiency you need the information much more frequently than that.

2. On using this book. In studying a particular topic, such as nuisance for example, proceed as follows.

(*a*) *Read straight through*, at your normal reading speed, the chapter on nuisance. Do not attempt to memorise at this stage, the purpose of which is to gain an overall general idea of what you are about to study. If possible, do a second reading in the same way.

(*b*) *Divide the chapter*, mentally or by pencilling in the margin, into sections *based on your optimum period of study*. Study the first section intensively, then turn the book over and attempt to recall what you have learned. Do this until you can make *two* perfect and unhesitating recalls. Study all the sections of the chapter in this way. Try to work with complete concentration and maximum efficiency for your optimum period, but stop and rest as soon as you reach the point of diminishing returns. Remember that complete concentration is a habit which can be acquired by regular practice.

(*c*) *Revision.* When you have thus mastered all the sections, work through the questions at the end of the chapter. These are purely factual, and intended only to test whether you have successfully memorised the subject-matter. References are given to the numbered sections of the chapter which contain the answers. For the sake of brevity, some of the questions are so worded that, strictly speaking, they can be answered "yes" or "no"; but, of course, you must always know the *reason* for such an answer. Do not conclude your study of the chapter until you can answer all the questions correctly and without hesitation.

(*d*) *Re-reading*. Read the chapter you have just studied, straight through, at your normal reading pace, as many times as possible. On no account be tempted to neglect this part of the work, which has the function, *essential to comprehension*, of relating the parts to the whole, so that what has been learned and memorised is also *understood*. Never attempt to learn law as a series of arbitrary and disconnected rules. Although memorisation is essential for success in examinations, it is never enough in itself. Success, both in examinations and in practice, requires *understanding*, not only of each part, but of how the parts fit together, and the relationship of each one both to the other parts and to the whole.

3. On examinations

(*a*) *Work*. There is no way of passing a serious examination without doing the work. If you do not do the work, you will fail. On the other hand, if you have done the work there is no need for anxiety, which merely consumes the energy needed for the job in hand. Therefore do the work and be confident. If you have enough brains to get into one end of a course, you have enough *brains* to get out of the other. But brains are not enough in themselves—you also have to *work efficiently*, both at learning the subject matter, *and* at learning the techniques of passing examinations.

(*b*) *Practice*. Passing examinations is a skill in its own right. The *only way* to master a skill is by *practice*. It is therefore essential to study and *practise* the art of writing examination answers. It is not enough merely to learn the subject; you must also learn to pass an examination in that subject. It is a common and costly mistake to think that the former subsumes the latter.

(*c*) *In the examination room*, decide at the outset which questions you are going to answer, and in what order, then stick to your decision. Do not be rushed and flurried into hurrying over this. If you know what you are going to do, you can go ahead and do it without residual and distracting anxieties. Taking a cool businesslike, professional approach to the job of being an examinee contributes at least as much towards examination success as does intellectual brilliance.

(*d*) *Plan the allocation of time* before you begin to write the paper. This plan should not be rigid, but should be followed to the extent of making sure that you write *full answers to the number of questions required by the paper*. It is particularly the fault of well-prepared candidates that they write such long answers to the first two or three questions that they have to write hurried and inadequate ones to the remainder, and so do less well than they should. Every reasonably well-prepared candidate knows far more than he can possibly put down in the time, so that *selection* and the *weighing of relative degrees of relevance* are of paramount importance. Speed and confidence in these skills can be developed only by plenty of practice. It cannot be too often or strongly emphasised that writing examinations is a *distinct* and difficult skill which must be *practised* to obtain the best results. It is a fact that examination performance can be significantly improved by *practising the skills involved*. So get hold of plenty of old papers and allocate regular time to practice. It will be time well spent.

(e) *Plan each answer before you start to write it.* Time thus spent is always well repaid. Candidates who spend the entire three hours in frantic scribbling are usually hard-working, well-prepared, unnecessarily nervous students who fail to do as well as they deserve. Remember that most law papers require more and shorter answers than those in subjects such as history and English. Law students have often studied and taken examinations in such subjects at school, and need to adjust their style. A good law style is concise and succinct almost to the point of being stacatto.

(f) *Always leave time to read through your answers* and make any necessary corrections. Many students have a great psychological aversion to doing this, but they should conquer it. People do strange things under stress. A misplaced or omitted negative or comma can entirely alter the meaning of a sentence, and the examiner can only take what you have written at its face value.

(g) *Answering problem questions.* These are often easier than they look, not least because the information given in the question stimulates the memory. However, if you can see the answer straight away, nevertheless have another look. There may be two versions of the answer, both correct, but one expected from average students and the other from potential honours candidates. If you fall into the latter category, make sure you write the appropriate version.

In doing problems, you may find it useful to adopt the following general tactics:

(i) Read the question very carefully and decide what it is about. Questions on negligence, for example, might also involve breach of statutory duty; those on nuisance, the Rule in *Rylands* v. *Fletcher*. Any question may touch on parties or remedies, additionally to its main subject-matter. If you feel any serious doubt about what is involved, avoid the question (unless it is compulsory).

If you decide to do a particular question, read it very carefully again. Remember that everything in it has been put there for a purpose—examiners do not go in for padding. So, for example, the question may include descriptive phrases such as "over 21"; "X's employer"; "an animal known to be nervous"; "a person of weak intellect." In your answer, you must either elucidate the significance of these or explain why you think they have no significance in that context. If something in the question is ambiguous, you must explain the nature of the ambiguity, the various interpretations of which it allows, and the effects of adopting each of them. Determine to have all such matters *clearly thought out, and arranged in the form of a plan* (see below) *before you start to write the answer*. If you simply start to write the answer from the first thought that occurs to you, and depend on being able to think out the order as you go along, the result will be a muddled and long-winded effusion which will get very little credit, *even though it contains all the relevant matter*. A problem question is intended to test, not merely extent of knowledge, but the lawyer-like ability to select and arrange material in the way most effective for the elucidation and explanation of the hypothetical case posed in the problem. For this purpose, a thirty-five-minute answer consisting of fifteen minutes' thinking and twenty minutes' writing (or even the other way round) will always do better than thirty-five minutes' disordered scribbling.

(*ii*) Jot down in list form the *principles of law* involved. Write alongside each the names of relevant cases and statutes, and *brief* notes on subject-matter, as *aides memoires*, so that you will not later forget to include those points in the answer. During your preparation you should practise the making of these outline plans. A planned answer is always much better than an *ad hoc*, slap-dash affair, hurled down in whatever order the thoughts occur to you.

Remember that you can cite a case by its facts alone, if you cannot remember its name—or write it, *e.g.* *?* v. *Hamilton* or *Dann* v. *?*. It is permissible to invent appropriate "facts" to illustrate a point, so long as you make it clear that you have done so. *Never* invent a fictitious name and try to pass it off as a real case.

(*iii*) Rearrange the principles you have listed, in the logical order demanded by the answer you are about to write. Then, continuing to observe the logical order, *apply these principles* to the facts given in the question. All problem questions are designed to test your ability thus to apply principles.

(*iv*) Pay the strictest attention throughout to *relevance*. Many students cannot resist the temptation to write everything they know about the matters involved in the question, regardless of relevance. You cannot afford to waste either your time or the examiner's.

(*h*) *Non-problem questions.* Many students avidly seize on these, under the mistaken notion that they *must* be easier than problems. As regards the "discussion" type of question, the opposite is more likely to be true. Also, many students interpret such questions to mean "Write what you know about . . ." The result is pages of atrocious waffle, which is as ill rewarded as it is ill written. *Never* waffle in law examinations, it is always fatal.

In general, "discussion" questions should be answered by stating the various possible views of the matter, followed by an evaluation of their merits, and (where the question clearly requires it) a final section stating your own conclusions. You must give authority and evidence for all your statements, and your conclusions must be seen to follow from their premises. Remember also to observe the convention of writing, *e.g.*, "it is submitted that" or "it therefore seems that," not "I think" of "in my opinion."

It is better to assume that questions which require no more than the accurate reproduction of memorised facts will be heavily penalised in respect of omissions and inaccuracies. The moral is to do such questions only if you are *sure* of the facts. If you are, write the answer as a series of short numbered paragraphs, rather than in narrative form. Use tables and diagrams where appropriate. The great value of such questions is that, *provided you know the answer perfectly*, it can be written down very quickly, thus saving invaluable time for more difficult questions.

(*i*) *Summary.* When taking examinations, your aim should be to produce accurate, relevant, logically developed, legibly written answers, which are as brief and concise as is consistent with adequate treatment of the questions. Such answers cannot be produced without *adequate practice before the examination and cool, methodical planning in the examination room.* These are quite as important for examination success as intellectual ability and extensive knowledge. This will continue to be the case until (a consummation devoutly to be wished) a thorough-going reform of the examination system takes place.

SPECIMEN TEST PAPERS

These test papers are intended to provide practice in answering examination questions. If done as complete papers, six questions should be attempted in three hours. When less than a full paper is attempted, time per question should not exceed thirty-five minutes.

It is again stressed that students should regularly practise examination technique. To facilitate short periods of practice, a number of miscellaneous questions have been added after the test papers.

London University LL.B. questions are indicated by *LL.B.* followed by the year.

Questions from the Law Society's Qualifying Examinations are indicated by *L.S.* followed by the month and year.

Answers should be based on the law at the time of your answer, not at the date of the question.

TEST PAPER 1

1. (a) "In my view, the maxim (*volenti non fit injuria*), in the absence of express contract, has no application to negligence *simpliciter* where the duty of care is based solely on proximity or 'neighbourship' in the Atkinian sense." (Diplock, L.J.) Discuss.
[*LL.B.*, 1966]

(b) "In trespass, as well as negligence, inevitable accident has no place." (Winfield.) Discuss. [*LL.B.*, 1966]

2. X is a worker employed in Y's iron foundry. A statutory regulation imposed upon employers requires certain safety barriers to be used in all foundries. Y provides these barriers and instructs X to use them. X fails to do so with the result that he and a fellow-worker, Z, sustain injuries. X is an experienced foundry-man, aware of the regulation and of the risks involved in dispensing with the barriers.

Advise (i) X and (ii) Z.

Would you change your advice if the statutory duty were imposed on X? [*LL.B.*, 1965]

3. Basil was employed by a company, and was a member of a union. The union had an agreement with the company that there would be no strikes. Disputes would be referred to arbitration.

Basil resigned his membership of the union, and the union representatives told the company that labour would be withdrawn if Basil were not dismissed. Basil was dismissed.

(a) Advise Basil whether he can successfully sue the union representatives for the loss of his employment.

(b) If one of the union representatives had not been a party to the agreement with the company that there would be no strikes, would your advice differ? [L.S., February 1965]

4. (a) What is meant by the publication of a defamatory statement?

(b) John Smith, clerk, aged 40, of Barnet, has never been convicted of a criminal offence. He sues for libel in respect of an account in the defendants' newspaper of the trial and conviction for bigamy of one John Smith, clerk, aged 40 of Barnet.

Advise the defendants. [LL.B., 1962]

5. Prima facie, an infant is liable in tort, but, where the tortious act is in substance a breach of contract, the infant is not liable in tort. Discuss this and give an example. [L.S., February 1965]

6. (a) Is the defendant's motive ever relevant in the tort of nuisance?

(b) A and B occupy adjacent premises. A poplar tree grows on A's ground, adjoining the boundary fence. The roots of the tree spread under the soil and interfere with B's horticulture. Without notifying A, B trenches deeply and cuts the roots on his side of the fence. The tree then falls on A's house, damaging the roof and injuring A's guests. Discuss. [LL.B., 1962]

7. Yvonne asked her accountant to call on her one evening to discuss business. Afterwards Yvonne tried to persuade him to stay all night, and when he refused she locked one of the two doors of her flat and threw the key out of the window. She alleges that he was not enthusiastic about escaping otherwise he would have discovered the other door before morning. What should be considered when advising Yvonne as to her liability for false imprisonment? [L.S., February 1966]

8. A chemical manufacturer, M, wishing to install a machine on an existing raised platform, refers the plans to his consulting engineer, E, who, without inspecting the platform, passes the construction as safe. M's installation contractor, C, is not satisfied that the platform is safe, but, after being informed of E's approval, proceeds to install the machine. The platform collapses, and the falling machine dislodges some chemicals stored in the next room, which unexpectedly combine into a corrosive mixture, causing serious skin damage to the storeman, F, an employee of M. Advise F. [LL.B., 1964]

1. Keith and George were employed by the same company. George wrote to Donald, a director of the company, making false and scandalous allegations about Keith's conduct and morals while he was away on business in Europe. Without seeking confirmation of the allegations Donald took the letter to the Chairman, and then to Keith's wife Helen.

(a) Would Donald be well advised to contest any action for defamation by Keith?

(b) Would the position be altered if (i) Donald had shown the letter to the Chairman because he realised it would be his opportunity to push Keith out, and get his job; (ii) Donald was Helen's uncle? [L.S., February 1966]

2. (a) In what circumstances can the maxim *res ispa loquitur* be applied?

(b) B, a builder, contracted with O to repair the chimney stack of O's house. While W and X, two of B's workmen, were dismantling part of the stack, a chimney pot fell and wrecked S's expensive motor-mower in the garden of an adjacent house. S hears that W has since won a fortune on the Pools. Advise S. [LL.B., 1964]

3. What must a plaintiff prove to establish trespass to land? [LL.B., June 1962]

4. Albert's gamekeeper, without Albert's knowledge, places an iron bar across what he believes to be Albert's private road. It is, however, a public road. Bertram, riding home in the dark on his new bicycle, collides with the bar and is injured. Has Bertram any remedy in damages against Albert and his gamekeeper? Would your answer differ if the gamekeeper had told Albert what he had done, and Albert had approved? [L.S., February 1965]

5. In a built-up area, Brown's bull-dog enters the next-door garden belonging to Smith and kills Smith's turkey and pet rabbit. Smith angrily drives the dog out of the garden into the road where the dog chases a passing car. The car swerves and overturns, and H, the driver, sustains injuries. Advise Brown as to his liability for these incidents. [LL.B., 1966]

6. F loses his umbrella, which G finds and, being unable to ascertain the owner, gives to his son, H, who is ignorant of the foregoing facts. F recognises the umbrella in H's possession and demands it. H refuses to give it up, stating that he got it from his father. F thereupon attempts to wrest the umbrella from H but H beats F over the head with it and F gives up the struggle.
Advise F. [LL.B., 1965]

7. Charles has piled earth full of chemicals against Edward's wall. The chemicals are slightly damaging the wall, and the ultimate damage may be extensive. Edward has from the start protested to Charles about it. The grant of an injunction would seriously affect the business of Charles while conferring little benefit upon Edward.

Advise Edward whether (*i*) an injunction could be granted in these circumstances and (*ii*) whether the court would award damages instead of an injunction.   [*L.S.*, February 1966]

8. X agrees with Y to store his (X's) cooker in Y's warehouse. Later, X sells the cooker to Z. Z informs Y that he has bought the cooker and proposes to build it into his new kitchen, for which purpose he needs the exact dimensions. Y carelessly gives Z the wrong dimensions, but refuses to part with the cooker pending authorisation from X. After ten days, Y releases the cooker to Z, who find that it is larger than he has been told, and incurs £50 expenses in re-adapting the kitchen to receive the cooker. Advise Z.   [*LL.B.*, 1964]

TEST PAPER 3

1. (*a*) Discuss, with illustrations from decided cases, the defence of lawful arrest in an action for false imprisonment. In what respects, if any, do police powers and duties as to arrest differ from those of a private individual?

(*b*) L, after lunching in a restaurant, suddenly notices that he is late for an appointment. In his hurry to leave he seizes the overcoat of another customer, M, mistakenly thinking it to be his own. M, who does not believe L's story, detains L and sends for the police. What tort, or torts, if any, have been committed?
          [*LL.B.*, 1966]

2. A pupil was walking along a school corridor during school hours when another pupil pushed a swing door towards him. He put out his hand to stop it and his hand went through the glass panel of the door, causing him severe injuries. When considering the question of liability in damages what points should be borne in mind?   [*L.S.*, February 1965]

3. Mrs S takes her daughter G, aged 4 years, to the local supermarket. Inside the entrance there is a prominent notice, reading "Danger, Work in Progress," which apparently refers to a roped-off cavity in the floor where tiles are being laid. While Mrs S is inspecting groceries, she steps backward, pushing over a support holding the rope, falls into the cavity, and breaks her right arm. Meanwhile, G has been attempting to climb up a pile of wire

baskets, which fall over with her, the edge of one of the baskets piercing her left eye. Advise Mrs S on the position of herself and G.

[*LL.B.*, 1962]

4. (Answer *either* (*a*) or (*b*), *not both*.)

(*a*) A, an estate agent of repute, is entrusted by B with the sale of B's house. B does not mention to A that the house has constantly required underpinning because of the nature of the soil. A could ascertain these quite easily, but fails to do so. Describing the house as "in sound condition throughout," A negotiates a sale to P. Soon after P pays the price and takes possession, the house collapses, injuring P and his wife, W.

Advise P and W.

(*b*) Discuss the problem of remoteness of damage in the law of tort. [*LL.B.*, 1965]

5. Outline the tort of procuring breach of contract, and give an example. [*L.S.*, February 1964]

6. An article in a magazine, which is edited and printed abroad, describes A as "a fraudulent house-agent, who robs the poor and ought to be in prison." The magazine is distributed in England by a company which supplies numerous periodicals to retailers. One of the company's legal advisers scans the periodicals for objectionable matter before distribution, but he has not the time to read the whole of the contents. A friend of A, having purchased a copy of the magazine at a bookshop, informs A of the reference to him, and A sues the company for libel. The company obtains evidence that A has defrauded three persons in the course of his business as a house-agent, but there is no evidence that any of them was poor or of any robbery. Advise the company as to their defence. [*LL.B.*, 1964]

7. "Two defences to actions of tort, (*a*) contributory negligence of plaintiff and (*b*) plaintiff a trespasser, are less effective against children of tender years than against adults." Discuss this statement, giving an example. [*L.S.*, February 1964]

8. "It is essential to liability under the Rule in *Rylands* v. *Fletcher* that the thing that does the mischief should escape from the area which the defendant occupies or controls." Discuss and explain this statement. [*L.S.*, August 1965]

MISCELLANEOUS QUESTIONS

LL.B.

1. (a) Distinguish conversion from detinue.

(b) X Co. send an art book to P, who had not solicited it, with a letter saying: "This splendid volume is shortly to be published at £7.7s. You may purchase it for £5.5s. by posting us your cheque for that amount within seven days. If you decide not to avail yourself of this exceptional opportunity, you may return the book to us without obligation." P ignored the letter, put the book outside his front door, where it was damaged by rain, and took no further action. Advise X Co. as to their rights, if any.   [1964]

2. The T Trade Union favours, upon moral grounds, a boycott of goods from the Republic of Pandemonia. F and G, officials of the Union, know that the A Company has contracts to deliver such goods to the retail trade. They inform A Company that, if it does not refrain from dealing in Pandemonian goods, the Union members employed by A Company will be instructed not to handle such goods. A Company thereupon advises its purchasers that it is unable to make further deliveries.

(a) Has A Company any remedy against (i) the T Trade Union; (ii) F and G?

(b) Have the purchasers any rights against F and G?   [1964]

3. R was severely injured by the negligent driving of S, and after seven days in hospital R died of his injuries. He left a widow, whom he had employed in his business at £15 a week, a son aged 19, who is in receipt of a State grant for university education, and adopted daughter aged 12. At the time of the accident R's expectation of life was 25 years; and he held an assurance policy by which £1,000 became due on his death. Discuss the extent of S's liability, if any.   [1964]

4. L attended a horse show as a guest of M, the owner of the ground. The only barrier between the spectators and the competitors was a line of plants in pots. At the entrance and interspersed in this line were notice boards reading, "Keep off the course. The proprietor accepts no liability for injury on or off the course." L, who had read one or more of these notices, was run down and injured by N, a rider in a race whose horse took a wider sweep than usual at a curve in the course and passed through the line of

pots, where L was standing off the course. L sued M for breach of the common duty of care, and N for negligence and trespass to the person. Consider any liability on the part of the defendants. [1964]

5. Discuss the rights, if any, in tort of D, F and H in the following circumstances.

(a) D is driving his car along the highway when an oak tree, growing on E's adjacent land, falls across the road and damages the car;

(b) F is cycling along the highway when he is caused to fall and injure himself by a football, which is kicked from the adjoining land of G by one of a number of boys allowed by G to play there;

(c) H is walking along the highway when he is injured by a window pane falling from a house occupied by I on a weekly tenancy from J.   [1964]

6. F causes enquiries to be made through his own bankers X & Co. as to the financial stability of two prospective customers, G and H, both of whom bank at the Z Bank. Z Bank has reason to know that G is bordering on insolvency and that H is conducting a sound and flourishing business. Z Bank negligently confuses the reports, giving an extremely favourable reference on G and the reverse on H. These reports are passed on by X & Co. to F, who thereupon gives extensive credit to G, resulting in heavy loss to F. F abstains from dealing with H. H, upon learning about the discreditable report on his affairs, is so distressed that he suffers a stroke. Advise (a) F, (b) H, as to his rights (if any) in tort. [1962]

7. Discuss the plaintiff's rights in the following circumstances:

(a) The plaintiff is dozing in a hammock in his garden, when the garden is entered by the defendant's cows. They trample the flower-beds and one of them, tossing its head, impales the plaintiff with a horn.

(b) The defendant's dog strays into the plaintiff's land, where it mutilates his ducks and bites his hand.

(c) The defendant's pet monkey is released by a mischievous boy. It drops from a tree on to the back of a cyclist on the highway, causing him to turn violently on to the footpath and to collide with and injure the plaintiff.

8. X is a workman in Y's factory. A statutory regulation provides that processing tanks of the type used in Y's factory must be fenced, so as to protect workmen from falling into them. There are no such fences in Y's factory. X has become addicted to inhaling intoxicating and poisonous fumes by putting his head over a processing tank, which is not necessary for his work. Both Y and X's fellow workmen are aware of X's addiction and Y has frequently warned X against this practice. On one occasion after prolonged inhalation, X is so dizzy that he reels into a fellow

worker, Z who falls and breaks an arm. X dies from the toxic effects of the fumes. Advise (a) X's wife; (b) Z. [1962]

9. Discuss the general conditions of liability on the part of the defendant for a tort committed against the plaintiff by the defendant's servant. [1962]

10. X negligently drives his car along a dockside. His car hits and injures a pedestrian, who in consequence has to have his hand amputated. The pedestrian is a celebrated pianist, earning £6,000 a year. X's car then swerves over the dockside into the open hold of a ship. Burning petrol from the car ignites a valuable cargo of furs, doing £30,000 worth of damage. A strong wind unexpectedly springs up and blows some of the ignited furs on to a neighbouring tanker, as a result of which it is completely destroyed by fire. The tanker cannot be replaced for less than £500,000. Discuss the extent of X's liability. [1962]

11. Compare the defences of fair comment and qualified privilege and discuss the meaning and effect of malice in connection therewith. [1966]

12. R owns an hotel and, for the convenience of its guests, authorises S to run a travel agency from a bureau in the lobby of the hotel building. S employs T, a reputable contractor, to refit and redecorate the travel bureau. T's trestles are so placed that a hotel guest, without being in any way careless, trips over one and breaks his leg. Advise the guest. [1966]

13. C, a chauffeur, employed by X, is permitted by X to drive a car owned by X to his, C's, home at the end of the day's work and garage it there overnight. Whilst backing the car out of the garage the next morning C runs over and kills his wife, W. Advise P & Q, the personal representatives of W, as to their rights of action if any. [1966]

14. F is under a statutory duty to provide and use safety boards in all roof construction works. F instructs an employee, M, who is experienced at this type of work, to draw the boards from the equipment store and then use them on a particular job. M, however, ignores the instructions and works on the roof without the boards. O, who is then engaged by F on the same job, falls between the rafters because of the lack of safety boards, and M, in a vain attempt to save O, also falls. Both men are injured. Advise F. [1966]

15. The N laboratory is carrying on experiments in nuclear fission. After an explosion in the laboratory, the reason for which is unknown, it is found that there is considerable radioactivity in the radius of five miles. The authorities, acting under permissive statutory powers, cause the population to be evacuated, cattle in

the contaminated area to be destroyed, and cattle in the neighbouring areas to be quarantined. Farmer Q, in the contaminated
area, loses his entire herd in this way. Farmer T, in the neighbouring area, is unable to market his cattle at the most profitable
time. K, a cattle-feed merchant, suffers serious business prejudice
for lack of a market for his merchandise. Consider whether Q, T
and K have any remedies. (Disregard the provisions of the
Nuclear Installations (*Licensing and Insurance*) *Act*, 1965.)   [1966]

16. "The truth is that the distinction between trespass and
case is obsolete . . . we divide the causes of action now according
as the defendant did the injury intentionally or unintentionally"
(Lord Denning, M.R., in *Letang* v. *Cooper*). Explain and discuss.
                                                                   [1965]

17. Dr D performs a minor operation on E, aged 21, the sole
support of his widowed mother, M. During the operation, Sister S,
misunderstanding what Dr D asks for, hands him the wrong
syringe, with which Dr D injects E, thereby causing E's death
later that day, after much pain. Advise M.   [1965]

18. T is the tenant of a factory building owned by P. Part of
the brick wall surrounding the building and being part of the
premises leased suddenly collapses, damaging Smith's car which
was illegally parked outside the premises in the adjoining street,
and injuring Curly, a child of six. At the time, Curly, without
asking T's permission, was playing inside the premises on some
ladders stacked against the wall, which fell to the ground when the
wall collapsed. T knew that children sometimes played on these
ladders, and chased them off the premises from time to time, but
was not aware of Curly's presence when the injury occurred.
    Advise Smith and Curly.   [1965]

19. K is instructed by L to drive L's van from London to
Edinburgh. Without L's knowledge K first drives to a place
twenty miles south of London to visit his sick mother; then, two
hours later, sets forth for Edinburgh. After driving for five miles,
K negligently collides with M's lorry, which is en route to South-
ampton loaded with goods for export belonging to X. Some goods
are damaged. The resultant delay causes X's goods to be shipped
late at considerable extra cost to X by way of (*i*) storage charges;
(*ii*) liquidated damages payable to the purchaser of the goods for
late delivery.
    Advise X.   [1965]

20. The body of a small child, believed murdered, is found in a
house in Fulham. A newspaper reports as follows: "Eustace
Blenkinsop, a Fulham barman, has been questioned for 3 hours by
the police regarding the dead child; he may be able to help their
enquiries." The man actually interviewed was one Eustace

Blenkinsop, a lorry-driver employed by brewers in Fulham, and living next door to the house where the body was found. His questioning lasted one hour and a half, but did not yield anything of value to the police. There is also another Eustace Blenkinsop, who is a barman living and working in Fulham, and well known in the district. Separate actions for libel are brought by the two Blenkinsops, each alleging as regards himself that the report bore the defamatory meanings that the plaintiff (a) murdered or probably murdered the child, or (b) was suspected or reasonably suspected of so doing.

Advise the newspaper. [1965]

21. A is riding his horse, which he knows to be a nervous animal, on his farm. The horse, for no apparent reason, suddenly bolts through a gap in the hedge separating A's land from B's and tramples B's vegetable beds. When C, an employee of B, tries to divert the horse, the horse kicks him.

Discuss. [1965]

LAW SOCIETY

1. Outline the general defences which may be pleaded in answer to an action for tort, assuming that the person sued has done the wrong alleged. [February 1965]

2. Indicate what Albert should establish to succeed in the following actions.

(a) Albert sues Celia for false imprisonment.

(b) Albert sues Yvonne for trespass.

(c) Albert sues Barbara for negligence. [February 1965]

3. In connection with the tort of negligence what is meant by "remoteness of damage"? [August 1965]

4. A grocer accused Helen in a loud voice of not having paid him for the previous week's groceries, and added that he did not want her as a customer in future. Several other customers in the shop heard this. Later the grocer called on Helen at her house and said that he had made a mistake. She had paid him after all.

(a) Advise Helen as to her remedies against the grocer.

(b) If the grocer's wife has been the only other person in the shop at the time of the accusation, would the position be affected? [February 1965]

5. Henry obtained money from Iris by fraud. Her brother-in-law assisted her to recover the money by legal action.

(a) Advise Henry whether the brother-in-law is liable to him in maintenance.

(b) Advise whether it would be maintenance for interested

manufacturers to assist each other in defending actions for infringements of patents.   [August 1965]

6. Colin lives in a terrace house, and complains that the occupier of the house on one side keeps about twenty barking dogs in his back yard, while on the other side several young people play musical instruments every evening. This noise is affecting Colin's health. Explain the principles that would guide a court in deciding whether legal remedies exist.   [February 1964]

7. Olive saw the rent collector coming down the street. When she heard a knock on the door she threw a bucket of water out of an upstairs window intending it for the collector. Unfortunately, it was not the collector but the vicar. What facts would you bear in mind when advising Olive as to her liability.

          [February 1964]

8. "The mere causing of actual loss to another is not necessarily a tort." Examine this statement and give an example of the kind of case referred to.   [February 1964]

9. What is the effect upon an action for tort of the death of (a) the tortfeasor and (b) the person injured?   [February 1964]

10. Albert's cattle have strayed onto Basil's land, and eaten cereal crops and grass. In addition they trampled on Basil's young child, seriously injuring him. Advise Basil what Albert must prove in order to escape liability for the damage done by his cattle.   [February 1964]

11. Albert was a passenger in Basil's coach. When Basil was driving along a mountain road the coach suddenly swerved and plunged over the side. Basil escaped injury. Albert sues Basil for his injuries, stating that all he knows is that he was a passenger in the coach when it fell.

(a) Explain the doctrine of *res ipsa loquitur* in relation to this.

(b) In what respects would your answer differ if Basil contends that the coach swerved because there was a defect in the steering which was difficult to discover, and that the coach was regularly serviced?   [February 1966]

12. Edward tells you that his neighbour Keith, with whom he is on bad terms, has a pear tree the branches on which overhang his garden, and seriously interfere with his amenities. Edward can reach the lower branches from his own garden, but to get at the upper ones he will have to go into Keith's garden, which he can easily do, because Keith is away. Explain the legal principles which are involved and advise Edward:

(a) if he can cut down the branches which he can reach from his own garden;

(b) if he can go into Keith's garden to cut down the upper branches;

(c) to whom the fruit and the branches would belong.

[February 1965]

13. "In an action for malicious prosecution the plaintiff must establish that the defendant prosecuted him without reasonable and probable cause." Discuss and explain "without reasonable and probable cause."   [February 1966]

14. Simon was going out one night when he almost fell over a motor cycle totally blocking the exit to his drive. He recognised the cycle as belonging to Charles, a visitor of his neighbour. Simon removed the cycle and put it outside his neighbour's house. Charles says Simon is liable for trespass to goods. Do you consider that this is so?   [February 1966]

15. When Alice's doctor was away on holiday another doctor called to see her daughter who had mumps. This doctor said the child could return to school. Alice said that her own doctor had told her that the child should stay away for a month. He replied, "Had he been drinking when he called?" Alice was upset at this remark and told her own doctor about it. Alice's doctor consults you about this. Advise him.   [February 1964]

16. Edward's apprentice was bitten and scratched by a pet monkey, and was not fit for work for several weeks. Advise Edward whether he has a right of action against the owner of the animal. In what respect would your answer differ if:

(a) the apprentice dies the same day;

(b) the apprentice only received a few scratches and returns to work the next day?   [August 1965]

17. (a) Jack, reading a prospectus of a company, and being impressed with certain statements therein, applies for and is allotted shares. Keith, having also read the prospectus and being equally impressed, omits to apply for shares at the time, but 3 months later purchases some in the open market. The statements on which they relied are false and fraudulent. Advise them whether they have any right of action for damages against the directors of the company, giving your reasons.

(b) Briefly outline what must be shown to establish liability in the tort of deceit.   [August 1965]

18. John telephoned Brenda and told her that her husband had been injured in Maureen's aeroplane when she crashed on landing. John added that previously they had both been drinking heavily at the club. Brenda was stricken with such fear that she received a nervous shock which has unbalanced her and made her ill. John was only playing a practical joke, and the story was untrue. Is

John liable to Brenda for causing her nervous shock? If Brenda knew John was a notorious joker, would your answer differ?

[February 1966]

19. Charles was cleaning his petrol-driven lawn mower in his garden shed when it burst into flames. He ran next door to the nearest telephone to call the fire brigade. On his return he discovered that he had forgotten his key and was locked out of the shed. The fire spread and damaged his neighbour's property. Is Charles immune from liability for the damage? [February 1966]

20. Albert inserts an advertisement in a newspaper stating that his goods are the best on the market and far superior to others sold in that town. He intended, and it was understood by those reading the advertisement, to mean goods sold by his rival, Desmond. Has Desmond any remedy against Albert in respect of this advertisement? [February 1965]

21. What are the liabilities of the owner in respect of damage done by:
   (a) his dog that has already bitten a tradesman, and
   (b) his tame monkey that would never hurt anyone?

[February 1965]

INDEX

A

Account, 22
Action on the case, 17
Act of a stranger, 86
Act of God, 12, 86, 108
Aliens, 173
Animals, 11, 23, 106, 110, 112
Apology, 135
Arrest, 37
Assault, 35
Assignment, 204

B

Bankruptcy, 173
Battery, 35
Breach of Contract, 163

C

Cattle trespass, 109
Causation, 74, 188
Chastisement, 38
Chattels, 99, 183
Children, 63, 71, 91
Consent, 51, 78, 135, 146
Conspiracy, 5, 148
Contract, 3
"Contract fallacy," 99
Contribution, 122, 176
Contributory negligence, 6, 7, 32, 52, 67, 78, 108
Control test, 115
Conversion, 5, 27, 29, 33, 183
Convicts, 173
Corporations, 170
Crown, the, 168

D

Damages, 21, 180
Damnum sine injuria, 4
Deceased persons, 175
Deceit, 5, 150
Defamation, 2, 127
Derry v. *Peek* (Rule in), 150
Detinue, 27, 33
Distress damage feasant, 21, 34
Distress for rent, 34
Dogs, 112
Donoghue v. *Stevenson,* 56, 99
Duty of care, 57, 59, 60, 90, 103

E

Ex turpi causa non oritur actio, 14

F

Fair comment, 135
False imprisonment, 35
Fire, 87
Force, 37
Foreign sovereigns, 169
Forms of Action, 2, 80
Fraud, 100, 150

G

General and special employers, 116

H

Highways, 45 *et seq.,* 110, 118
Husband and wife, 160, 174

229